JACQUES BOUSQUET

MANNERISM

THE PAINTING AND
STYLE OF THE LATE
RENAISSANCE

BRAZILLER

Translated by
SIMON WATSON
TAYLOR
from the French

*The illustration on the jacket
of this book is an adaptation in grisaille of a detail
from The Rape of Persephone by Niccolò dell' Abbate in
the Musee du Louvre*

Libraby of Congress Catalogue Card Number: 64-13415

Published 1964 by arrangement

with F. Bruckmann KG, Munich, Germany

No part of the contents of this book may be reproduced

without the written consent of the publisher

George Braziller, Inc., 215 Park Avenue South, New York 3, New York

Printed in Germany

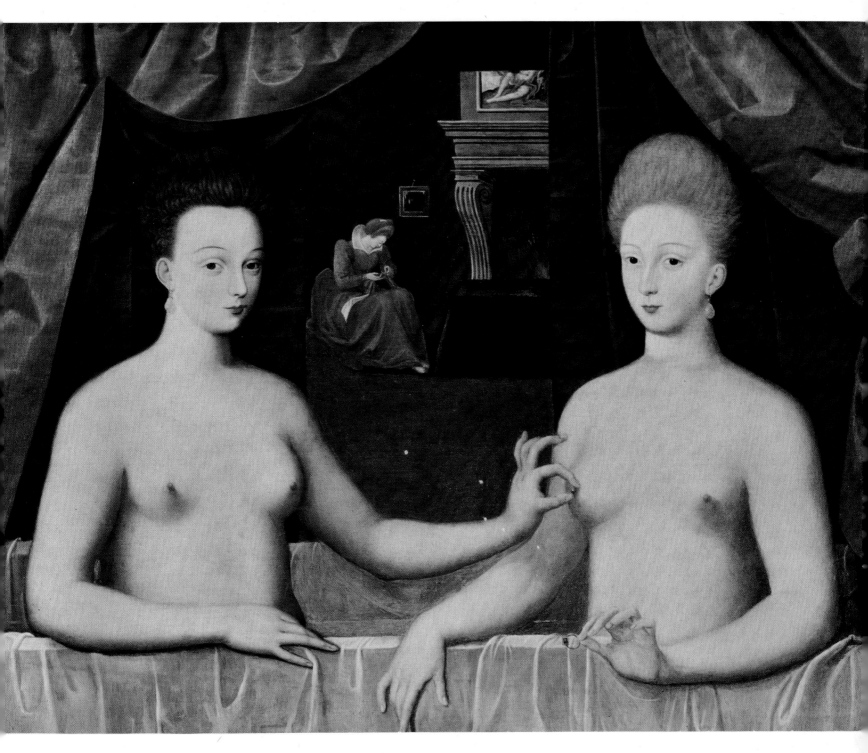

TABLE OF CONTENTS

Selections from
mannerist poetry

I

GIOVANNI DELLA CASA

O DOLCE SELVA *solitaria amica*
De' mi pensieri sbigottiti, et stanchi;
Mentre Borea ne' di torbidi, et manchi,
D' horrido gel l'aere, et la terra implica;
Et la tua verde chioma ombrosa, antica,
Come la mia, par d'ogni 'ntorno imbianchi,
Hor, che'n vece di fior vermigli, et bianchi,
Ha neve, et ghiaccio ogni tua piaggia aprica;
A questa breve, et nubilosa luce
Vo ripensando, che m'avanza; et ghiaccio
Gli spirti anch'io sento, et le membra farsi:
Ma più di te dentro, et d'intorno agghiaccio;
Che' più crudo Euro a me mio verno adduce,
Più lunga notte, et di più freddi, et scarsi.

O GENTLE WOOD, *solitary friend*
Of my downcast, tired thoughts,
While the North Wind in the short, gloomy days
Fills the air and earth with horrid frost,
And your green, shady, ancient foliage,
Like mine, seems on every side whitened,
Now, that instead of white and red-hued flowers
Your every sunny hillside has snow and ice,
By this brief and cloudy light
Which pushes me forward, I go thinking again,
I feel ice forming in my limbs and on my breath,
And with even more ice within and around you
My winter brings me an even rawer East Wind,
Longer nights, and shorter, colder days.

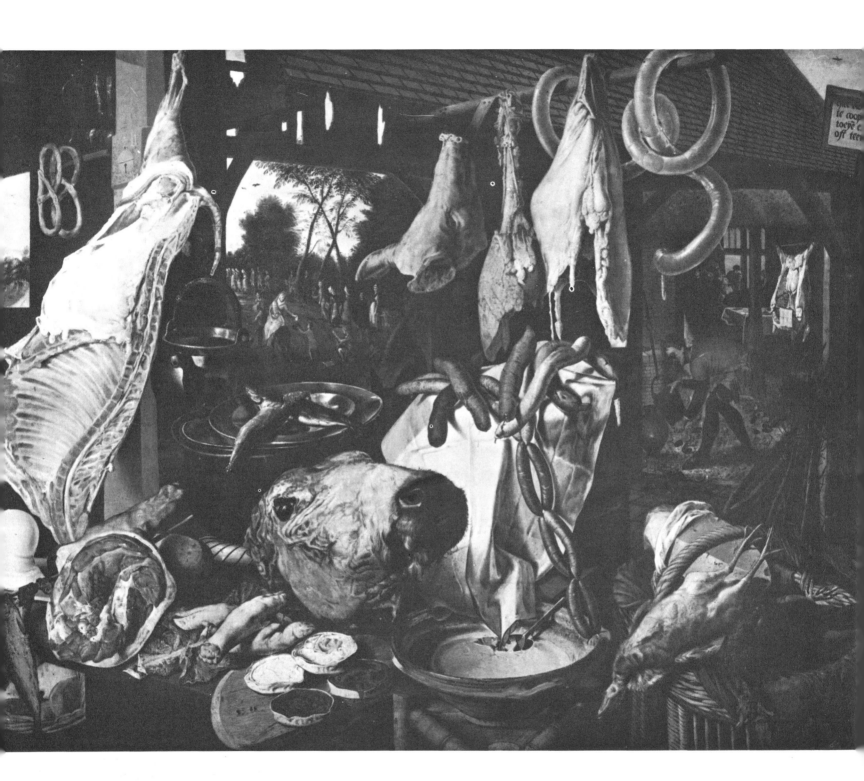

Le Menu de Manduce

Pain blanc,
Pain mollet,
Choine,
Pain bourgeoys,
Carbonnades de six sortes,
Longes de veau rousty froides, sinapisés de pouldre
Zinziberine,
Fressures,
Fricassées, neuf espèces,
Pastez d'assiette,
Grasses souppes de primes,
Souppes de Leurier,
Chous cabutz à la moulle de boeuf,
Salmiguondins.

Andouilles capparassonnées de moustarde fine,
Saulcisses,
Langues de boeuf fumées,
Saumates,
Fricandeaux,
Boudins,
Cervelats,
Saulcissons,
Jambons,
Hure de sangliers,
Venaison sallée aux naveaulx.

Esclanches à l'aillade,
Pastés à la saulce chaulde,
Coustelettes de porc à l'oignonnade,
Chappons roustiz avecques leur degout,
Lievres, Levraux,
Perdrix, Perdriaux,
Faisans, Faisandeaux,
Becasses, Becassins,
Hartolans,
Cochons au mouts,
Risses, Chevreaulx,
Espaulles de mouton aux cappres,
Pieces de boeuf royalles,
Poictrines de veau,
Poulles bouillies et gras chappons
au blanc manger.
Gelinottes
Cailles, Cailleteaux.
Porcespicz.
Pastez de lardons,
Pieds de porc au sou,

Fromaiges,
Peches de Corbeil,
Artichaulx,
Guasteaux feueillettez,
Cardes,
Beuignetz,
Tourtes de seize façons,
Guauffres, Crespes,
Pastez de coings,
Caillebottes,
Neige de Creme,
Myrobolans confictz,
Hippocras rouge et vermeil,
Tartres, vingt sortes,
Confictures seiches et liquides,
soixante et dixhuyt especes,
Dragée de cent couleurs.

Arans blans bouffiz,
Arans sors,
Sardines,
Anchoys,
Salades cent diversités,
de cresson, de Obelon, de la couille à l'envesque,
de responses, d'aureilles de Judas
(c'est une sorte de funges issans des
vieux Suzeaulx), de asperges, de
chevrefeuel: tant d'autres.

Huytres en escalles,
Lamproyes à saulce d'Hippocras,
Barbeaulx,
Rayes,
Casserons,
Huytres frittes,
Petoncles,
Languoustes,
Truites,
Poulpes,
Limandes,
Gougeons,
Barbues,
Brochetz,
Palamides,
Roussettes,
Oursins,
Vielles,
Ortigues,

Anges de mer,
Lempreons,
Soles,
Poles,
Moules,
Homars,
Chevrettes,
Seiches,
Rippes,
Tons,
Excrevisses,
Palourdes,
Chatouilles,
Anguilles,
Anguillettes,
Tortues,
Serpens, id est,
Anguilles de boys,
Cancres,
Escargotz,
Grenoilles.
Merluz salés,
Stocficz,
Oeufs fritz, perduz, suffocquez,
estuvez, trainnez par les cendres,
iectez par la cheminée,
barbouillez, gouildronnez, etc.
Papillons,
Lancerons marinez.

Riz,
Mil,
Gruau,
Beurre d'amendes,
Neige de beurre,
Pistaces,
Fisticques,
Figues,
Raisins,
Escherviz,
Millorque,
Fromentée,
Pruneaulx,
Dactyles,
Noix,
Noizilles,
Pasquenades,
Artichaux.

The Menu of
Manduce   FRANÇOIS RABELAIS
GARGANTUA AND PANTAGRUEL
BOOK 4, CHAPTERS 59 AND 60

White bread
Brown bread
Carbonadoes, six sorts
Sweetbreads
Fricassees, nine sorts
Gravy soups
Cold loins of veal with spice
Zinziberine
Marrow-bones, toast and
Cabbage
Hashes
Chitterlings garnished with
Mustard
Sausages

Neat's tongues
Hung beef
Scotch collops
Puddings
Cervelats
Hams
Powdered venison with turnips
Leg of Mutton with shallots
Lumber pies with hot sauce
Roast capons basted with their
own drippings
Fawns, deer
Hares, leverets
Partridges and young
partridges
Plovers
Dwarf-herons
Wood-hens

Fat kids
Shoulder of mutton with
capers
Sirloins of beef
Breast of veal
Pheasants and pheasant poots
Woodcocks
Snipes
Bacon pies
Soused hog's feet
Parmesan cheese
Gold-peaches
Artichokes
Olives
Thrushes
Geese, gooslings
Hedgehogs
Fritters

Crisp wafers
Quince tarts
Curds and cream
Preserved mirobolans
Comfits, one hundred colours
Fresh herrings, full roed
Salads, one hundred varieties
of cresses
(sodden hoptops, bishop's-cods,
celery, chives, rampions,
jew's-ears, sparagus,
wood-bind,
and a world of others.)
Red herrings
Anchovies
Oysters in the shell
Barbels, great and small
Fried oysters

Prawns
Lamprels
Golden carps
Flounders
Gudgeons
Pikes
Rochets
Sea-bears
Crayfish
Shrimps
Porpoises
Trout, not above a foot long
Sea-breams
Soles
Mussels
Lobsters
Great prawns
Fresh cods

Dried melwels
Eel-pouts
Tortoises
Serpents, i. e. wood-eels
Crab-fish
Snails and whelks
Frogs
Eggs, fried, beaten, buttered,
poached, herdened, boiled,
broiled, stewed, sliced,
roasted in the embers,
tossed in the chimney, etc.
Rice, milk and hasty pudding
Buttered wheat
Water gruel and milk porridge
Pistachios, figs, raisins
Dates, filberts
Parsnips and artichokes

Quelle odeur sens-je en cette chambre?
Quel doux parfum de musc et d'ambre
Me vient le cerveau resjouir
Et tout le cœur espanouir?
Qu'est-ce donc? je l'ay descouvert
Dans ce panier rempli de vert:
C'est un *Melon*, où la Nature,
Par une admirable structure,
A voulu graver à l'entour
Mille plaisants chiffres d'amour...
Baillez-le-moy, je vous en prie,
Que j'en commette idolâtrie:
O! qu'elle odeur! qu'il est pesant!
Et qu'il me charme en le baisant!
O dieux! que l'esclat qu'il me lance,
M'en confirme bien l'excellence!
Qui vit jamais un si beau teint!
D'un jaune sanguin il se peint;
Il est massif jusques au centre,
Il a peu de grains dans le ventre,
Et ce peu-là, je pense encor
Que ce soient autant de grains d'or;
Il est sec, son escorce est mince;
Bref c'est un vray manger de prince;
Mais, bien que je ne le sois pas,
J'en feray pourtant un repas...
Non, le cocos, fruit délectable,
Qui luy tout seul fournit la table
De tous les mets que le désir
Puisse imaginer et choisir...
Ny le cher abricot, que j'ayme,
Ny la fraise avecque de la crème,
Ny la manne qui vient du ciel
Ny le pur aliment du miel,
Ny la poire de Tours sacrée,
Ny la verte figue sucrée,
Ny la prune au jus délicat,
Ny mesme le raisin muscat
(Parole pour moy bien estrange),
Ne sont qu'amertume et que fange
Au prix de ce *Melon* divin,
Honneur du climat angevin...
O manger précieux! délices de la bouche!
O doux reptile herbu, rampant sur une couche!
O beaucoup mieux que l'or, chef-d'œuvre d'Apollon!
O fleur de tous les fruits! O ravissant *Melon*!

The Melon

What odour accosts me in this room?
What charming scent of musk and amber
Comes to delight my mind and sense
And to rejoice my heart?
What may it be? I find it now
In this green-leaf-bedecked basket:
It is a Melon, wherein Nature,
By a most admirable design
Has wished to mark on its round surface
A thousand pleasant love signs...
Make it agape for me, I pray,
That I may commit idolatry:
O! what odor! and how heavy!
How it charms me as I inhale it!
O gods! may the lustre that it wafts to me
Confirm its inner excellence!
Was ever such glorious hue perceived?
Suffused by richest, deepest yellow,
Its firmness reaches to its center,
The seeds its stomach holds are few,
And yet those few, I really think
Are far more likely grains of gold;
Its rind is dry and smooth and thin;
A meal it is, fit for a prince;
But, though I am not so exalted,
I shall make of it a meal...
No, not the cocoanut, delectable fruit
Which, alone, furnishes the table,
With all the viands which desire
May first imagine and then choose...
Nor the dear apricot, which I love,
Nor the strawberry white with cream,
Nor the heavens' very manna,
Nor honey's pure and limpid essence,
Nor yet the sacred pear of Tours,
Nor the sweet green fig,
Nor the plum's juicy fragrance,
Nor even the muscat grape
(However strange for me to say this)
Are more than bitterness and mire
Compared with this divinest Melon,
Glory of the Angevine climate...
O precious repast! succulent morsel!
O sweet reptile rampant in leafy couch!
O! better far than gold, Apollo's masterwork!
O flower of fruits! O ravishing Melon!

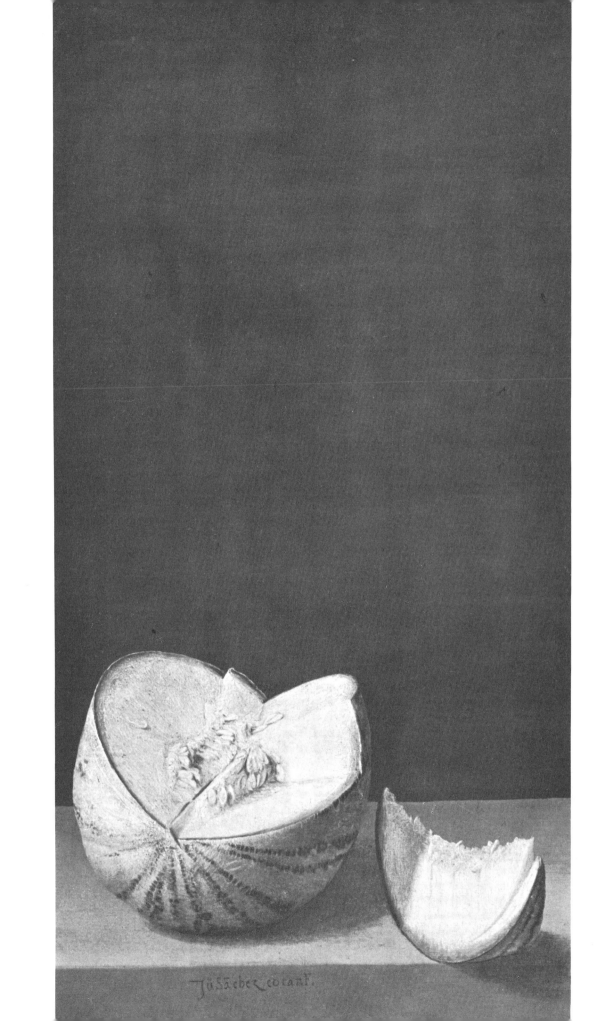

Remy Belleau   Les amours et nouveaux eschanges des pierres precieuses, vertus et proprietez d'icelles

Voila ce que je scay des pierres que Nature
Brasse dedans les flancs de ceste Terre dure:
Reste à dire sans plus le lustre clair et beau
Qui la pierre embellit et qui farde sa peau.
Telle est donc la couleur, quelle en est la matiere,
Car s'elle est pure et nette en sa masse premiere,
Le lustre en sera net, mais s'elle a de l'obscur
Elle sera meslee, et brune d'espesseur,
Mais sur tout la chaleur qui donne la teinture
A la matiere mesme est la cause en Nature
Qui donne la couleur, la grace et le beau teint
Aux pierres, dont la glace et le visage est peint.

Aussi selon l'aspect du Soleil et des terres,
Et des metaux divers où s'engendrent les pierres
S'imprime la couleur, autre estant de l'erain,
Que de l'or, ou du fer, du cuivre ou de l'estain.
Car où le Soleil bat de sa flamme ordinaire,
Là les pierres se font de couleur verde et noire:
Aux lieux sombres et frais le rouge pourprissant
Donne teinte à la pierre, à l'esclat rougissant:
D'un suc fort detrampé et d'une humeur trespure
Le Crystal prend couleur, et la roche plus dure
Du Diamant se teint d'un suc et d'une humeur
Moins claire et plus brunette, et plus basse en couleur:
L'Emeraude se peint d'une humeur verdoyante,
Du rouge le Rubis à la peau flamboyante,
L'Iris du Crystalin, du violet pourprin
L'Amethyste au beau teint, du bleu le Saphystrin:
Le suc fort bigarré fait l'Agathe et l'Opalle,
La Chrysolithe tient de l'humeur jaune et palle…

Here follows what I know about the stones
Sprinkled by Nature in the Earth's hard flanks:
Now we shall speak of the bright, lovely lustre
That beautifies the stone and tints its surface.
The color is the very substance itself,
For when this is pure and clear in its first mass
The lustre will be clear; if clouded
The color will be dull and brown to view.
But in all these, the heat which gave its hue
To the prime substance is the fact in Nature
Endowing color, grace and lovely hue
To the stones' glossy painted faces.

So, following the aspects of the Sun and earth,
And of the divers metals whence the stones first sprang,
The color prints itself, differently than with ores
Such as gold or iron or copper or tin.
For where the Sun beats down with fiery heat,
There the stones' coloring is green or black:
In cool and shady places a purplish red
Makes the stone blush brightly:
The moistest essence and the purest humor
Give to the Crystal its color, and the Diamond's harder rock
Is tinted with an essence and a humor
Less clear, brownish, darker, too, in color:
The Emerald's glow springs from a verdant essence,
The Ruby's surface shines with blazing red,
Crystal is rainbow-hued, the lovely Amethyst
Is purplish violet, the Sapphire blue:
A mottled essence conjures Agate, Opal,
While that of Chrysolite is yellow, pale…

Rémy Belleau   Amorous propositions and new comments concerning precious stones, together with their virtues and properties

What is

Mannerism?

The Legend of Mannerism

Mannerism is the artistic expression of an epoch, the artistic style which prevailed in the art of all Europe for roughly one hundred years, from about 1520 to about 1620. The Mannerist period was perhaps the richest and most diverse period in the whole history of European painting: it produced many great masters and a host of first rate artists of enormous talent and imagination who worked in the cities and courts throughout Europe. The history of art, however, has been curiously unjust toward Mannerism. For a long time it recognized neither the extent of the Mannerist movement nor its historical significance, and still less the true stature of the movement's participants.

Following an erroneous but tenacious tradition, Mannerists were held to be only those Italian artists of the period from 1520 to 1600 who painted "alla maniera di Raffaello" or "alla maniera di Michelangelo." That is to say, "after the manner of Raphael" or "after the manner of Michelangelo." And by this it was implied that these two great artists had carried art to such a degree of perfection, that the painters of the following generations suffered from a feeling of inferiority and, with varying degrees of servility and clumsiness, resigned themselves to academic imitation of the styles of the renowned masters.

This interpretation of Mannerism is quite contrary to the facts. One has only to look at a few works by those Italian painters who flourished during the first half of the sixteenth century, whom the history of art invariably classifies as Mannerists—Parmigianino, Jacopo da Pontormo, Rosso Fiorentino, Lelio Orsi, Angelo Bronzino, and Domenico Beccafumi—to realize that one can accuse them of anything one likes execpt academicism. Far from copying their predecessors of the High Renaissance, the Mannerists are characterized by a frenzied pursuit of new means of expression, delighting in linear distortion, unusual compositions, new color schemes, and unwonted themes. Often their works suggest the boldest artistic movements of our own epoch—Cubism, Expressionism, and Surrealism. It is difficult to understand how anyone could ever have come to label them as imitators and conformists.

The legend that dubbed artists Mannerist, because they painted "alla maniera" of Raphael or Michelangelo, thus implying that these artists were merely belated followers and ungifted imitators of their great predecessors, was based in the first place upon a confusion of meaning. The fact is that the word *maniera* originally carried with it no stigma and certainly no suggestion of imitation. For Vasari, the author of *The Lives of the Most Eminent Architects, Painters and Sculptors* (Florence, 1550) the word *maniera* was more or less synonymous with style. For Vasari, to have *maniera* was to have style, or as we would say today, to have artistic individuality. Certainly Vasari esteemed above all else the *gran maniera* of Michelangelo, but there is nothing to suggest that this was for him the only possible *maniera*. Thirty-four years later, another writer, Raffaello Borghini, in his treatise *Il Riposo* (Florence, 1584), employed the word *maniera* in the same definitely positive sense. For example, he regretted the absence of *maniera* in the work of certain artists. It was only much later, toward the end of the seventeenth century, that *maniera* began to take on the sense of uninspired technical competence and studied imitation of the masters. This new interpretation appeared for the first time, it would seem, in Pietro Bellori's *Le vite de' pittori ...moderni* (Rome, 1672), a treatise on the lives of the Italian artists of the late sixteenth and seventeenth centuries. This pejorative meaning of the word *maniera* soon acquired widespread currency, lending its new sense to the foreign derivations of *maniera (maniéré, maniériste* and *maniérisme* in French; Mannerist and Mannerism in English; *manieriert* and *Manieriertheit* in German). From that time on Mannerism became another word for academicism, hollow affectation, and artificiality. It became more than an art historical term, it became an insult. The *Grand Larousse du XIXᵉ siècle* defines Mannerism as a "defect in the artist who abandons himself to the mannered style *(genre maniéré)*."

This misinterpretation, like all misinterpretations, was not purely gratuitous. It was the later seventeenth century critics, who, championing the classical cause, originally launched the idea that Mannerism, an eminently anti-classical style, was a phenomenon of decadence. The nineteenth century with its respect for established values repeated this judgment quite uncritically. The history of art was taught in terms of a cyclical development in which a period of perfection was always followed by a period of decadence. One simply became used to thinking that, after the piously venerated great masters of the beginning of the sixteenth century, art had suffered a kind of eclipse. Even a mere thirty or so years ago, art history leapt lightly from the chapter headed "Renaissance," which closed at 1520 with the death of Raphael, to the chapter headed "Baroque" which started around 1620 with Rubens. Between these two dates, except for the great Venetians, Michelangelo, Pieter Bruegel the Elder, and El Greco, who were treated as isolated exceptions, this period of the history of art was uncharted territory. It appeared as a confused and swarming scene compounded of mediocre artists, insipid imitators of the High Renaissance, belated Gothics, and bizarre minor masters.

In the museums, Mannerist pictures, when not simply stacked away in the basement, were relegated to the darkest corridors or hung high up on the walls. And even when they were displayed to some effect, they had become invisible, so to speak. It had been so firmly drummed into people's minds that Mannerism was worthless that one did not even look at these paintings, but simply walked by without seeing them. A hundred of the richest, most glorious and most significant years in the history of art had vanished as completely as the lost civilizations of ancient Asia or pre-Colombian America.

The Rediscovery of Mannerism

It was not until the third decade of the present century that the history of art or, to be more exact, a few art historians rediscovered these hundred lost years. The restless and disordered era following the First World War was predisposed to show understanding for the mental confusion and disquiet of the Mannerist epoch. In his *Kunstgeschichte als Geistesgeschichte* (1928), Max Dvořák was the first to assign—or rather to reassign—a positive meaning to Mannerism and to realize that Mannerism was not simply an Italian school but an entire European movement, in which artists as different as Bruegel and El Greco were involved. This conception was developed authoritatively between the two World Wars by the work of Frederick Antal, Hermann Voss, Hans Hoffmann, Nikolaus Pevsner, Werner Weisbach and Walter Friedlaender. The *Encyclopedia Italiana* in 1934, and the *Grosse Brockhaus* in 1936, devoted important articles to Mannerism which they defined as the dominant European style between the High Renaissance and the Baroque.

Mannerist painters who had fallen into anonymity or long been forgotten—Luca Cambiaso, Arcimboldo, Antoine Caron de Beauvais, Georges de La Tour, Monsù Desiderio, and Baugin, for example—were gradually rediscovered. Suddenly an interest in Mannerism became fashionable. The Surrealists perceived the aspects of Mannerism which partially reflected their own preoccupations, and the French review *Minotaure* reproduced works of the Mannerist artists Lucas Cranach the Elder, Urs Graf, Giovanni Stradano, and Arcimboldo. The Paris International Exhibition of 1937, and another exhibition held in Paris at the Wildenstein Gallery two years later, revealed to the public the refined eroticism of the Mannerist painters of the School of Fontainebleau.

After the Second World War, exhibitions devoted to Mannerism succeeded each other ever more rapidly: *Französische Phantastik* at Vienna, 1946; *Desiderio* at the Ringling Museum, Sarasota, Florida, and the Galleria dell'Obelisco, Rome, both held in 1950; *The Art of Mannerism* at the Arcade Gallery, London, 1950; *Fontainebleau e la Maniera Italiana* at Naples, 1952; *Aufgang der Neuzeit* (German culture and art from the death of Dürer to the Thirty Years' War), at Nuremberg, 1952; *From Pontormo to El Greco* at the John Herron Art Museum, Indianapolis, 1954; *Arcimboldo* at Rome, 1955; *Luca Cambiaso* at the Palazzo dell'Accademia, Genoa, 1956; *Pontormo e il primo Manierismo Fiorentino* at the Palazzo Strozzi, Florence, 1956. Significantly, the Council of Europe entitled its 1955 exhibition at the Rijkmuseum, Amsterdam, *The Triumph of Mannerism*. After three centuries of obscurity, Mannerism is today one of the epochs which most intrigues and interests art lovers in general, and it now appears as the artistic epoch of the past most akin to our own.

Definition of Mannerism

After all we have said about the unjustified contempt in which Mannerism was long held and about its reappearance on the scene, it may perhaps be appropriate at this stage to define rather more precisely what Mannerism is. This is not such an easy undertaking. No school of painting in the sixteenth century labelled itself "Mannerist;" Mannerism, like Baroque, Rococo or Romanticism, is a term invented after the event and can be interpreted by anyone as he pleases, extending or limiting the concept according to his whim.

There is no lack of definitions. Some confine the Mannerist movement to the school of Italian painting of the mid-sixteenth century; others see it as a cultural phenomenon affecting the whole of Europe, prolonged well into the seventeenth century and finding expression in literature just as much as in the visual arts. Some view Mannerism simply as an intermediate stage between High Renaissance and Baroque; while others consider it to be, on the contrary, an essential moment in the development of Western culture. For some it is a return to the Gothic style; for others it is the beginning of a movement leading to the classicism of 1800; for yet others Mannerism is anti-classicism.

However, everyone is more or less agreed that Mannerism has something to do with *maniera*, and equally, everyone is prepared to include among the Mannerists a certain number of Italian painters who commenced their careers around the second and third decades of the sixteenth century. This includes such artists as Parmigianino, Jacopo da Pontormo, Rosso Fiorentino, Angelo Bronzino, Daniele da Volterra, Domenico Beccafumi and Lelio Orsi. It appears to me that a valid method for defining Mannerism would be to take this minimal common agreement as the base for discussion, and leaving aside all theorizing, attempt to discover from the works of these artists what is in fact the *maniera* of Mannerism. In this way we may discover more concrete and less arbitrary characteristics in Mannerism. This will enable us subsequently to examine whether these characteristics are shared by other painters

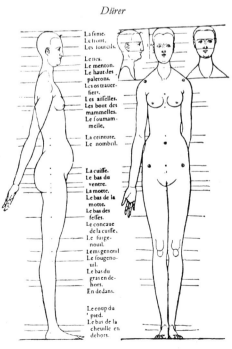

Dürer

25

outside Italy, or are applicable to other cultural forms, and thus to determine as objectively as possible the extent and the essential meaning of the Mannerist phenomenon.

The first observation to be made is that the Mannerists—even if we restrict this name solely to the mid-sixteenth century Italian painters—do not have a *maniera* but rather a whole host of *maniere*. We here cite a few which are particularly evident:

— extreme clarity of contours, lustrous forms, sculptural painting (Bronzino, *Venus, Cupid, Time and Folly*, page 151);

— a tendency toward cubism (Rosso, *Moses Defending the Daughters of Jethro*, page 99);

— use of geometric forms (Orsi, *Allegory of Christ and the Church*, page 107);

— deformation, elongation of the figures (Pontormo, *The Visitation*, page 93); plays of perspective (Parmigianino, *Self Portrait in a Convex Mirror*, page 116); and acromegaly, the strange enlargement of parts of the body (Pontormo, *Seated Nude*, page 113);

— serpentine line (Bronzino, *The Annunciation*, page 112);

— exaggerated or "mannered" gestures (Bronzino, *Saint John the Baptist*, page 86; Beccafumi, *Christ in Limbo*, page 171);

— harsh metallic colors (Bronzino, *Venus, Cupid, Time and Folly*, page 151);

— imaginative, evocative atmospheres, such as stormy twilights (Orsi, *Christ on the Way to Emmaus*, page 155).

Mannerism, then, is not characterized by a manner, but rather by the preoccupation with "manner," or style as we would call it today. Parmigianino, Pontormo, Rosso, Bronzino, and the others are artists who cultivate style, who place the accent less on what they are saying than on the manner of saying it. The so-called classical painters of the High Renaissance —above all Raphael—set out from the postulate that there exists a perfect style, a style owing nothing to the artist's individuality, to his working technique or to the fashions of his times, but an eternal style which was equally valid for the Greece of Pericles, the Rome of Augustus or Italy of the early sixteenth century. It was this eternal style, this ideal realism, this "classical" style which Raphael and his contemporaries believed to have determined. But styles only constitute different ways of expression, and there is no sense in asserting that one of these ways of expression is truer than the others. Various modes of expression are neither more nor less true in themselves, they are just different. The achievement of the Mannerists was precisely that they realized there was no one style but an infinity of styles. Mannerism was above all the awareness of style as such and in this respect it has a direct relationship to the whole of modern art.

If a preoccupation with style be the most salient characteristic of Mannerism, it becomes clear that the term cannot be restricted to a few Italian artists active in the mid-sixteenth century. This preoccupation with style characterizes all European painting from about the third decade of the sixteenth century into the first quarter of the seventeenth century. And this is equally true of Dutch, Flemish, French, German, and Spanish painting, as well as Italian. We shall see that those diverse stylistic expressions which we have noted in the works of the Italian Mannerist appear likewise in painting outside of Italy.

Clarity of contour and sculptural painting first appeared in the Netherlands at the beginning of the sixteenth century, Jan Gossaert Mabuse and Maerten van Heemskerck being the most typical representatives of this trend. In the work of the painters of the School of Fontainebleau, female bodies were so precisely delineated and elegantly contoured that they often give the impression of sculptures in wax. By the beginning of the seventeenth century,

The Spread of the
Mannerist Style
Throughout Europe

this "manner" was being adapted to the depiction of still lifes. Osias Beert, Clara Peeters, Evaristo Baschenis, and Baugin painted objects, fruits, and edible delicacies with such meticulous precision that these inanimate things acquired an aura of eternity.

In the use of geometric forms the Germans went much further than the Italians. Albrecht Dürer and Erhard Schön had made geometric studies which were unquestionably cubist even before the Italians Daniele da Volterra, Rosso Fiorentino, or Luca Cambiaso produced their works showing a cubist tendency. In Germany also Wenzel Jamnitzer engraved a series of amazing polyhedrons, and Lorenz Stoer created veritable geometric landscapes. This same cubist tendency appeared in France in the works of Jean de Gourmont, and later in the works of Georges de La Tour.

The elongation of the human figure and the use of the serpentine line were not confined solely to Parmigianino, Pontormo, and Bronzino. They were also characteristic traits of the School of Fontainebleau. This tendency is strong in the works of El Greco in Spain. Effects of elongation were also exploited by Hendrick Goltzius and Joachim Wtewael in the Netherlands, Hans Rottenhammer and Bartholomeus Spranger and all the other painters of the court of Rudolf II at Prague, as well as by Jacques Bellange who worked in Lorraine.

The same applies to linear deformations and distortions. One of Albrecht Dürer's pupils, Erhard Schön, specialized in anamorphosis (images depicted in such a way as to render them unrecognizable unless viewed from a specific angle). Such tricks of perspective were tremendously popular throughout Europe into the middle of the seventeenth century. A taste for acromegalic deformations is very evident in the work of Maerten van Heemskerck and Lucas Cranach the Elder.

Mannerist gesticulation is nowhere more apparent than in the works of certain Dutch masters. The study of posture dominates the art of Bartholomeus Spranger and the whole school of Haarlem, as well as the schools of Utrecht and Prague.

Everywhere artists sought in their coloring the new, the bold, or the exquisite. Heemskerck's color effects were both as subtle and as daringly new as those of his Italian contemporaries. Like Bronzino, Frans Floris and Marten de Vos made use of very crude, almost acid tints which hover on the verge of vulgarity but leave an exquisite impression of freshness. Certain portraitists, such as Adriaen van Cronenburg and Ludger Tom Ring the Younger exploited the effects of a juxtaposition of only two or three arrestingly pure colors.

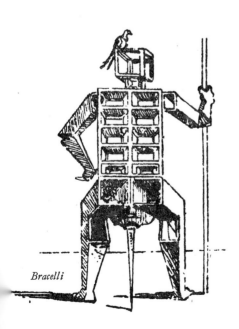

Bracelli

Finally, a concern with the evocation of atmosphere was shared by painters everywhere in the sixteenth and early seventeenth centuries. The painting of night scenes began in the Netherlands with Geertgen tot Sint Jans and Dirk Vellert, triumphed in Italy with Luca Cambiaso and Caravaggio, and returned to the north with Gerrit Honthorst and Georges de La Tour. Fires in the night were a regular feature of Flemish painting, from Hieronymus Bosch to Pieter Bruegel the Younger. Impressions of stormy twilights are to be met with in the works of Nikolaus Manuel Deutsch and Albrecht Altdorfer even before they appear in the paintings of such Italian masters as Dosso Dossi, Lelio Orsi, or Tintoretto, and they reappear in Spain with El Greco.

The common denominators of all European art in the Mannerist epoch are by no means limited to stylistic forms. The themes which preoccupied European painters between 1520 and 1620 were equally widespread. Every artist from Rosso to Spranger made great use of mythology, a theme which appears banal to us today but which, in the context of the emergence from the Middle Ages, must have provided a most powerful source of inspiration for all poetic artistic expression. Northerners and Italians shared the same taste in subject matter for everything strange, eccentric and fantastic. They all cultivated ambiguity and were not afraid of the mysterious and the macabre. Both northerners and Italians delighted in erotic subjects, and in the works of both there can be seen a strong current of perversion: equivocal young boys, lewd old women, lascivious old men, scenes of incest and provocative, sadistic representations of virgin martyrs were most common throughout European art in the sixteenth century. Both Italians and northerners made use of fantastic architectural and natural settings. These enchanted dream worlds appear in the works of Italian artists such as Tintoretto and Niccolò dell'Abbate, as well as in the paintings of Albrecht Altdorfer, Joachim Patinir, El Greco, Antoine Caron de Beauvais or Monsù Desiderio.

If we are to call the painters of the Florentine school of about 1520 such as Parmigianino, Pontormo and Rosso Mannerists, is it not logical to give the name Mannerists to all the European painters who, from about 1520 to about 1620, developed the same "manners?" The painters in Switzerland, the Flemish and Dutch painters of the 1520's known as Romanists, the Danube School, the School of Fontainebleau, Tintoretto and his studio, El Greco, the School of Haarlem, the School of Utrecht, and the School of Antwerp of about 1600, the painters of the court of Lorraine, the School of Augsburg, the group of painters who worked for the Emperor Rudolf II in Prague, many of the followers of Caravaggio, and the northern still life painters of the early seventeenth century all constitute, together with the Florentine painters of the 1520's and the generation of artists which succeeded them in Florence, varieties of a vast European movement dominated by the quest for style and by the poetic strangeness of the themes adopted.

A movement as vigorous as Mannerism naturally embraced more than one form of artistic expression.

Mannerist Architecture, Sculpture and Literature

Architecture throughout Europe during the sixteenth and early seventeenth century shared certain basic principles of design and decoration which clearly constituted a Mannerist architectural style. The Palace of Charles V at Granada by Pedro Machuca (active from 1517–1550) and the sacristy of San Lorenzo in Florence by Michelangelo are both works of Mannerist architecture. In its play with form, Mannerist architecture reveals the same preoccupation with style which we have noted in the painting of the epoch. We will here limit ourselves to one stylistic analogy between Mannerist architecture and painting. The use of ambiguous forms and a play of perspective was as common in architectural design as it was in painting. The curious effect produced by the spiral staircase of the architect Vignola (1507–1563) in the Palazzo Farnese at Caprorola near Rome, and the ingeniously foreshortened perspective of the stage of the Teatro Olimpico in Vicenza by Andrea Palladio (1508–1580) are typical examples. Even the false perspective colonnade in the Palazzo Spada at Rome, although executed as late as the mid-seventeenth century by the great Baroque architect Francesco Borromini, is typically Mannerist in conception.

Sculpture of the Mannerist period shared very closely the stylistic principles and idiosyncracies of the painting of the epoch. Some of the most important figures of the Mannerist movement were both painters and sculptors. Certainly much of the sculpture of Michelangelo may be classified as Mannerist. The stucco decorations of Rosso Fiorentino at the Palace of Fontainebleau are of a style similar to his paintings. These stuccos by Rosso had a great formative influence upon the painters among his following. So close was the relationship between sculpture and painting that when we say Mannerist painting is sculptural, we might equally add that Mannerist sculpture has often a draughtsman-like quality. The works of

ALEXANDER M. DARIVM VLT: SVPERAT
CÆSIS IN ACIE PERSAR: PEDIT: CM. EQVIT
VI RO XM. INTERFECTIS. MATRE QVOQVE
CONIVGE. LIBERIS DARII REG: CVM M. HAVD
AMPLIVS EQVITIB: FVGA DILAPSI. CAPTIS.

many Mannerist sculptors find perfect parallels in the works of Mannerist painters with whom they were associated. The delicate elegance of the nymphs of the French sculptor Jean Goujon (active 1540–1568) recall the paintings of Primaticcio with whom he worked at Fontainebleau. The sculptor Giovanni da Bologna (1524–1608) worked at the court of the Dukes of Florence with Bronzino, and his bronzes are comparable in their elegance to the painted figures of Bronzino. The bronzes of the Dutch sculptor Adriaen de Vries (about 1560–1627), vie in erotic power with the paintings of Bartholomeus Spranger, who like de Vries was working at the court of Rudolf II in Prague.

The literature of the epoch is also permeated with Mannerist tendencies—an important fact which has only recently been given due attention. Throughout Europe, the period stretching from the close of the fifteenth century to the mid-seventeenth century is characterized by a series of literary movements which accentuate *style*. The late *rhétoriqueurs,* the *Pléiade* group and *Les Précieux* in France, *Marinismo* in Italy, *culteranismo* and *conceptismo* in Spain, euphuism and concettism in England, *Sinnspiel* and *Schwulst* in Germany, were all movements which cultivated verbal acrobatics. Rare words, metaphors, circumlocutions, inversions, antitheses, assonances, unusual rhythms were in favor, and in general a greater interest was shown in the "manner" of expression than in the idea expressed. All these features are essentially Mannerist.

There is such a fundamental difference between the basic forms and methods of painting and literature that it is difficult to base a far-reaching comparison on these general grounds. On the other hand, the themes utilized allow one to perceive in detail the very close relationship between writers and artists. In both categories, we find the same avid interest in mythological subjects, the same underlying melancholia, the same preoccupation with the strange, the bizarre, and the occult, the same encyclopedic curiosity about the individual features of the universe, its animals, its plants and its natural phenomena, the same erotic disquiet and, more than disquiet, not infrequently perversion and sadism. The writers of this period, Jacopo Sannazaro, Ariosto, Francesco Berni, Tasso, Rabelais, Ronsard, Rémy Belleau, Théodore d'Aubigné, Girard de Saint-Amant, Camões, Góngora, Spenser, Shakespeare, Webster, Milton, Friedrich von Spee, and Andreas Gryphius are all Mannerists to a greater or lesser extent. In literature as in painting, Mannerism provides the common stylistic denominator of a period which would otherwise defy classification.

The Place of Mannerism in the Development of European Culture

The rediscovery of Mannerism entails a radical revision of the history of European art.

Hitherto, Mannerism has always been treated negatively, as an anti-classicism, a reaction to the immediately preceding classicism of the High Renaissance, or as an intermediary period between the High Renaissance and the Baroque. Now, however, it presents itself as an eminently positive phenomenon, indeed as a phenomenon which is far richer, broader and more stable than either the Baroque or the classicism of the High Renaissance and in addition a phenomenon which is far more clearly defined than either of these.

All the elements of Romantic art and of Contemporary art are already embodied in Mannerism. It is infinitely closer to us today than the Baroque. In fact it is now the Baroque which appears to us as a short lived event in the development of Western culture, a pause between Mannerism and Romanticism.

Equally, it is not difficult to see that the Mannerism of 1520's was a direct continuation, not of the Middle Ages, as Dvořák thought, but of the era of disquiet and change which followed the Middle Ages. The undulating lines of early fifteenth century sculpture, the extravagances of the so-called Manueline architectural style in Portugal, the expressionism of Matthias Grünewald and Hieronymus Bosch, the surrealist precision of Roger van der Weyden and Hugo van der Goes, Signorelli's gaunt, angular male nudes, Botticelli's elegant delicacy, Mantegna's tricks of perspective… what are all these if not Mannerism before its time? The Italian classicism of the early 1500's was a fleeting moment between the Mannerism of the fifteenth and sixteenth centuries. Moreover, was not the classicism of the early 1500's itself simply one manner among others? Oswald Spengler, in his *The Decline of the West*, includes classicism—consciously studied classicism based on the works of antiquity—among the manifestations of the decadence of a civilization. The word decadence implies a debatable value judgment, but it seems fairly evident that classicism as a deliberate archaism is the sophistication of an epoch that has outlasted its original impetus. All conscious classicism is really pseudo-classicism. Mannerism concerns itself with style or, more precisely, styles: the ephemeral classicism of 1500 could very well be one style among others in the vast repertory of styles that is Mannerism.

Flotner

In addition, the frontier between the classicists of 1500 and the Mannerists of 1520 is extremely fluid. Leonardo was one of the inventors of light and color effects, the celebrated *sfumato*; Michelangelo is held to be the father of sculptural painting and the *linea serpentina* (serpentine line); Raphael, in his paintings for the Vatican Loggie, launched the fashion for "grotesques." So we see that the three principal painters of the High Renaissance were already involved in what was to be the Mannerist adventure. The classicism of 1500, as well as the Baroque of a later era, shows itself to be a particularly unstable phenomenon lacking well defined frontiers, whereas the historical importance of Mannerism asserts itself firmly. Far from being a brief gap between High Renaissance and Baroque, Mannerism constitutes the basic factor in the history of late fifteenth, sixteenth and early seventeenth century art.

Viewed in this new perspective, the general development of European culture takes on a far simpler and more coherent appearance. It is now possible to see that the period of the late Middle Ages, or if one prefers, the Early Renaissance, Mannerism, Romanticism and, beyond Romanticism, Expressionism, Symbolism, Surrealism, and other modern movements, constitute a single phenomenon, characterized by the quest for style. The phrase "quest for style" inevitably implies a diversity of styles. The unity of art, from the fifteenth century to our own times, lies in the rapidity of change: a new style scarcely has time to establish its supremacy before it finds itself out of date, and so the quest for something new starts all over again. This perpetual change may be interpreted variously as freedom or restlessness, as originality or instability. It is true in a certain sense that modern art is anticlassical. However, in this respect it is in opposition not to the pseudo-classicisms—the synthetic classicisms—of the early 1500's or the period about 1660, but to that time of genuine equilibrium in Western civilization represented by the twelfth and thirteenth centuries. Until about the twelfth century, the forces (ideas, feelings, aspirations) which molded Western civilization had not yet achieved an adequate form of expression. The possibilities of Western civilization still outdistanced their means of expression. This is perceptible, for example, in Romanesque sculpture and painting which one can describe either as technically clumsy or, on the other hand, as teeming with possibilities. Romanesque art of the eleventh and twelfth centuries is, as has frequently been said, an archaism, but it also gives the impression of constantly leading up to an unrealized objective—its forces converging upon a still undiscovered formula. Whence its impression of simplicity, cohesion and perfect stylistic unity. Between the twelfth and the thirteenth centuries there arrived the moment when the *means* of expression of the culture more or less caught up with the *need* for expression. This moment was not identical in the different arts, and for architecture and sculpture it came rather earlier than for painting. But as soon as a system of culture acquires certain elements of maturity, every aspect of that culture is influenced thereby. The moment of maturity is an ideal point, a narrow crest behind which the opposite slope falls away sharply. With the onset of the fourteenth century, we can find elements in Western culture symptomatic not of decadence (such a value judgment is, we repeat, perfectly arbitrary) but of post-maturity. Thus contrary to the situation in the Romanesque period, in the twelfth and thirteenth centuries it was the means of expression which overreached the intentions of the culture. During the period of pre-maturity, specifically that of Romanesque art, the relative poverty of the means of expression ruled out any diversity. All available energies were converging toward the still undiscovered formula, resulting in an extremely compact and stable style. But once the principal theme becomes dominant, a culture can continue to survive only by varying this theme. During the period of pre-maturity, unity is the essential virtue and any originality would seem diabolical or crazy, while in the period of post-maturity maintenance of unity would betoken stagnation and death. The differences which were yesterday's heresies are tomorrow's symbols of progress and vitality. This is true of all aspects of civilization, applying equally to its spiritual, social, economic, as well as artistic existence. Until the twelfth or thirteenth century, Western art existed and thrived through a process of concentration. From about the fifteenth century onwards, it existed and thrived through a process of self-renewal which involved in a certain measure the constant overturning and dispersion of its own entity. Change, originality, freedom were thenceforward the rules of cultural continuity.

The rhythm of change has obviously not been uniform between the fifteenth century and the present day, and it is precisely the differences of rhythm which permit us to chart the successive stages of this long period of change.

During the fifteenth century occurred a period of liberation of technique and an avid interest in experimentation. In another sense this liberation may be considered the conquest of realism. A brief pause occurred at the very end of the fifteenth and beginning of the sixteenth century. An almost semi-superstitious admiration for Greco-Roman masterpieces, the desire to rival the models of antiquity, channeled artistic expression into the search of a single absolute. Diversity and experimentation were arrested. But the pause of the High Renaissance was very brief. Soon antiquity itself was once again simply a new theme with variations. From the 1520's onward the movement of freedom and experimentation regained momentum, producing that explosion of diversity, that exaltation of formal, intellectual and moral freedom —permissiveness, even—which we call Mannerism.

Then came a second pause. In every field, religious, political, social, and cultural, the forces of tradition attempted to stabilize Western civilization. In the field of art, this reaction showed itself in the shape of the Baroque classicism of about 1660. For a century or so, order gained the upper hand over freedom, rules over originality, will over imagination.

However, the forces of change were by no means dead. Throughout the later seventeenth and early eighteenth centuries, we can detect their secret activity beneath the thin veneer of classicism. By the middle of the eighteenth century they had returned to the surface with the pre-Romantic movement and have retained a dominating position ever since. The great number of schools which have succeeded each other during the last hundred years—Romanticism, Realism, Symbolism, Naturalism, Expressionism, Cubism, Surrealism, and Abstractionism—provide the quite unequivocal sign of the triumph of the forces of motion. Of course, Romanticism, Symbolism, Surrealism, etc. are not simple different names for Mannerism, but they are, like Mannerism, distinct moments of one same continuity. To be unaware of Mannerism is to condemn oneself to being unaware of this continuity of change which is the outstanding fact of Western culture during the last five centuries.

The rehabilitation of Mannerism is not, then, simply one of those ephemeral fashions which are so frequent in art appreciation. On the contrary, it is a real revolution in the history of art, which henceforth presents itself in an entirely different perspective.

This new perspective has thrown open a vast and hitherto scarcely inventoried treasure house. It has enabled us to discover, during the course of the last few decades, the true dimensions of artists such as Nikolaus Manuel Deutsch, Albrecht Altdorfer, Jan Gossaert Mabuse, Maerten van Heemskerck, Lucas van Leyden, Rosso Fiorentino, Domenico Beccafumi, Hernando Yañez, Jacques Bellange and so many others who, although never totally forgotten, had nevertheless been relegated to places far below their worth. With this new light on Mannerism we have also been able to rediscover a whole host of talented painters who really had been forgotten, such as Jean de Gourmont, Antoine Caron de Beauvais, Luca Cambiaso, Giuseppe Arcimboldo, Monsù Desiderio, and Baugin. But the reader has only to glance through the biographical dictionary at the end of this volume to get some idea of the incredible number of Mannerist painters who are seldom or never mentioned in standard histories of art. Who, outside of the specialist, knows the names of Bracelli, Lucas de Heer, Adriaen van Cronenburg, Sebastian Stosskopf, Lorenz Stoer, Benedetto Pagni, or Jacopo Zucchi? Yet, as the reader may judge by studying the works reproduced in this volume, each of these painters is more than a mere artist of talent: he has brought something genuinely original to the enrichment of culture.

There is also no doubt that besides these excellent Mannerist artists already recovered from oblivion there remain many more who are still completely unknown. One has every reason to believe that private collections and provincial museums hold many surprises in store for us. It is one of the special charms of Mannerism that it still allows us the pleasure of discovery.

Selections from
mannerist poetry
II

EDMUND SPENSER »THE FAERIE QUEENE«

There he him found all carelessly displaid,

In secrete shadow from the sunny ray,

On a sweet bed of lillies softly layd,

Amidst a flock of Damzelles fresh and gay,

That round about him dissolute did play

Their wanton follies and light meriments:

Every of which did loosely disaray

Her upper partes of meet habiliments,

And shewd them naked, deckt with many ornaments.

And every of them strove with most delights

Him to aggrate, and greatest pleasures shew:

Some framd faire lookes, glancing like evening lights;

Other sweet wordes, dropping like honny dew;

Some bathed kisses, and did soft embrew

The sugred licour through his melting lips:

One boastes her beautie, and does yield to vew

Her dainty limbes above her tender hips;

Another her out boastes, and all for tryall strips.

Book II, Canto 5: 285–302

*M*OSTRA IL BEL PETTO le sue nevi ignude,

Onde il foco d'amor si nutre e desta:

    Parte appar delle mamme acerbe e crude,

Patre altrui ne ricopre invida vesta:

    Invida, ma s'agli occhi il varco chiude,

L'amoroso pensier già non arresta;

    Che non ben pago di bellezza esterna,

    Ne gli occulti secreti anco s'interna.

TORQUATO TASSO GERUSALEMME LIBERATA

*H*ER BREASTS, two hills o'erspread with purest snow,

Sweet, smooth and supple, soft and gently swelling,

    Between them lies a milken dale below,

Where love, youth, gladness, whiteness make their dwelling;

    Her breasts half hid, and half were laid to show;

Her envious vesture greedy sight repelling:

    So was the wanton clad, as if thus much

    Should please the eye, the rest unseen the touch.

TORQUATO TASSO   JERUSALEM DELIVERED

Canto IV, verse 31

LE BEAU TETIN

Tétin refaict, plus blanc qu'un œuf,
Tétin de satin blanc tout neuf,
Tétin qui fais honte à la Rose,
Tétin plus beau que nulle chose
Tétin dur, non pas Tétin, voyre,
Mais petite boule d'Ivoire,
Au milieu duquel est assise
Une Fraise, ou une Cerise
Que nul ne voit, ne touche aussi,
Mais je gage qu'il en est ainsi:
Tétin donc au petit bout rouge,
Tétin qui jamais ne se bouge,
Soit pour venir, soit pour aller,
Soit pour courir, soit pour baller:
Tétin gauche, Tétin mignon,
Tousjours loin de son compaignon,
Tétin qui portes tesmoignage
Du demourant du personnage,
Quand on te voit, il vient à maints
Une envie dedans les mains
De te taster, de te tenir:
Mais il se fault bien contenir
D'en approcher, bon gré ma vie,
Car il viendroit une autre envie.
O Tétin ne grand ne petit,
Tétin meur, Tétin d'appetit,
Tétin qui nuict et jour criez:
Mariez moy tost, mariez!
Tétin qui t'enfles, et repoulses
Ton gorgias de deux bon poulses,
A bon droict heureux on dira
Celluy qui de laict t'emplira,
Faisant d'un Tétin de pucelle,
Tétin de femme entière et belle.

CLÉMENT MAROT   41

Clément Marot   The Lovely Breast

Charming breast, whiter than egg-shell,
Breast of fresh white satin,
Breast which puts the Rose to shame,
Breast that nothing earthly matches,
Firm Breast—why, no, not Breast
But little Ivory globe,
With on its center poised
A Strawberry or a Cherry
Nor seen nor touched by any man,
Yet I will wager it is thus:
Breast, then, with rose-red tip,
Breast which never bestirs itself
Either in coming or in going,
Either in running or in dancing:
Sweet and delicate left breast
Standing ever apart from its playmate,

Breast which amply recommends
The individual's other parts—
When they behold you, many feel
An itching in their hands
To fondle you, to hold you cupped:
But they must all foreswear
To reach you, however great the urge,
For fear a different itch assail them.
O Breast that is not big or small,
Breast so ripe, so appetizing,
Breast which, night and day, cries out!
Marry me soon, marry me!
Breast which swells so that each breath
Adds two inches to your bosom,
Well may we say he will be happy
Whose fortune is to fill you full of milk,
Making of a pure young virgin's breast
The Breast of a woman, whole and beautiful.

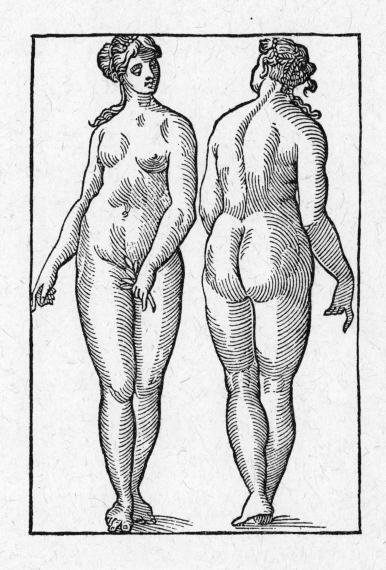

La fiera gente inospitale e cruda
alla bestia crudel nel lito espose
  la bellissima donna così ignuda,
come natura prima la compose.
  Un velo non ha pure, in che richiuda
i bianchi gigli e le vermiglie rose,
  da non cader per luglio o per dicembre,
  di che non sparse le polite membre. LUDOVICO ARIOSTO

L'ORLANDO FURIOSO CANTO X, VERSE 81

And thus the caitives left her all forlorne,
With nothing but the rocks and seas in sight,
  As naked as of nature she was borne,
And void of succour, and all comfort quite.
  No vaile of lawn as then by her was worne,
To shade the damask rose and lilies white,
  Whose colours were so mixt in every member,
Like fragrant both in July and December.

Esprit des beaux esprits, vagabonde inconstance,
Qu'Eole, roi des vents, avec l'onde conçut,
Pour être de ce monde une seconde essence,
Reçois ces vers sacrés à ta seule puissance,
Aussi bien que mon âme autrefois te reçut.

. . .

Doncques, fille de l'air, de cent plumes couverte,
Qui, de serf que j'étais, m'a mis en liberté,
Je te fais un présent des restes de ma perte,
De mon amour changé, de sa flamme déserte,
Et du folâtre objet qui m'avait arrêté.

Je te fais un présent d'un tableau fantastique,
Où l'amour et le jeu par la main se tiendront,
L'oubliance, l'espoir, le désir frénétique,
Les femmes et les vents ensemble s'y verront.

Les sables de la mer, les orages, les nues,
Les feux qui font en l'air les tonnantes chaleurs,
Les flammes des éclairs plus tôt mortes que vues,
Les peintures du ciel à nos yeux inconnues
A ce divin tableau serviront de couleurs.

Pour un temple sacré je te donne ma belle,
Je te donne son cœur pour en faire un autel,
Pour faire ton séjour tu prendras sa cervelle,
Et moi, je te serai comme un prêtre fidèle
Qui passera ses jours en un changé immortel.

O spirit of lovely spirits, inconstant wraith,
Whom Aeolus, king of winds, fashioned from foam
To be a second essence of this world,
Receive these verses sacred to your power,
Just as I once received you in my soul.

. . .

So, feather-covered daughter of the air,
Who gave me freedom, bondsman that I was,
I give you as a gift my loss's remnants,
My altered love, its flame now almost quenched,
the playful thing who held me in her thrall.

I give you as a gift a most strange picture,
Depicting love and play, each hand in hand;
Forgetfulness, and hope, and crazed desire,
Women and winds shall meet in this frame.

Sands of the sea, tempests and floating clouds,
The fires that harbinger the sky's hot thunders,
Lightning flashes no sooner seen than gone,
The sky's paintings unknown to human sight,
All these will serve as colors for this picture.

I give you my fair one for a sacred temple,
Give you her heart as altar to be used,
For your abode you shall possess her brain,
And I shall be a faithful priest to you
Passing his days in an immortal change.

The Social
Background
of Mannerism

An Age of Change

Style of a hundred manners, consecrated to diversity, Mannerism was the product of an age of change.

During the last decade of the sixteenth century, a great Italian poet and philosopher, the Dominican Tommaso Campanella, wrote: "Our century contains more history in its hundred years than the entire world in its previous four thousand years..." He was not exaggerating. In the space of a hundred years, the very forms of the earth, the sky and time itself had been entirely transformed, the social order had been destroyed, and the truth of the Christian religion called into doubt. All this may seem unexceptional by today's standards, but in that age the impact must have been staggering. We cannot possibly understand the thought and art of the sixteenth century unless we can recreate in our minds the atmosphere of confusion and upheaval in which the men of this era lived. This atmosphere naturally affected most deeply those who were most sensitive to it: the writers and the artists.

In 1492, Columbus landed on an island on the other side of the Atlantic Ocean. This discovery of the New World was only the first in a whole series of discoveries which were to occur at intervals throughout the sixteenth century. In 1513, Vasco Núñez de Balboa sighted the Pacific Ocean. In 1519, the soldiers of Cortés entered the Aztec capital and were dazzled by its glory. In 1532, Pizarro, making his way down the west coast of America, stumbled upon a whole new civilization, the Inca empire. In 1542, Cabrillo, marching northward, reached California, and thought it to be Eldorado. Between 1534 and 1542 Jacques Cartier explored Labrador and the estuary of the St. Lawrence; and in 1585, Raleigh set foot in Virginia.

In the East, the achievements of explorers were no less astonishing. In 1498, Vasco da Gama saw the fabulous land of India for the first time. In 1509, Affonso d'Albuquerque took over Malacca, opening the approaches to the kingdoms of Pegu, Champa and Siam to the Portuguese. In 1540, some Portuguese pirates made a raid upon the coast of Nanking; in 1551, Francis Xavier arrived in Kyoto.

To achieve some idea of the amazement and almost sacred awe experienced by those living at the time of these heroic exploits, one has only to turn to the stirring saga of Camões's *Os Lúsiadas* or Mendes Pinto's *Peregrinaçao*. Pinto, half merchant, half pirate, spent twenty years in the Far East. From 1537 to 1558 he visited Siam, Cambodia, China and Japan. For Pinto, the Far East was a world so different from the one to which he was accustomed that it might equally well have been a dream world. Quite naturally, he wrote of his adventures in just the sort of tone one might use to recall one's dreams. His book often gives the impression of being a fairy-tale rather than a traveller's journal.

One can well understand that those who remained home must also have dreamed while reading the voyagers' accounts, studying the prints which reproduced landscapes and scenes of life in these distant lands, handling the precious stuffs, the curious objects, and the unknown substances brought back by the travellers. For sixteenth century man, these voyages opened wide the gates of the marvellous.

At the same time, while the voyagers were enlarging the earth, the astronomers were expanding the sky. In 1543, Copernicus's *De Revolutionibus Orbium Coelestium* appeared. As Montaigne commented in his *Apologie* for Raimon Sebond, all at once we find that the sky and stars have stopped "rocking to and fro" and that it is the earth which moves. In 1610, Galileo made use of a theory of a Dutch optician, Hans Lippersheim, to invent a telescope capable of enlarging surfaces nine hundred times. With this he was able to see Jupiter's satellites, Saturn's rings, and the Milky Way, each of its innumerable stars a world analogous to our own solar system as described by Copernicus. Galileo expressed his wonder and astonishment in his *Sidereal Messenger,* which was greeted enthusiastically by Campanella and Kepler, and which had enormous repercussions. We are so used to the Copernican vision of the universe that it is difficult for us to imagine the shock which this discovery must have entailed for the intellectuals of the time. We can get some impression of it, however, by considering the opposition it encountered. When in 1616 the Holy Office forbade Galileo to teach that the earth moved around the sun, it was defending not only a passage in the Bible but also man's traditional idea of the world.

Cambiaso

At the same time that man was exploring terrestrial and celestial space, he was also in the process of discovering the past. Although the initial impetus to humanism had been given during the fifteenth century, it was not until the sixteenth century that the extension of printing and teaching allowed the cultured classes in general to study and absorb the work of the classical authors. History, which had hitherto been a sealed book, suddenly took on a familiar appearance, and man started to acquaint himself with the adventure of humanity. This new consciousness of history was only one aspect of a far more generalized process of establishing domination over time. Clocks, which were still very rare at the end of the fifteenth century, came into general use among the aristocracy and the bourgeoisie from about 1550 onward. In the new iconology, the clock became the attribute of Temperance and Prudence. A drawing in the Musée du Louvre attributed to Veronese, *The Triumph of Virtue over Vice,* even makes the clock the symbol of virtue: the good use of time depends upon its being exactly measured. The calendar too was at last gradually unified. In France, for example, the beginning of the year had previously varied from province to province—in one district it might be Christmas, in another the Feast of the Annunciation, in yet another, Easter. By a decree of Charles IX in 1564, the beginning of the year was finally fixed throughout the kingdom as being the first of January. This was followed in 1582 by Pope Gregory XIII's great reform, in which he re-established a concordance between ecclesiastical and true chronology, and determined for posterity a more accurate lunar cycle. Thus history, the clock, and the calendar combined to endow Europe with a unified sense of time—the very basis of modern life.

It may be seen then that the Mannerist era was marked by extremely comprehensive changes in every field. In the field of technology, for example, the sixteenth century was marked by positive progress in the mineral and metallurgical industries. Between 1510 and 1630 the production of iron in Europe doubled. A rapid increase in the number of windmills and water-mills resulted in the use of more efficient sources of non-animal energy. The era witnessed inventions of scientific instruments and discoveries in mechanics. The pulley, microscope, and telescope were invented and investigations were made into suspension and transmission systems, the motion of projectiles, and the laws of hydrostatics. In the economic field, the opening up of overseas markets initiated a tremendous expansion in commerce, while the inflow of precious metals facilitated trade. Financial capitalism appeared on the scene in the shape of joint stock companies, stock exchanges and public credit. In the social field, the bourgeoisie established itself finally as the dominant social class of the new era. One banking family, the Medicis, became sovereign princes, while another, the Fuggers, were powerful enough to decide imperial elections. In the political field, feudalism gave way to absolutism, and the doctrine of realism elaborated by Machiavelli compelled recognition.

An era dominated by such a fever for change was not likely to be overly respectful toward religious traditions. Certainly heresies had flourished throughout the Middle Ages, but in the last analysis they had all finally been defeated. In the sixteenth century however, a heresy managed not only to survive but to establish itself firmly. But the victory of the Reformation signified more than the triumph of Luther's particular ideas; it was equally the triumph of the spirit of diversity. Lutheran theology was only one form of a vast movement of free thought which included widely divergent tendencies: natural philosophers such as Pietro Pomponazzi, Jerome Cardan and the whole Paduan school, Christian communists such as Thomas Münzer, the Anabaptists, and Tommaso Campanella, sceptics such as Étienne Dolet and Montaigne, critics of the Scriptures such as Erasmus and Johann Reuchlin, sensualists such as Bernardino Telesio, and syncretists such as Giordano Bruno. In a certain sense, Luther's Reformation was already a Counter-Reformation, since it stabilized religious tradition by retreating to a more easily defensible position, but the fact remains that it gave a tremendous impetus to the dispersion of Christianity. Unity of faith was now a thing of the past and the era of religious diversity began. With the schism between Protestantism and Roman Catholicism, the way was open for every form of intellectual daring.

The Reformation, political and social shifts, humanism, and astronomical and geographical discoveries were closely linked phenomena sharing an identical spirit of change. It is this spirit which characterizes the century better than any particular doctrine. Mannerism too was part of this spirit. In every ideological field, Western civilization was passing from the era of stability to the era of movement.

| Civilization of Movement and Contradiction | An era of great changes is always complex. Civilization does not advance at the same pace on every front: the approaching future jostles the retreating past, while the most delicate progress may still be tainted with barbarism. Hence these inexplicable contrasts, this reckless exuberance, this strange diversity with which the Mannerist age confronts us. It was the age of sensuality. Rabelais sang the praises of food and drink; Aretino codified erotic pleasure in a work illustrated by Giulio Romano; the courtesan became an essential element of society; the female body was an idol sung by poets in its most intimate details and invoked by painters as their central theme. Yet it was also the age of mysticism, the age which gave us the *Castillo interior* of Saint Theresa of Avila, the *Cantico espiritual* of Saint John of the Cross, the *Méditations* of Jean de Sponde, Jean-Baptiste Chassignet's *Méspris de la Vie*, English metaphysical poetry, the religious eclogues of Spee and Silesius, the diaphanous Virgins of Luis de Morales (known as the "divine" Morales), and El Greco's ecstatic saints. |

It was the age of lust for life. Navigators launched themselves haphazardly onto unknown seas. Handfuls of men departed to conquer immense empires on the other side of the world. Merchants gambled their entire fortunes on a single speculation. The humanists stuffed themselves with learning. The princely courts, hotbeds of intrigues, duels, and passionate love affairs, were overflowing with a life and optimism, symbolized in the paintings and sculptures of innumerable sporting gods and heroes which adorned the princely palaces and gardens. On the other hand, it was an age of anxiety. Modern melancholia was born in these times. Dürer, Michelangelo, Pontormo, Dosso Dossi, Giovanni della Casa and Emperor Rudolph II were all essentially melancholic types. Christian existentialism, with its doctrine of justification by faith, was created, and so was the first romantic hero, Hamlet.

It was the age of Platonism (Pietro Bembo, Jean du Bellay, Edmund Spenser), but it was also one of the periods during which women were the least respected (see Brantôme and the Italian storytellers). When a place was captured, rape was the order of the day and any city desirous of escaping this fate had to pay a special indemnity. In France, during the Wars of Religion, the troops had the habit of taking captured women along behind them; Strozzi, cousin of Queen Catherine de' Medici, widow of Henri II, is reported to have ordered drowned in the Loire eight hundred Protestant women whom the French soldiers had brought with them for amusement, and who were becoming a nuisance.

It was a time of renewal for the ideals of chivalry (Ariosto, Tasso) but it was equally the epoch of Machiavellian politics and double-dealing.

It was the age of the triumph of homosexuality. A painter glorified himself with the surname Sodoma; a king, Henri III, appeared at parties dressed as a woman; the greatest poets —Shakespeare and Michelangelo—wrote marvellous sonnets to their male lovers. Yet at the same time it was the age of Genevan puritanism and the prudery of the Counter-Reformation.

The Mannerist period was an age of delicacies and refinements. The fork was invented; courtiers perfumed themselves; manuals of etiquette proliferated; pastoral poetry and art was much in vogue. But it was also an age of the most fearsome brutality; torture was raised to one of the fine arts. The works of the Italian storytellers and the Elizabethan dramatists reflect this compassionless cruelty.

This epoch also witnessed the birth of rationalism. Some people questioned the authority of Aristotle, others wanted to trust nothing except experience, yet others even went so far as to criticize the Scriptures. But it was equally an age of fantastic credulity. Witch-burning was at its peak (one hundred in one year in the diocese of Como alone); books on demonology abounded; sovereigns such as Catherine de' Medici, Francesco I of Florence, and the Emperor Rudolph II were enthralled by alchemy and astrology.

Solis

Mannerism, Art of an Age of Evasion

Mannerist art shares in these contradictions and expresses them. It would thus be dangerous to explain this art by a single factor or by a single series of factors, for such an approach would allow us to perceive only one aspect of reality.

A widespread viewpoint treats Mannerism as a phenomenon of evasion by art, a dream renouncing an intolerable reality. The beginning of the sixteenth century was in fact a moment of crisis for Italy. The discovery of the sea route to India by way of the Cape had diverted the Far East trade from Mediterranean. Almost simultaneously, the Protestant revolt (in 1521, Luther solemnly burned the Papal Bull in Wittenberg) had called into question the primacy of Rome. Thus, in the spiritual as well as in the material field, Italy saw her power and prestige gravely jeopardized. More seriously still, her very liberty was threatened by the opposing greeds of the Holy Roman Emperor Charles V and François I of France. In 1527, the Imperial troops sacked Rome, and for more than three centuries Italy was destined to remain to all intents and purposes a foreign colony.

The capture of Rome in particular appeared to contemporaries as a sign of the times. Charles, Duc de Bourbon, Constable of France, who was in command of the Imperial forces, was mortally wounded in the attack. The soldiery, left to its own devices, broke out in unbelievable excesses. Palaces and churches were ruthlessly pillaged; priceless artistic treasures were destroyed; convents became the stage for cruel orgies. The Protestant German mercenaries, rigged out in sacred adornments, amused themselves by performing sacrilegious masquerades. Cardinals were paraded ignominiously through the streets while their tormentors rained blows upon them. The basilica of St. Peter's was turned into a stable. François Guichardin reported that the city was filled with the cries of raped Roman ladies and nuns, and that unfortunates were being systematically tortured to force them to reveal possible hidden treasure. To crown these horrors, plague broke out. The glorious dream of the Renaissance crumbled in a scene from hell and Erasmus could write: "In truth, this was not the end of a city but the end of a world."

Many artists died from ill-treatment or from disease. Those who survived retained nightmarish memories of their experiences. Rosso not only lost all his possessions, his paintings, drawings and engravings, but was forced by the victorious enemy to help clear goods out of warehouses, half naked, like a slave. Parmigianino, slightly more fortunate, escaped actual physical maltreatment, but he too was completely stripped of his property. Vincenzo da San Gimignano after untold perils succeeded in escaping from Rome and regaining his natal town of San Gimignano, but died there soon after from fatigue and depression. Giulio Clovio, taken prisoner by the Spanish, vowed that if he survived he would take holy orders; he eventually entered the religious brotherhood of Regular Flagellants in Mantua. Baldassare Peruzzi, robbed and beaten, escaped with great difficulty and arrived in Siena clad only in a shirt. Giovanni Antonio Lappoli was in the same state of disarray when he contrived to flee from the holocaust, and Vasari relates that he barely recovered from the shock of his terrible experiences.

According to those who view Mannerism as an art of evasion, it was in this atmosphere of catastrophe that Mannerism was born. Likewise it is considered to have spread to the rest of Europe in the wake of the disquiet created by the division of Christianity, the perpetual wars, the intellectual servitude imposed by absolutism and the Counter-Reformation, and the uneasiness of the economy due to the influx of New World money. Like Romanticism two centuries later, Mannerism would thus constitute a phenomenon of evasion. Refinement, subtlety, pastoral idylls, chivalry, erotism, and occultism were just so many compensations for the disappointments of real life. Disgusted with the world, the artist simply withdrew into himself and lived and worked in his ivory tower.

This explanation of Mannerism as an evasion seems to find confirmation in the treatises on aesthetics which appeared towards the end of the sixteenth century, notably Raffaello Borghini's *Il Riposo* (1584), Giovanni Battista Armenini's *De Veri Precetti della Pittura* (1587), Giovanni Paolo Lomazzo's *Idea del tempio della pittura* (1590) and Federigo Zuccaro's *Idea de' Pittori, Scultori ed Architetti* (1607). All these works applied the Platonic theories of the *Idea* to art, and proclaimed that beauty did not reside in exterior objects but in the artist's mind and soul. Thus creating a work of art should never be reduced simply to copying nature ("They make me laugh," wrote Armenini, "those who think that everything natural is good"). Nature for the artist was merely the pretext for exteriorizing the *Idea* of beauty which the artist already possessed within himself. Given that God had created a pre-established harmony between man's ideas and the aims of the universe, according to Platonic philosophy it followed that the artist's idea does coincide to a limited extent with reality. But the way to encounter reality in its profoundest, truest essence was not to waste one's efforts in vain imitation of exterior aspects. The artist must look inward, into his own soul, to find the *disegno*

Vanni

interno (as Zuccaro called it), the pre-existing interior design which he was then to embody on canvas or in marble. As Michelangelo said: "One paints with the brain, not with the hand" ("Si pinge col cervello, non con la mano"). The work of art is a pure creation by man, paralleling the universe which is a creation of God's.

This idealist theory of art found in the writings of the sixteenth century is indeed evidenced by many of the stylistic phenomena of Mannerist painting. The tendency to abstraction of forms in certain works by Rosso and Daniele da Volterra or in the cubist drawings of Luca Cambiaso are certainly examples of a *disegno interno*. The primacy of artistic vision over reality is powerfully demonstrated in Pontormo's expressionistic deformations, or the surrealistic dream-like worlds created by Monsù Desiderio. Generally, *maniera*, or style and originality, are concepts which enter easily into the idealist theory of art.

It is pertinent to remark, however, that this idealist aesthetic was evolved during the closing years of the sixteenth century and the very early years of the seventeenth century, when Mannerism had long been established and was already on the decline. More than the spirit of the 1520's this aesthetic theory reflects the abstract and reactionary climate of the Counter-Reformation and the triumph of absolutism.

It is equally pertinent to note that the idealist theoreticians were often not painters themselves. Borghini was a theologian, and Armenini, the author of a rather unimpressive painting of the *Assumption*, abandoned art for the priesthood.

If it behooves us to mistrust the explanation which artists themselves give of their own work, how much more warily still should we approach the explanation made on their behalf by others. These philosophically oriented systematizations only too often involve preoccupations wholly divorced from art.

The late sixteenth century idealist theories of art do help us to understand certain aspects of Mannerism, especially its preoccupation with style. It would be absurd to disregard them. But we should still be careful not to confuse Mannerist art with the theories of Lomazzo or Zuccaro. Even though certain Mannerist painters shared these ideas, ideas are one thing and painting is another. The excessive importance which many historians today ascribe to the idealist theories of about 1600 tend to sanction the impression that the Mannerist artist was an introverted individual and that Mannerist art lacks contact with reality. In other words Mannerism was above all an art of evasion. It is unquestionable that evasion was an important aspects of Mannerism but it does not account for Mannerism's vitality, its love of life, its sensuality, its independence, or its curiosity about the universe. The sack of Rome in 1527 does not explain the Mannerism which flourished in Antwerp during an era when that city was at the peak of its prosperity. The decline of Italy in the sixteenth century does not explain the very marked Mannerist tendencies already evident in Italian art in the late fifteenth century. Mannerism is essentially a complex phenomenon and any simple explanation is a false explanation, or an incomplete explanation. Although it is important to emphasize Mannerism's idealism and studied search for evasion, it is equally important to bear in mind its optimism, belief in progress, and spirit of revolt.

The naturalist current during the sixteenth century was at least as strong as the idealist, Platonic current, and historically it is more important because it constituted an innovation. An epoch is characterized by what it initiates, not by what it carries over from previous epochs. The first master of naturalist thought was Pietro Pomponazzi (1492–1525), the most illustrious representative of the philosophical school of Padua. In his *De Immortalitate Animae*

Mannerism,
Art of an Age of Progress

(1516), under the pretext of analyzing the possible thought processes of a philosopher lacking the light of Revelation, he demonstrated that the intellectual soul (which cannot think without images) is not separable from the sentient soul and must consequently disappear together with the latter; man has no supernatural end, his end is humanity. His *De Naturalium Effectuum Admirandorum Causis*, published in 1556, affirmed that the laws of the universe are immutable, gave natural explanations to miracles and prodigies, and rejected demonology and sorcery as superstitions. François Rabelais—an admirer of Pomponazzi—proclaimed in his *Quart Livre* (1552) that nature is goodness and anti-nature is evil. Jerome Cardan (1501–1576), one of the founders of algebra and mechanics, described in his *De Coelo* the intimate ties binding soul and body. Bernardino Telesio (1509–1588), who is often classed among the Platonists, was nevertheless the author of a book with the significant title *De Natura Rerum*; he believed that the soul is corporal, and that animals as well as men possess souls.

None of these philosophers, of course, ever openly professed free thought. But their adversaries—Protestant as well as Catholic—certainly did not allow themselves to be convinced. In 1536, Calvin, in his *Christianae Religionis Institutio*, accused the Paduan philosophers of teaching "that religion had anciently been contrived by the cunning and subtlety of a few people, so that by this means they might keep the simple populace in a state of modesty." Ten years later, in his *Treatise concerning scandals*, Calvin attacked Rabelais and other jokesters: "These dogs," he wrote graciously, "...find it easy to say that all religions have been forged in the brains of men, that we hold there to be a God because it pleases us to believe so, that the hope of life everlasting is designed to amuse idiots, that all that one speaks of Hell is said in order to terrify small children."

Thanks to their relative prudence and to powerful patrons, Pomponazzi, Cardan, and Telesio managed to escape the stake. But at the close of the century, in the climate of the Counter-Reformation, repression hardened and free thought began to acquire its martyrs. We will mention just two cases. Giordano Bruno (1548–1600) was a Dominican who upheld a sort of naturalist pantheism, and preached the coming of a universal religion from which all fanaticism would be excluded. He led an adventurous existence which took him through the whole of Europe, pursued continually by the indiscriminate persecutions of Catholics, Anglicans, Calvinists, and Lutherans. Finally, after six years of imprisonment in Venice, he was transferred to Rome and handed over to the tribunal of the Holy Office, but he still refused to repudiate his writings and was burnt at the stake. Lucilio Vanini (1585–1619), a defrocked Carmelite, a talented physician and brilliant conversationalist, attacked authority by means of irony: his wittiness anticipated Voltaire. But an overly enthusiastic work, *De Admirandis Naturae Arcanis* (1616) caused his downfall. He was condemned by the Parliament of Toulouse to have his tongue cut out and to be burnt alive. At the stake, just before the executioner's pincers tore out his tongue, he cried out his atheism.

Despite repression, atheism made steady progress at the beginning of the seventeenth century. The proof of this lies in the increasing number of apologetical works. In France, for example, a single year—1624—saw the appearance of Father Garasse's *Curious doctrine of the Wits of this Day* and Father Mersenne's *Impiety of Deists, Atheists and Libertines of this Day*... Mersenne claimed that there were fifty thousand atheists in Paris in 1624. Doubtless he was exaggerating, but it is quite certain that free thought did exercise a powerful influence on French intellectual life of the period: the two of the best writers of the final phase of Mannerism in France, Théophile de Viau and Cyrano de Bergerac, were both freethinkers.

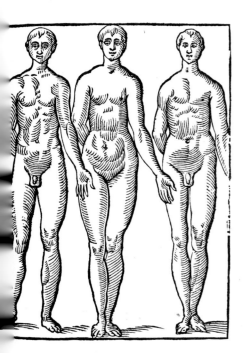

An unequivocal sign of the naturalism of the Mannerist era lay in the fresh interest brought to bear by intellectuals upon the problems of man's material situation in this temporal world. Since the start of the Reformation, several of Luther's disciples had proclaimed that the religious reformation should be accompanied by a social revolution. One of these, Thomas Münzer, founded an egalitarian community at Altstedt in 1523, in which the members' possessions were shared equally among all, following the practice of the early Christians. Münzer taught that Jesus Christ had set all men free; therefore it was unthinkable that there should be serfs. He believed that the Gospel was incompatible with a class society in which some had all and others nothing, and he preached the establishment of a "Fraternal City" from which exploitation and falsehood would be utterly banished. These doctrines spread with lightning speed. The inhabitants of Mülhausen in Franconia, stirred up by the preaching of a former Cistercian monk, Heinrich Pfeffer, drove their magistrates out of town and called on Münzer for help. Münzer drew up a charter in twelve articles for the town, a most curious document anticipating most of the principles of the French Revolution of 1789. By the end of 1524, a large part of southern Germany was in a state of insurrection, and Münzer succeeded in mustering a peasant army of forty thousand men. But Luther, far from applauding this attempt to establish the reign of God upon earth, declared that "neither injustice, nor tyranny can justify rebellion" and called upon the secular arm to act against the seditious mob: "Now," he exclaimed, "has come the time of naked steel, the time of wrath... Therefore, beloved Lords, deliver us, save us, exterminate..." The beloved lords had no need at all of such spiritual encouragement; Catholics and Protestants buried religious differences to make common cause against the present danger, and in 1525 the bands of peasants, lacking arms and military skill, were literally exterminated at Frankenhausen.

The subsequent repression was atrocious. Nevertheless, Münster's followers, the Anabaptists (so-called because they believed in the necessity of a second baptism when the person had become adult and could choose his religion) multiplied throughout southern Germany and then spread their influence northward, as far as Kiel and Riga, Sweden and the Netherlands. In 1534, two Dutch Anabaptists, John of Leyden (Johan Beuckelszoon) and Johan Matsys, seized the town of Münster from its bishop-prince and set up a kind of communist theocracy. The town was not retaken by the episcopal troops until eight months later. John of Leyden was captured, paraded throughout Germany in an iron cage, then torn to death with red-hot pincers.

A great number of naturalist sects had existed in the Netherlands since the fifteenth century—the Men of Understanding, the Adamists, the Society of the Poor, and the Picards. All these sects looked forward to the return of the Golden Age, the reopening of the terrestrial Paradise, and a reconciliation between spirit and flesh. They often practiced nudism as a symbol of original innocence, and sometimes even polygamy. These sects must inevitably have had a great influence upon Flemish art of the period. It seems fairly certain, for example, that Hieronymus Bosch was an Adamist, and that his *Garden of Delights* (Madrid, Prado) was conceived as an altar-piece for an Adamist chapel. In the prevailing atmosphere of religious turmoil Anabaptism found a fertile soil. In Antwerp, a working-class roofer named Loiet founded an Anabaptist church about 1525, which recruited most of its members from among artisans but also included a few noblemen. In 1545, Loiet was burnt at the stake.

Peasant revolts had occurred throughout the Middle Ages. The new factor in the sixteenth century was the alliance between progressive ideas and popular revolts. Tommaso Campanella was the most striking example of this alliance. A Dominican monk from Naples,

PAX

BEATI PACIFICI QVONIAM
FILII DEI VOCABVNTVR

he had become an admirer of Telesio's philosophy, endorsing in particular the latter's pan-physical naturalism. But he did not restrict himself to theorizing. In 1599 he attempted to provoke an uprising in Calabria against Spanish domination, and to found a theocratic republic whose principles he set out in his *City of the Sun* (written in 1602, published in 1623). Campanella's original idea was that society must be revitalized by a more just and more rational economic organization. In his words: "There are seventy thousand souls living in Naples, and yet there are hardly ten or fifteen thousand workers among this number. And thus these latter wear themselves out and kill themselves for work which is beyond their powers to perform. In the City of the Sun, labours being equally allocated, no one will work for more than four hours a day." This work moreover, far from being a curse, would be a pleasure since everyone would work according to his vocation, in whatever field he was most competent. It is not surprising that the nineteenth century reformers, Saint-Simon, Charles Fourier and Louis Blanc, hailed Campanella as a precursor of socialism.

The Calabrian plot failed. Campanella was thrown in prison and spent the next twenty-seven years in irons. He was interrogated by torture no less than seven times, and one particular session of torture lasted for thirty-five hours. Campanella not only survived these torments but even composed some admirable verses during his captivity. It is worth quoting his sonnet on the People:

"The People is a fickle, brutish animal, ignorant of his strength, enduring blows and heavy burdens. He lets himself be lead by a feeble child whom he could knock down with a single push.

"But he fears this child and obeys his every whim; he does not know how much he is feared, nor that his masters are preparing for him a stupefying potion.

"How unbelievable! He strikes himself and chains himself with his own hands; he fights and dies for a single coin from among the many he has himself given the king in taxes.

"Everything between heaven and earth is his, but he does not know it..."

This revolutionary agitation in the sixteenth century is sufficient evidence that the Mannerist era was not, as some historians believe, simply an era of evasion. It was in fact also an era of faith in the future of humanity. In looking at Mannerist painting, we must bear in mind that it is the product of a century exhilarated by the discoveries of its explorers, a century to which Copernicus had opened up the infinite riches of the heavens, a century ardently curious about the variety and dissimilarity of the universe. As Montaigne put it, it was a century enamoured of human justice and progress. When considering the art of the Mannerist period, one should remember that at the same moment of history, Campanella dared to present man as "a second god..., for he commands the depths, ascends into the sky without wings, counts all moving bodies and measures them..., understands the nature of the axis and fixes its laws, like a god." To neglect this aspect of the sixteenth century is to fail to appreciate the basic elements of joyous sensuality, rich variety, independence, and even insubordination in Mannerism. Let us repeat once again that Mannerism is not a simple phenomenon; it is idealism, but it is also naturalism; it is evasion, but it is also joy of life and hope in the future.

Having reviewed the broad historical influences working on Mannerist art, it is perhaps appropriate at this stage to examine the particular conditions under which it developed.

In times of stability, culture tends to retain its traditions over a considerable period of time, and finally diffuses itself evenly through the different strata of society, bringing its works of art more or less within the reach of all; the artist works for the masses as much as for the

**Mannerism
and the Princely Courts**

upper classes. In times of change, however—of which the Mannerist era is an example—culture is in a state of constant development and modification, so that a particular form of art does not have the time to popularize itself before it is succeeded by another form. Under these circumstances, the cultural division between different social groups within a nation becomes considerable and culture becomes almost exclusively an *avant-garde* culture, accessible only to a minority or minorities. Restricted groups of enlightened amateurs, with whom the artist often has direct contact, obviously have a far greater influence on him than would a larger public. Mannerism was strongly marked by the fact that it was not only an art directed toward a minority, but specifically an art emanating from princely courts.

The sixteenth century princely court was a highly selective, closed society, a sort of artificial paradise into which nothing vulgar or displeasing was allowed entry. Often, the princely palace was situated outside the town, in a forest or rural retreat (the Palazzo del Té, Hesdin, Fontainebleau, Pratolino, and the Villa d'Este are good examples). In any case, it was isolated from the outside world by gardens, which surrounded it with an enchanted landscape in which man's imagination enriched the existing beauties of nature. For instance, the visitor wandering down the park walks of Hesdin (the residence of Maria of Austria, Regent of the Netherlands) would find himself confronted with all sorts of surprising or terrifying spectacles: *trompe-l'œil* illusions, automatons, and grotesque or macabre statues. Fontainebleau possessed, among other marvels, a fairy grotto—the work of Bernard Palissy—encrusted with shell-work, stalactites, marble, as well as agate and other precious stones. In the gardens of Pratolino, nine miles from Florence, one could admire artificial grottoes, hydraulically operated automatons, and the statue of a giant in whose hollow stomach several men could easily stand together. An Englishman, Fynes Moryson, who visited Pratolino at the end of the sixteenth century, described with astonishment "a cave solidly built but constructed artificially in such a way that, on entering, one has the impression that great blocks of stone are about to tumble onto one's head; when one turns on a faucet certain statues of nymphs, driven by water pressure, emerge from the cave, then disappear into it again, as though they were alive, and without the water being visible; in this cave, too, which appears as though it were on the point of falling into ruins, are to be found statues of all kinds of animals, the strangest that I have ever seen." The ruins of Prince Orsini's park at Bomarzo near Viterbo, with statues of giants and monsters, give a good idea of the "world apart" which a Mannerist residence constituted.

In this world apart there moved a humanity apart, a humanity perfumed and painted, adorned with jewelry, clothed in fabrics woven from gold and silver thread, people whose lives were one long holiday compounded of balls, tourneys, plays and banquets. But the courtier did not differ from ordinary mortals merely in his dress and his luxury. Baldassare Castiglione has left us, in his *Cortegiano* (1528), a long list of the talents which a good courtier should possess. The courtier was versed in all the sports (riding, fencing, wrestling, swimming); he had, in addition to strength and skill, acquired grace and elegance of movement by practicing dancing and gymnastics. But physical training was not enough: "I desire," wrote Castiglione, "that our courtier should be more than averagely instructed in belles-lettres..., that he should know not only the Latin language, but also Greek..., that he should be well versed in the works of the poets... and, furthermore, that he should be proficient in writing both prose and verse, principally in the vernacular; in addition to the satisfaction which this will bring him, he will thus always have a subject of conversation with the ladies who, in general, adore these things. I should not be satisfied were my gentleman not also musician, able not only to read a score but also to play several instruments. There is also one thing which I consider of great importance and which our gentleman should on no account neglect: that is a talent for drawing and a knowledge of painting."

These requirements were by no means fanciful. Every sixteenth century gentleman knew how to sing in parts the complicated polyphonic compositions of the time. Many were competent to take their place in amateur orchestras or quartets. A Paduan musician, Antonio Rota, prospered by giving lute lessons to the gentry. Henry VIII of England and Mary Stuart both composed attractive airs for the lute. Every gentleman was also something of a poet: François I wrote some charming ballads and Charles IX corresponded in verse with Ronsard. It appears that the princes themselves began studying drawing only at the beginning of the seventeenth century: Louis XIII made some competent sketches, and Prince Rupert was a master of mezzotint engraving. From the sixteenth century onward, however, *dilettanti* abounded in Italy, and many noblemen were also amateur painters. Several monarchs devoted themselves to a study of the sciences. Duke Francesco I of Florence and Emperor Rudolph II both spent much of their time in their laboratories or private museums. All the princes collected books, antiquities, and contemporary paintings.

But what typified court life above everything else was good manners. Our modern rules of good breeding were first elaborated and codified in the princely courts of the sixteenth century. In a little book destined to create an extraordinary impact, *Il Galateo* (1558), Giovanni della Casa—who was also one of the finest Mannerist poets—explained to a young gentleman how he should behave in society. He advised him not to overeat, to cough and sneeze as silently as possible, not to blow his nose into his table napkin, to satisfy his physical needs discreetly and, above all, never to talk about them, not to laugh too loudly, not to make grimaces while speaking, not to raise his voice immoderately, to walk lightly, not to swing his arms, to dress according to the fashion but soberly, not to make extravagantly prolonged compliments, and not to use coarse language. These recommendations may seem to us today to be rather superfluous, but they clearly were not superfluous at the time: *Il Galateo* was translated into every European language and was followed by innumerable imitations.

There is more than a verbal affinity between good manners and Mannerism. They both take for granted a preoccupation with ritual and with established manners, a certain negation of reality because of its inherent coarseness, a certain effort to construct artificially a strictly human world. Good manners and Mannerism belong to the same moment of civilization, the moment when man, having fulfilled his immediate needs, began to seek refinement. It is natural that good manners and Mannerism should have been born in the same era and in the same social environment.

The princely courts were, so to speak, the forcing houses of Mannerism. The Papal courts of Clement VII (pope from 1523 to 1534) and Paul III (pope from 1534 to 1549) employed Parmigianino, Rosso Fiorentino, Giulio Romano, Perino del Vaga, Daniele da Volterra, Giorgio Vasari, and Bacchiacca. From Rome, Giulio Romano went to Mantua where he had a large following in his works for the court of Federigo II, Gonzaga. Jacopo da Pontormo, Angelo Bronzino, Giorgio Vasari, Poppi, Jacopo Ligozzi, and a great many others worked for the Dukes of Florence. The Duke of Urbino employed Girolamo Genga, Giovanni Battista Franco, and Taddeo Zuccaro. Bartholomeus Spranger, Hans von Aachen, Matthäus Gundelach, Josef Heintz, Giuseppe Arcimboldo and Joris Hoefnagel all worked at the court of the Emperor Rudolf II at Prague. Philip II of Spain called a group of Italian Mannerists to work for him, including Luca Cambiaso, Pellegrino Tibaldi, and Federigo Zuccaro. The School of Lorraine, which included Jacques

Callot, Jacques Bellange, and Claude Deruet, flourished at the court of the Dukes of Nancy. The School of Fontainebleau is remarkable as a pure creation of the French kings of the House of Valois. In 1530 François I called Rosso Fiorentino to work for him at Fontainebleau. In 1532 Rosso was joined by Francesco Primaticcio, who held the position of first importance at Fontainebleau after the death of Rosso in 1540. In 1552 Niccolò dell'Abbate arrived at Fontainebleau, and together with Primaticcio decorated the Gallery of Ulysses in the Palace. The French sculptor Jean Goujon, as well as the most important French painters, Jean Cousin the Elder and Antoine Caron de Beauvais, formed their style on that of Rosso and Primaticcio. Antoine Caron de Beauvais and the so-called Master of Flora worked with Primaticcio and Niccolò dell'Abbate in the Gallery of Ulysses. Among the many other French artists who were formed at Fontainebleau, we should mention the painter of many elegant female portraits who is perhaps to be identified with François Bunel the Younger.

We have mentioned only the most remarkable cases, but the list could be extended with many secondary courts which played an important role in the Mannerist movement. It is difficult to establish a classification with so changeable and cosmopolitan a movement as Mannerism, but it does seem that the least misleading classification is in terms of the courts at which the painters worked.

Certainly, the princely courts did not create Mannerism, but they greatly helped it to develop and they had a tremendous influence on it. It was these princes and prelates who assured the triumph of a profane art which, by its very nature, was far more versatile than religious art. It was these patrons who created the whole climate of distinction, elegance, and concettism in which Mannerism grew up. It was they, above all, who authorized the extraordinary moral liberty—one might well say license—of sixteenth century art. The courts were above the law and above current morality. Sexual perversion—which was one of the essential characteristics of Mannerism—could never have been treated openly had the princes themselves not condoned scandalous conduct. At the court of Henri III, the ladies-in-waiting of the Queen Mother, Catherine de' Medici, presided over the details of a banquet naked under diaphanous robes which left their breasts uncovered. At another banquet, during the same reign, the guests all dressed in garments of the opposite sex, men masquerading as women, and women as men. The equivocal flowers of Mannerism sprang from this rich, decaying soil, and flourished.

However strong the influence of aristocratic minorities upon Mannerism may have been, one should nevertheless not forget the role played by other classes of society.

The fifteenth century had seen the constitution of the bourgeoisie as an independent social class, distinct from both the common people and the nobility. By the beginning of the sixteenth century, there already existed a great number of bourgeois citizens who were no longer semi-uncouth upstarts, but could boast of a family tradition and several successive generations which had enjoyed ease and luxury. They had built richly furnished, sumptuous residences for themselves in the great trading cities. They had acquired seats in the town councils, their sons attended the universities, and their business dealings with foreign countries gave them access to international culture. A new aristocracy—the aristocracy of money—was in the process of being born. In many cases, especially in the Netherlands and Italy, it was already eclipsing the real nobility. The discoveries of maritime explorers brought in new commodities, opened up new markets, and hastened the flow of precious metals to Europe (the annual production of silver, which was about two tons in 1500, had increased tenfold by 1550). Thus, the

Mannerism
and the Bourgeoisie

means of exchange were multiplied and an intense commercial activity was set in motion, the chief beneficiary of which was the bourgeois. Huge commercial and financial fortunes were founded at this time, and certain dynasties of merchants became as powerful as the princely families.

The classical example is that of the Fuggers of Augsburg. Originating as a modest weaving enterprise in Augsburg, the house of Fugger started turning its activities toward commerce during the fifteenth century. The Fuggers travelled to Venice to buy cotton, silk, and spices which they then resold in Germany, the Netherlands, and Denmark. They soon added banking to these activities, specializing in exchange and credit operations. From the beginning of the fifteenth century, the Fuggers were the Vatican's principal bankers. It was they who assumed the responsibility of transferring to Rome the sums of money collected in northern Europe for "Peter's Pence." It was they who established the sale of indulgences, incurring the wrath of Luther who, playing on the words "Fuggerei" and "Wucherei," made their name synonymous with usurer. In 1519, it was Jacob Fugger—head of the house since 1510— who financed the election of Charles v as Holy Roman Emperor. Since the votes were available to the highest bidder, François i of France, who was the wealthiest of the candidates, felt sure he would win the contest. But François i reckoned without the cunning of Charles v, who offered letters of exchange from the Fugger bank, payable only if he himself was elected. Jacob Fugger hazarded the sum of 850,000 florins in this operation—a fabulous amount for those times. When the Emperor created difficulties about repaying him, he was perfectly justified in writing to him, in 1523, that "it is known and evident that Your Majesty would not have obtained the Roman crown without me." But Fugger himself was at the head of a veritable financial empire. He had branches of his bank throughout Germany, as well as in Rome, Venice, Antwerp, and Lisbon. Apart from the mines of central Europe, he owned the concession for the quicksilver deposits in Almaden and the silver mines of Guadalcanal. Unable to pay his debts, Charles v ceded to Fugger the farm-rents of the lands of the *Maestrazgos* (orders of chivalry) in Spain, so that Fugger found himself in control of almost a third of Spain's territory. A chronicler of Augsburg, Clement Senders, wrote with pride: "The names of Jacob Fugger and his nephews are known in all kingdoms and lands and even in pagan countries. Emperors, kings, princes, and lords have sent him ambassadors, the Pope has acknowledged him and greeted him as his very dear son, cardinals have risen at his approach."

This family of financial princes led a truly princely existence. They owned palaces crammed with pictures, tapestries, gold plate and jewelry, antiquities and exotic objects. They maintained private zoos supplied with animals by their own overseas trading expeditions. They possessed vast aviaries and aquariums, described admiringly by Montaigne in the *Journal* of his voyage to Italy. They were enlightened patrons of the arts: they had their bank in Venice decorated by Giorgione, and the one in Rome by Perino del Vaga. The Fuggers surrounded themselves with humanists and artists. Thanks to them, Augsburg became one of the capitals of European Mannerism, the "Swabian Rome."

The Fuggers, however, were simply the most distinguished members of a whole clan of businessmen and financiers who, behind the façade of emperor, kings, and princes, were fast becoming the real masters of Europe: these families had names such as Welser, Rehlinger, Imhoff, Tucher, Salviati, Strozzi, Grimaldi, Chigi, Kleberger and Van Spangen. Like the Fuggers, most of them were intelligent amateurs who not only commissioned Mannerist works for themselves, but what is more important still, introduced a taste for such painting among the bourgeoisie. Ultimately each one of the great commercial centers also became an artistic center. The artistic schools of the princely courts were now supplemented by the groups or schools of artists who worked in these wealthy cities: the School of Nuremberg with Albrecht Dürer, Hans Baldung Grien and, later, Wenzel Jamnitzer; the School of Augsburg with Christoph Amberger, Hans Rottenhammer, and Georg Pencz; the School of Antwerp, or more accurately, the Schools of Antwerp (the first, at the turn of the century, with the so-called Romanists, the second, around 1600 with the circle of Jan Bruegel the Elder); the School of Utrecht with Abraham Bloemaert and Joachim Wtewael; the School of Haarlem with Karel van Mander, Cornelis Cornelisz van Haarlem, and Hendrick Goltzius. There is no doubt that many of these artists also worked for the courts, and that on the other hand, many court artists also belonged to a city school. Nevertheless, however complicated the interrelationship may have been, it is unquestionably possible to distinguish in Mannerism, running alongside the aristocratic trend, a specifically bourgeois trend, particularly in Germany, Switzerland, and the Netherlands. This bourgeois Mannerism was, generally speaking, more extremist than the courtly variety. It was both closer to the whimsical oddness of the dying Middle Ages and to the eccentricities of the yet unborn Romantic movement. Elegance of gesture is often so exaggerated here that it becomes affectation (as in the work of Herri met de Bles or Cornelis Engelbrechtsz). In some works by Pieter Aertsen, Jan van Hemessen, and Joachim Beuckelaer, expressionism is transformed into a systematic vulgarity, which reminds one of some of the German Expressionist painters of the 1920's. The erotic element often becomes very crude, sometimes obscene, as for instance in some works of Urs Graf, Barthel Beham, or Georg Pencz. Subtlety easily degenerates into a bookish pedantry, indulging in ultracomplex symbolism and obscure anecdote. There was a pronounced tendency to glorify everyday objects; hence the many kitchen scenes and still lifes. Finally, as has happened throughout the history of art, bourgeois civilization, being essentially an urban civilization, began to feel a tremendous need for escape into nature. From this era and this social environment there sprang the first pure landscape artists: Joachim Patinir, Jan Bruegel the Elder, Gillis van Coninxloo, Gillis Mostaert, Paul Bril, and Roland Jacobsz Savery.

Mannerism and the People

During the sixteenth century, there existed a small number of cultured members of the working class who played a more important role in the development of art than may be imagined. The great mass of the people, consisting of the peasantry, was of course completely excluded from any culture, let alone that promulgated by the Mannerists. But among the apprentices and journeymen living in the large towns at that time, there existed a true proletarian élite.

The most original religious movement of the sixteenth century, Anabaptism, was conceived among the urban proletariat, and its prophets and leaders were workers. Many workers made great efforts to acquire learning, some with remarkable success. It may suffice to mention the example of a certain Thomas Platter, from a peasant family, who was first a servant in Alsace, then a rope maker in Basel. He became so fired with enthusiasm for humanism that without aid he learned Latin and Greek and became a distinguished Hebrew scholar. One should also remember that many painters were of modest origin. Jan Gossaert Mabuse was the son of a bookbinder, Jean Bellegambe the son of a cooper, Sodoma the son of a shoemaker, Salviati the son of a weaver; Girolamo Genga, in his youth, was an apprentice wool-stapler, and Girolamo da Carpi a plasterer; Maerten van Heemskerck, Giorgione, and Pieter Bruegel the Elder all belonged to peasant families; Domenico Beccafumi herded sheep as a child. We may well conjecture that the work of these artists reflects, to some extent, the invironment from which they emerged.

LUDGER TOM RING THE YOUNG
Three Peacoc
Munster, Landesmuseu

66

The populus of the towns also had a certain influence on the evolution of taste. Certainly, sixteenth century workingmen had not the opportunity to really become acquainted with contemporary painting, since most of the artistic output of the time was hidden away in princely palaces or the mansions of the wealthy middle class. It should be remembered however, that it was these laborers who formed the bulk of the audience at the frequent parades, triumphs, and carnivals which were such important events in the town life of the epoch, and were also important factors in molding the forms and feelings of Mannerism.

For the carnival of 1511 in Florence, for instance, Piero di Cosimo prepared a spectacle of the Triumph of Death. The triumphal car was draped in black cloth with skulls and cross-bones painted on it, and was drawn by coal-black oxen. Within the car stood a colossal figure of Death, scythe in hand, while around him were covered tombs which opened from time to time, and from which emerged figures disguised as skeletons. After the chariot, the train of the dead followed with horsemen shrouded in black, mounted upon the most miserable horses that could be found. The horses were led by attendants wearing death's head masks, and bearing black torches or waving large black standards. The whole spectacle was accompanied by funereal music. "The novelty and the terrifying character of this lugubrious spectacle," reported Vasari, "filled the whole city with awe and admiration. Although at first sight one would not have thought it appropriate for the carnival, yet, because of its novelty...it gave no small pleasure to the people. For, just as they sometimes prefer sharp and bitter food, so in their pastimes, they are attracted to horrible things." Allegory, strangeness, and a taste for the macabre—this popular masquerade surely contained a few of the elements which characterize Mannerism.

The most celebrated Mannerist artists worked for these popular spectacles. Andrea del Sarto, the sculptor Baccio Bandinelli, and Jacopo da Pontormo all decorated allegorical chariots for the masquerade organized by the religious brotherhoods of Florence to celebrate the election of Leo X in 1513. The chariot representing the Golden Age, designed by Pontormo, was particularly admired. Unfortunately, the child representing the Golden Age—the son of a baker who had been paid ten crowns to play the role—died soon afterwards from the effects of the gold paint with which he had been covered from head to foot. The solemn entry of Leo X during that same year was the pretext for further popular celebrations, for which Francesco Granacci invented a new type of entertainment in which a cavalcade was interspersed with short theatrical scenes. For the celebrations of the marriage of Francesco I de' Medici to Johanna of Austria (1565), Vasari prepared a series of allegorical chariots, the sketches for which are preserved in the Uffizi at Florence. Even funerals were the occasion for sumptuous artistic spectacles. The Academy of Painters and Sculptors in Florence executed a catafalque of extraordinary magnificence for the funeral of Michelangelo in 1564, to which each artist contributed the best of his talents. Such a vast crowd jostled to glimpse this marvel that it was necessary to leave it in position for several weeks.

Florence specialized in allegory, while in Rome, popular spectacles were less refined, but there too they bore the stamp of the bizarre. For the annual carnival in Rome, it was the habit to organize races run by old men, children, donkeys, and buffaloes, tournaments between young girls, and other similarly outrageous games. In Venice, the canals were used to full advantage, and the spectacles featured nymphs and tritons swimming around gilded vessels. At the festival of the *Sempiterni* in Venice in 1541, a huge round structure symbolizing the universe was constructed on the Grand Canal, and a floating ballet was organized inside it.

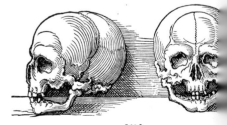

In Paris, where the religious miracle plays had been forbidden in 1548, the great popular spectacles were now the royal entries into the city. Among the artists who worked in preparation for these events in France should be mentioned above all Antoine Caron de Beauvais. But nowhere were such royal entries more splendidly mounted than in the Netherlands. When Charles v made his entry into Antwerp in 1521, two hundred painters contributed to the erection of a triumphal archway which was greatly admired by Albrecht Dürer, who was staying in the town at the time. "This work," he noted, "is composed of four hundred arches, each one forty feet wide, spaced along each side of the street where the royal procession is to pass. The disposition is very beautiful and the arches are each to have two platforms upon which dramatic performances will be enacted. All this is most beautiful and most splendid and the whole cost, in work of carpentry and of painting, is four hundred florins." When the young king appeared, escorted by five hundred mounted nobles clad in velvet and silk, a file of young women drawn from the cream of society advanced to meet him. They represented the nymphs and nereids of a mythological triumph, and as such, were almost naked, wearing simply a diaphanous gauze around their loins. As he passed along this line of pretty girls, Charles v modestly lowered his eyes, but Dürer was less prudish and wrote to his friend Melanchthon that this scene recalling pagan antiquity had filled him with enthusiasm. No doubt it was appreciated equally by the boisterous folk of Antwerp.

The humble villagers and townsfolk flocked to these spectacles and derived the greatest pleasure from them. Thus they were not completely cut off from Mannerist art. They certainly helped to influence it, as every public influences the works designed for it. Nor were these ordinary citizens completely cut off from Mannerist literature. Let us bear in mind that the pit audience which applauded *Romeo and Juliet* and *Hamlet* was composed essentially of artisans, journeymen, and craft apprentices. It is true that the pit comprised only a part of the public, but it was an important part, and the author was bound to take it into account. The constant success which Shakespeare's plays encountered in the theaters of London, while the gay wits of the time remained cool in their reaction, is proof enough that the ordinary townsfolk were quite capable of appreciating what was best in Mannerist literary production.

Painting Becomes a Liberal Profession

In this era of general change which constituted the Mannerist epoch, the social situation of the artist was also undergoing a decisive evolution. The painter of the Middle Ages was an artisan, the member of a corporation or guild. In the fifteenth century, a few painters doubtless won great honors, but the great majority of artists still led an extremely modest and unobtrusive existence. During the sixteenth century, however, painting, previously considered a manual trade, became a liberal profession. Often Mannerist artists were men of a high culture and by no means simple craftsmen. Many were not limited to a single technique or talent: Rosso, Giorgio Vasari, Pellegrino Tibaldi and Salviati were architects as well as painters; Michelangelo was not only sculptor, painter and architect, but also the foremost poet of his day. According to Vasari, Correggio sang and played the lute "divinely," and Parmigianino was as talented in music as in painting.

In reaction to the guilds which left them little field for individualism, artists had begun to form brotherhoods. These were religious or charitable associations usually placed under the patronage of Saint Luke, and they were organized on a considerably more liberal basis than the guilds. During the second half of the sixteenth century the first academies were formed, which served to emancipate the artist from the servitude of the guilds and raised painting from a craft to the rank of a liberal profession.

The first of these early academies was the *Accademia del Disegno* of Florence. It was founded in 1561 by the Grand Duke Cosimo I de' Medici, at Vasari's suggestion, to provide training for young artists and to permit the artists to sever connections with the guilds. This academy had as its patrons Michelangelo and the Grand Duke himself. The president was Vincenzo Borghini, a critic and not an artist. Most of the members of the *Accademia del Disegno* were painters but it also included some eminent noble and ecclesiastic amateurs. In 1571 members of this academy received an official dispensation from belonging to a guild and obeying guild regulations.

It is important to note at this point that because Mannerist artists formed academies, we are not justified in accusing them of academicism in the sense that this word now has for us. The concept of academicism which was formed in reference to the pedantic and stultified art of the official national academies cannot be applied to Mannerism. The very foundation of these official academies post-dates Mannerism: the first national academies were not formed before the latter part of the seventeenth century. Eventually the authority of these official bodies reduced the teaching of art to a stale formula. Too closely associated with the authorities and the theoreticians, they systematically gave protection to an official style which was mediocre, priggish and devoid of imagination. It must be borne in mind that in forming academies the Mannerist artist had quite different aims, namely to win the artist greater freedom than he had known in the guilds and a more respected social and professional standing. The *Accademia del Disegno* in Florence, and more assiduously still the *Accademia di San Luca* in Rome, founded in 1593 by Federigo Zuccaro, served above all to further the social evolution of the artist. Thus, even if it is historically valid to trace the origin of the later, national academies of art back to Vasari and his generation, one must realize that the future evil consequences of the academies were totally unforeseen by the Mannerist artists, and the concept of "academic art" is diametrically opposed to the Mannerist love of freedom and diversity.

The artist's material circumstances kept pace with his new social standing. The most esteemed artists of the sixteenth century could command very high prices for their work. Raphael was paid 1,200 gold ducats for each of his *Stanze* in the Vatican; Michelangelo received 3,000 ducats for his ceiling in the Sistine Chapel; the Emperor Charles V gave Titian 1,000 crowns (crowns and ducats were equivalent at that time) for each picture he commissioned from him; Vasari received 2,000 ducats for his murals in the great hall of the Palazzo Vecchio in Florence. In addition, most artists of any importance held sinecures involving prebends or pensions: Benvenuto Cellini was a pontifical mace-bearer, Bramante and Sebastiano del Piombo were secretaries of the Seal of the Papal Bulls; Rosso had a fixed annual income of more than a thousand crowns from his prebend as canon of the Cathedral of Paris, together with the other offices bestowed on him by François I; Giulio Romano received a 1,000 ducat annual stipend from the Duke of Mantua; Vasari, at the Court of Florence, had an annual salary of 456 ducats; Paul III allotted Michelangelo a sum of six hundred crowns a year, payable out of a special toll set up on the river Po. These were considerable sums for that era. By way of comparison, it is of interest to note that in Rome in 1542 the steward of a princely house was paid only 120 crowns a year, the physician one hundred crowns, and the chaplain twenty-four crowns in addition to his upkeep. Many of the artists we have mentioned were thus in a position to lead lives of considerable luxury. Federigo Zuccaro had a palace constructed for himself. According to Vasari, Rosso "lived more like a prince than a painter." Francesco Primaticcio, created Abbé de Saint-Martin de Troyes, was a *grand seigneur* who was in a position, in his turn, to play the rôle of patron toward other less fortunate artists.

The artist had now become a gentleman. Julius III remarked that he would gladly have deducted several years from his own life if he could have added them to those of some great artist. Paul III declared, when Benvenuto Cellini was brought before him accused of murder, that such a man was above the laws. The artists, for their part, were fully conscious of their privileged status, and so permitted themselves considerable independence. On one occasion, Julius II had had Michelangelo expelled from the papal palace when he dared to raise the subject of payment. Michelangelo returned home and wrote to the Pope as follows: "Most Blessed Father, I have this morning been expelled from the palace on orders from your Holiness; therefore I am advising you that from now on, if you wish me, you will seek for me elsewhere than in Rome." Salviati, discontent because Pius IV had assigned some additional artists to assist him in his decoration in the Sala Regia of the Vatican Palace, abandoned the work he had so far accomplished and left for Florence without further word. That powerful figures should have tolerated and pardoned such behavior indicates sufficiently the extraordinary change that had taken place in the artist's social status.

The ennoblement of the artistic vocation, the rise in the value of works of art, the respect, even adulation which now surrounded the artist, were the outward and visible signs of a fundamental change in the concept of art and the artist. Hitherto painting was a craft learned through apprenticeship, but in the Mannerist period with rise of the romantic concept of genius, one was born a painter and each work of art was consequently a sort of miracle. It was these somewhat imprecise ideas that formed the basis of the speculations of such idealist theoreticians as Giovanni Paolo Lomazzo and Federigo Zuccaro, to whom we have already referred. According to their theories the spirit which conceived was more important than the hand which drew. A picture was considered to be an original vision rather than a material success. Far more important than any idealist theorizing was the very real triumph of originality and individualism. This whole volume is really a prolonged study of the originality of Mannerist painting. We wish at this point to demonstrate that lives of the painters of this epoch showed the same originality and individualism which so strongly characterized their works. This was the moment of history when the type of artist so celebrated by Romanticism first appeared on the scene: absent-minded, bohemian, eccentric, a willing scoffer at bourgeois respectability, but very often too, a recluse and a melancholic. Vasari's *Lives* are filled with examples of the curious ways of the Mannerist painters. Cristofano Gherardi was so careless of his appearance that he often put on his costume back to front, with the hood hanging down his chest; Duke Cosimo, having come across him dressed in this manner, had a robe of the finest cloth designed for him, which was exactly the same right side out, wrong side out, back and front. Piero di Cosimo, one of the precursors of Mannerism, flatly refused to allow his house to be swept or cleaned. He ate at any hour, whenever he felt hungry, and his garden was a wild jungle in which no branch was ever cut nor weed uprooted. The habits of certain Mannerist artists are not unsimilar to the behavior attributed to the Greenwich Village "beatniks" of today, or the self-styled existentialists of Saint-Germain des Prés. Vasari relates that the painter Jacopo da Sandro, known as Jacone, "had brought together a company or rather a band of friends who, under pretext of philosophy, lived like pigs, never washed their hands, faces, hair or beards, never cleaned out their rooms, made their beds once every other month, used cartoons for their paintings as table-cloths and drank only straight from the bottle, a way of life which they considered extremely distinguished."

Sodoma was not only a pederast but gloried in the fact, and moreover had a mania for animals. Vasari describes how "he loved to fill his house with all manner of curious beasts:

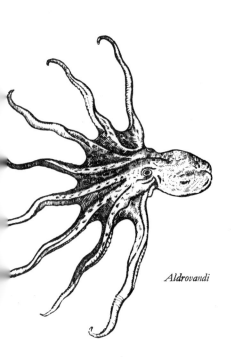

Aldrovandi

badgers, squirrels, monkeys, pumas, dwarf donkeys, Barbary goats, jackdaws, hens, tortoises, indeed anything which fell into his hands. He also had a crow which he had taught to imitate his voice, especially to answer the door, and many visitors, hearing it, imagined that it was the voice of its master. The other animals were so well trained that he was able to keep them always by his side, and his dwelling, with all these animals roaming at liberty, resembled a veritable Noah's Ark." Animals seem to have been one of the special weaknesses of the Mannerists. The sculptor, Giovanni Francesco Rustici, is reported to have kept a tame porcupine, an eagle, a talking crow, and a collection of snakes. Rosso, while he was living in Florence, owned a baboon of which he was very fond. The baboon, which was as mischievous as it was intelligent, enjoyed playing pranks on the monks of the adjacent monastery of Santa Croce. The monks finally lost patience and brought Rosso before the courts, but nothing could induce him to part with his pet, and so he took it with him to Rome to seek its fortune there.

Even the artists' amusements contained an element of the bizarre which was sometimes thoroughly disquieting. The banquets organized in Rome by the Company of the Caldron or the Company of the Trowel have remained famous because of their extravagance. One of these feasts for example, described in Vasari's *Life of Giovanni Francesco Rustici*, had for its theme the marriage of Persephone and Pluto. The banqueting hall represented Hades, being dimly illuminated, with fearsome paintings hanging on the walls, while the tables were draped in black, the servingmen disguised as devils, and the music consisted of the screams of the damned. The food offered corresponded to the setting: "The meats were decorated to resemble all sorts of animals of repugnant appearance, serpents, toads, lizards, spiders, scorpions, bats, while beneath this decoration lay the most delicious foods. They were presented to the diners on coal shovels, and a devil poured choice wines into crucibles of the type used for melting glass and which here were turned into drinking receptacles... and for dessert, were several sugar confections molded to resemble the bones of dead men."

There is usually but a single step from extravagant oddity to melancholy. According to some contemporaries, Parmigianino had become totally enthralled by alchemy and spent much time hovering over his furnaces. Toward the end of his life, he became increasingly strange and melancholic. He neglected his appearance and "allowed his beard to grow long and unkempt, which made him resemble a savage rather than a gentleman." Jacopo da Pontormo had a horror of public holidays and of crowds. "One could not imagine a more solitary man," said Vasari; "he lived in a sort of hovel... The only way to gain access to the room in which he slept and worked, was by climbing a ladder which he used to draw up after him so that no person might come upon him unannounced." Piero di Cosimo also lived in the strangest possible manner. His daily nourishment consisted of hard-boiled eggs. So as not to waste his time in the kitchen, he used to prepare four or five dozen at a time, piling them in a basket to have sustenance of a kind for a fortnight. He could not stand the cries of children, the sound of coughing, or the chanting of monks. Thunder terrified him, and in order not to see the flashes of lightning, he threw his cloak over his head and huddled up in a corner. On the other hand, rain enchanted him and "he loved to watch the water streaming off the roofs and splashing on the ground." Giulio Clovio reported in one of his letters that El Greco habitually shut himself up in his room, closed the curtains and sat there for long periods in the dark, allowing his imagination free rein. Rosso committed suicide in a fit of nervous depression.

All these characteristics distinguish the Mannerist artist from the Medieval artist. The latter formed part of a society whose ideology he submissively reflected, whereas the former was an individualist who created in solitude, and consequently had to bear upon his own shoulders the whole weight of human anxiety. The Medieval artist gave expression of spiritual calm to a civilization sure of its faith, and both ideas and style were pre-ordained for him. For the Mannerist artist all was possible, and his terrible liberty, the key to his originality, exacted the price of inevitable anguish. Here is to be found the close affinity which, passing over the Baroque and Classical interludes, links Mannerism with the culture of the last two centuries, with the pre-Romantic *mal de vivre*, with the nineteenth century's spleen, and with Existentialism's profound despair.

Mannerism, a Cosmopolitan Movement

Like all very individualistic cultures, Mannerism was also a cosmopolitan culture. In many cases it is difficult to say to which school a particular Mannerist painter belongs. Rosso was born in Florence, formed his style on a study of Parmigianino's design, worked first in Rome, then in Venice, and finally went to France, where he may be said to have founded the School of Fontainebleau. How is one to classify such an artist: among the Italians (and then which Italians?) or among the French? The same problem exists in classifying Bartholomeus Spranger. He was born in Antwerp, became the pupil of Jan Mandyn in Haarlem, studied later in Paris, worked for three years in Rome where he belonged to the Mannerist group brought together by Cardinal Alessandro Farnese, and ended his days at the courts of Maximilian II and Rudolph II where he became the most typical painter of the School of Prague.

These are just the most striking examples of a cosmopolitanism which characterized the entire culture of the era. No period saw more constant and consistent travel by artists than did the sixteenth century. Most of the better known painters from the northern countries lived in Italy for varying periods, sometimes at length. Bernard van Orley, Jan van Scorel, Michiel Coxie, Jan Gossaert Mabuse, Maerten van Heemskerck, Frans Floris, and Bartholomeus Spranger, for example, all worked in Rome at some time. Albrecht Dürer made two visits to Venice, from 1494 to 1495, and from 1505 to 1507, during which periods he collaborated with Titian and Giorgione in decorating the Fondaco dei Tedeschi. Jan Stefan van Calcar and, later, Monsù Desiderio lived in Naples. Denis Calvaert settled in Bologna. Often the Northerners who settled in Italy became so acclimated, they were known principally by their Italianized names. This is the case with Giovanni Stradano (Jan van der Straet) and Pietro Candido (Pieter de Witte), both of whom established themselves in Florence, and also with Ludovico Pozzoserrato (Lodewijk Toeput from Mechlin) who worked in Venice.

But Italy was not the only focal point of travel and immigration. Between Flanders and Holland there was a constant and indeed complex exchange of artists. Many Flemish painters, including Abraham Bloemaert, Jan Massys, Joachim Wtewael, and Lukas de Heere, spent some time in France. Italians such as Pellegrino Tibaldi, Federigo Zuccaro, Luca Cambiaso, Giovanni Battista Castello and Lazzaro Tavarone worked in Spain. And the greatest "Spanish" painter of the sixteenth century, who called himself El Greco, was really a Cretan named Domenikos Theotokopoulos, whose style was formed at Venice. Two of the most striking "English" Mannerist painters, Hans Eworth (Ewoutsz) and Isaac Oliver, were in fact foreigners, born respectively in Antwerp and Le Havre.

The development of engraving techniques furthered this cosmopolitanism as much as, and perhaps even more than, the artists' constant travel. Hitherto, the study and appreciation of a particular artist's style depended entirely on the possibility of seeing the original works wherever they might happen to be. What chance had a painter, living in Cologne in the fourteenth century, to acquire any idea whatsoever of the style of Giotto? Stylistic exchanges did indeed occur between different countries, but they were necessarily both slow and indirect.

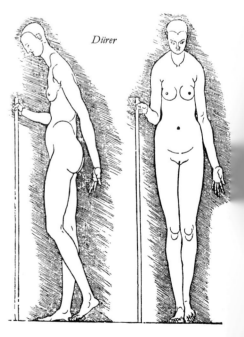

Dürer

The development of the art of print making (woodcuts, engravings and etchings) permitted the production of a large number of copies of a work of art at a moderate cost, in a form which was easily distributable. By this means artistic notions were exchanged extremely rapidly from one end of Europe to the other. As a young man Albrecht Dürer was strongly influenced by the engravings of Andrea Mantegna. And if we are to believe Vasari, Dürer's prints were destined, in turn, to lead Jacopo da Pontormo to change his style. The prints made after the works of Raphael by Marcantonio Raimondi spread the knowledge of Raphael's style throughout Europe. Similarly, works of Parmigianino were made known through prints by Gian Jacopo Caraglio, Giulio Bonasone, Fantuzzi, and Domenico Beccafumi. A whole group of engravers, notable among them René Boyvin, Fantuzzi, and Jacques Ducerceau popularized the style of the School of Fontainebleau.

Woodcuts and engravings circulated throughout the world, and everywhere they gave rise to imitations. A picture was recently discovered in a private collection in the Canary Islands, executed by a Flemish painter who had been exiled there, which is a transposition of an engraving by Jan Muller, *The Feast of Belshazzar,* after a drawing by Melchior Bocksberger. In Brazil, a late sixteenth century fresco was recently proven to show the influence of an engraving by René Boyvin after a painting by Rosso. Flemish prints reached as far as Japan, where they were copied by local artists. These facts may give one some indication of the degree to which engraving processes must have assisted the spread of new ideas and themes within Europe itself. Stylistically and iconographically, art was suddenly tremendously enriched by this exchange. This enrichment was one of the fundamental factors in the birth of Mannerism. Artists who had been bound by rigid national formulas only a few decades previously, began to realize that there existed an infinity of styles and an extraordinary quantity of themes. Confronted by a multiplicity of different manners, each sought to develop a new, personal manner. The diversity of what already existed naturally provoked originality and boldness—everything became possible.

Mannerism was not born in any one specific country. It resulted, rather, from a general awakening, simultaneously in all countries, to the variety of European art. In order to gain a clear perspective of the matter, it is important to dispose once and for all of the legend that casts Mannerism as a style of purely Italian origin, or more specifically, the style of the Florentine artists of the 1520's, which subsequently spread throughout Europe. Certainly, the innumerable Flemish, French, and German artists who went to work in Italy could not help being influenced to a greater or lesser extent by the Italian manner, but they exercised an equal influence on the Italians. By 1520, northern artistic concepts were exerting as much influence in Italy as were Italian concepts in the northern countries. Michelangelo, it is true, condemned the Flemish style. According to him, it was overly concerned with details, and presented a proliferation of objects, of which one alone would have sufficed to make a good picture. But his strong attack upon Flemish painting confirms that it was generally held in high esteem in Italy at that time. After Michelangelo, Albrecht Dürer was without doubt the most admired and imitated artist in Mannerist Italy. Aretino and Cellini speak of him admiringly. Sabba da Castiglione in his *Ricordi* (1546) hails him a "divine." Giulio Romano possessed a Dürer self-portrait which he prized above all else. Dürer's prints directly influenced or inspired paintings by Andrea del Sarto, Jacopo da Pontormo, and most of the great Venetian painters of the sixteenth century.

The various schools and centers of Mannerism did not develop their specific facets of Mannerism in isolation. These centers were above all centers of exchange. Mannerism, an eminently cosmopolitan and international movement, can only be understood within the context of European civilization as a whole. Therefore, in surveying the different aspects of Mannerist style and the themes of Mannerist art, we shall not attempt to distinguish between schools. Rather we shall try to find the techniques of design, color and composition, and the ideas, obsession and dreams which are common to all schools of Mannerist artists. Such an approach, by respecting the unity of the Mannerist movement, is the most effective way to demonstrate the primary place which this movement holds in the history of Western art.

Selections from
mannerist poetry
III

Nella notte di natale

Felice notte, ond' a noi nasce il giorno
di cui mai più sereno altro non fue,
che fra gli orrori e sotto l'ombre tue
copri quel Sol, ch'a l'altro sol fa scorno!
Felici voi, ch'in povero soggiorno,
pigro asinello e mansueto bue,
al pargoletto Dio le membra sue
state a scaldar co' dolci fiati intorno!
Felici voi, degnate a tanti onori,
aride erbette e rustica capanna,
ch'aprir vedete a mezzo 'l verno i fiori!
Così diceano, a suon di rozza canna,
innanzi al gran Bambin chini i pastori;
e sudo l'elce e'l pin nettare e manna.

Giovanni Battista Marini

On Christmas Night

Happy night, whence for us day is born
Than which never there was any more serene,
Night, which among horrors and under your shadows
Shelters that Sun which puts to shame the other sun!
Happy are you, who in a poor wayside abode,
Slow donkey and gentle ox,
Are warming the little infant God
With your sweet breath around him!
Happy are you to be worthy of so many honors,
Dry straw and rustic hovel,
Who see the flowers opening in the midst of winter!
So say the shepherds by the music of their rough, unpolished pipes,
Bowing down before the great Child.
And the pines and ilexes sweat nectar and manna.

…Llegó, y, a vista tanta
obedeciendo la dudosa planta,
inmóvil se quedó sobre un lentisco,
verde balcón del agradable risco.
Si mucho poco mapa les despliega,
mucho es más lo que, nieblas desatando,
confunde el Sol y la distancia niega.
Muda la admiración, habla callando,
y, ciega, un río sigue, que - luciente
de aquellos montes hijo -
con torcido discurso, aunque prolijo,

tiraniza los campos útilmente ;
orladas sus orillas de frutales,
quiere la Copia que su cuerno sea
- si al animal armaron de Amaltea
diáfanos cristales ;
engarzando edificios en su plata,
de muros se corona,
rocas abraza, islas aprisiona,
de la alta gruta donde se desata
hasta los jaspes líquidos, adonde
su orgullo pierde y su memoria esconde…

LUIS DE
GÓNGORA

LAS
SOLEDADES

-liff ascended he

-rtain feet obedient to his sight)

-bile stood, above a mastic tree,

-a balcony upon the pleasant height.

-gh much a little map unfolds, more still

-more—is that which now dissolving mists

-un confounds and distances deny;

-• Wonder speaks by silence, her blind eye

-vs the river, son of that same hill,

-e prolix discourse twists

-olent to tyrannize the plain.

Its borders lined with many an orchard lawn,
If not with flowers stolen from the Dawn,
The stream flows straight while it does not aspire
The heights with its own crystals to attain;
Flies from itself to find itself again,
Is lost; and searching for its wanderings,
Both errors sweet and sweet meanderings
The waters make with their lascivious fire;
And, linking buildings in its silver force,
With bowers crowned, majestically flows
Into abundant branches, there to wind

Mid isles that green parentheses provide
In the main period of the current's course;
From the high cavern where it first arose,
Until the liquid jasper, there to find
All memory lost and forfeited all pride.

Luis de Góngora, The Solitudes,
"First Solitude", Verses 190–211

81

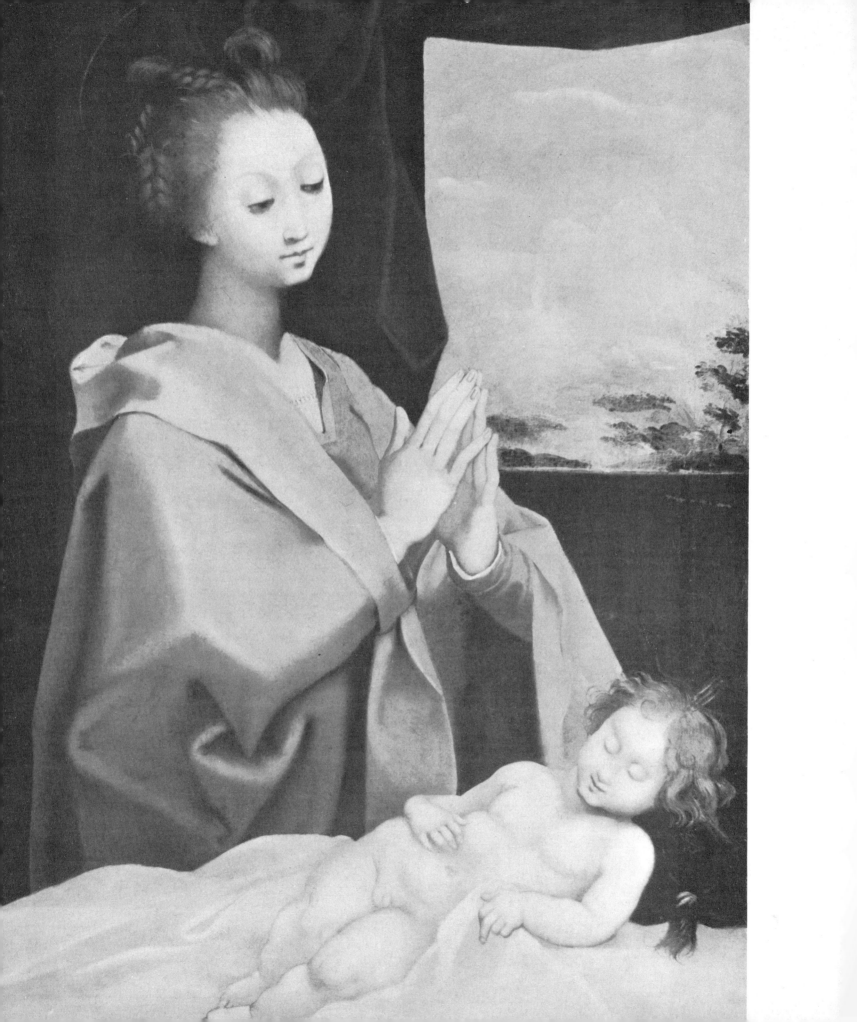

Christ's Little Lullaby

Sleep, great councilor of the world,
Our bridegroom, Son, and even Father,
Eyja, Eyja,
Bed and lair in which you're borne
Have I now laid out for you,
Sleep, most precious child!
Eyja, Eyja,
Sleep and rest,
Sleep, sleep, beloved heart!

Sleep, my crownlet! Light and life,
I will give you all that you hold dear,
Eyja, Eyja,
Sleep, you treasure-trove of boon;
Let me feed you, let me lave you
At the meager cradle here!
Eyja, Eyja,
Sleep, sleep, you my glory and repose.

Garlands on your little crib,
Flowers decking you from head to toe,
Eyja, Eyja,
Sleep, you joy, our heart's desire,
Sleep, soul's paradise,
Sleep, you precious manna!
Eyja, Eyja,
Sleep and rest,
Sleep, sleep, Saviour of the world.

Chriſt-Wiegenliedlein

Schlaf, du großer Weltberater,
Bräutigam, Sohn und selbſt auch Vater,
Eya, Eya,
Bett und Lager, das dich träget,
Hab ich dir zurechtgeleget,
Schlaf, du schönſtes Kindelein!
Eya, Eya,
Schlaf und ruhe,
Schlaf, schlaf, trautes Herzelein!

Schlaf, mein Krönlein! Licht und Leben,
Was dir lieb, will ich dir geben,
Eya, Eya,
Schlaf, du Ausbund aller Gaben;
Laß dich speiſen, laß dich laben
Bei der armen Krippen hier!
Eya, Eya,
Schlaf, schlaf, du mein Ehr und Ruhen!

Ich will dir dein Bettlein zieren,
Ganz mit Blumen überführen,
Eya, Eya,
Schlaf, du Luſt, die wir erwählen,
Schlaf, du Paradies der Seelen,
Schlaf, du wahres Himmelbrod!
Eya, Eya,
Schlaf und ruhe,
Schlaf, schlaf, Heiland aller Welt!

Paul Gerhardt

Aspects
of Mannerist
Style

Clarity of Line

ANGELO BRONZINO
Saint John the Baptist
Rome, Galleria Borghese

In the variety of styles which make up Mannerism, there is no more general or more immediately perceptible characteristic than the extreme clarity of the line. Whether it is a question of the single figure, as in Angelo Bronzino's *Saint John the Baptist*, or of very complex compositions filled with scrupulously recorded details, such as Ludger Tom Ring's *Marriage at Cana*, one is struck by the clarity of the outline and by the perfect "cleanness" of the painting. In the pages that follow, we shall discuss a few particularly significant examples, but almost all the works of art reproduced in this volume could equally well illustrate the linear purity which is one of the common denominators of Mannerist painting. It is typical that even those Mannerist painters who made use of the subtle play of atmosphere, such as Rosso, Domenico Beccafumi, or Adam Elsheimer, did not permit a dispersion of contours in their work. Of course, precision of line is not the prerogative of Mannerism. The Sienese primitives, for example, also used extremely clear, sharp delineation of form. This emphasis on linear pre-

LUDGER TOM RING THE YOUNGER
The Marriage at Cana
Berlin, Former Staatliche Museen

cision, however, is one of the stylistic factors which distinguishes Mannerism from the style of the High Renaissance which immediately preceded it and from the Baroque which immediately followed it.

This difference between the style of the High Renaissance and Mannerism becomes clear if one compares a detail of drapery by a High Renaissance painter, such as Raphael, with a similar detail in a Mannerist painting such as *The Resurrection,* by Cecco del Caravaggio of about 1600. In Raphael's works, one nearly always encounters undefined areas of drapery filled with broad strokes of flat paint. In the sleeve of the angel's robe in *The Resurrection* by Cecco del Caravaggio, on the other hand, not a single fragment of the cloth is left undefined. This is not simply to say that the design of Cecco del Caravaggio's painting is more detailed than a work by Raphael. In fact, if one observes the breeches of the soldier in the center of *The Resurrection,* it will be noted that there are very few details of design. Yet no single part of this area is left undefined in its surface contours.

The contrast between the linear precision of Mannerism and the chromatic pictorialism of Baroque painting is so clear it hardly requires emphasis. Even the uninitiated can perceive at first glance that a nude by Hans Bock the Elder belongs to a different stylistic category from a nude by Rubens or Rembrandt.

Purity of contour and controlled power of linear design provide one of the surest guides to the affiliations of artists between 1520 and 1620. They separate the authentic Mannerists from painters who, like many of the Venetians, notably Titian, remained outside the movement. This same criterion is equally valid in identifying the fifteenth century precursors of Mannerism, such as Sandro Botticelli, Luca Signorelli, Andrea Mantegna, Carlo Crivelli, Cosimo Tura, Roger van der Weyden, and Hugo van der Goes, or its belated continuers, such as Georges de La Tour, the Flemish followers of Caravaggio, or the northern still life painters of

the early seventeenth century exemplified by Osias Beert, Clara Peeters, Stosskopf and Baugin. The perfection of linear contours in Mannerist painting quite clearly lacks the emotion which emanates from the vibration of color in the work of Titian, Rubens, Delacroix, Turner, or Renoir. It is true that linear clarity is capable of falling into coldness. In fact certain Mannerist works, such as Benedetto Pagni's *Allegory of the Fame of the Medici* or Lukas de Heere's *Seven Arts in Time of War*, would seem to announce the academicism of the nineteenth century in their frigid delineation. On the other hand the painting of the great colorists had is own inherent danger of excessive emotionalism. When looking at the Rubens collection in the Prado in Madrid or the Turners in the Tate Gallery in London, one may experience deep enthusiasm or a certain repulsion, according to one's personal taste, but whatever the reaction one will certainly not remain indifferent. Such heights and depths of emotion are quite foreign to Mannerist painting. A Mannerist painting might well appear cold and leave us indifferent. The emphasis upon design as opposed to color is indicative of the ascendency of the cerebral over the emotional. The full appreciation of Mannerist painting does indeed demand a certain cerebral participation on the part of the observer. On the other hand the Mannerist artist's complete mastery over design gave him the liberty to play with this design, bestowing his work with an extra and obvious element of beauty: it is exactly this beauty of line and precise contour which constituted Mannerism's arresting elegance and exquisiteness of detail.

DANIELE DA VOLTERRA
The Beheading of John the Baptist
Turin, Galleria Sabauda

Emphasis on design makes Mannerism an essentially representational and intellectual art. The risk here is of falling into mere illustrative or literary invention, and Mannerism by no means escapes these pitfalls. Many Mannerist nudes come close to a pornographic imagery, and many of its allegories are tainted with pedantry. But the masterful graphic technique of Mannerism also allowed its artists to transcribe images of boundless imagination, strange dreams and bizarre fantasies. Thus, together with Surrealist painting, which is also an eminently graphic, linear painting (Salvadore Dalì, Paul Delvaux, Fabrizio Clerici and Léonor Fini), Mannerism is the art capable of opening for us most widely the doors into other worlds.

Sculptural Painting

The Mannerist emphasis upon line is closely linked with the vast strides made in the development of engraving during the sixteenth century. By copying prints (an essential exercise for every young artist of that era), and by making engravings from paintings, artists learned to give full definition to contours and volumes. The prints by Albrecht Dürer, Marcantonio Raimondi and his disciples, the engravers of the School of Fontainebleau such as René Boyvin, Fantuzzi, and Jacques Ducerceau, or those by Hendrick Goltzius and Jan Muller exercised an immense influence on Mannerist painting.

The influence of sculpture on painting was equally strong. Many of the principal Mannerist painters—first and foremost Michelangelo—were also sculptors, and Mannerist painting in general always maintained a close relationship with sculpture. A letter from Benvenuto Cellini to his friend Benedetto Varchi, dated the 28th of January 1546, well expresses the aesthetic ideas of the mid-sixteenth century on this subject: "I maintain," he writes, "that of all the plastic arts sculpture is seven times the greatest, for the reason that a statue must possess eight angles of vision, all equally good... It is recognized today that Michelangelo is the greatest painter ever known, from ancient or modern times, simply because he derives all that he knows of painting from a meticulous study of the methods of sculpture. And today I know of no one who approaches so closely this artistic truth but the skillful Bronzino."

JAN MULLER
Rape of a Sabine
Engravings after wax figures by
Adriaen de Vries

BRAHAM JANSSENS
llegory of Voluptuousness
ussels, Musée d'Art Ancien

BRAMANTINO
Ecce Homo
Lugano,
Thyssen Collec

In a great number of Mannerist paintings the artist has wished to imitate or rival sculpture by multiplying the angles of vision. According to Vasari, Giorgione maintained that painting was superior to sculpture, because in painting it was possible to apprehend with a single glance all the aspects of a figure without having to walk around it. To demonstrate his thesis, Giorgione "painted a nude figure seen from the rear; at the feet of this figure was a limpid pool which reflected the figure's front; on the right, the polished metal of a breast plate of a suit of armour gave a lateral view of the figure, while on the left side, a mirror allowed one to see the other flank." This painting by Giorgione is lost. The Musée du Louvre, however, possesses a portrait of a man by Girolamo Savoldo which is perhaps a free copy after the lost painting by Giorgione. Unfortunately the canvas in the Louvre is too dirty to allow a satis-

94 factory reproduction, but the *Allegory of Voluptuousness* by Abraham Janssens, illustrated here, is a work of similar inspiration. It will be noted that the sculptural monumentality of the forms in Janssens' painting is accentuated by the reflection of the head in a mirror. Jan Mul-

95 ler's engravings of the *Rape of the Sabines* attempt to demonstrate a similar idea by representing the same image first in full-face and then from behind. Muller's engravings were in fact made after wax figures by the Dutch sculptor Adriaen de Vries.

Often too, Mannerist artists actually sought in their paintings to evoke the texture of the sculpted substance. The head in Abraham Janssens' *Voluptuousness* is a clear attempt to imitate marble in paint. Dürer's *Portrait of the Financier Kleberger* gives one the impression of being a waxwork, while the *Ecce Homo* by Bramantino reproduces a sculpture in wood.

Cubism and the Expression of Volume

The exaltation of line coupled with the accentuation of volume sometimes resulted in a true cubist expression of form. Rosso's *Descent from the Cross* (Volterra, Pinacoteca) dating from 1521, clearly shows a desire to reduce the human form to its geometrical structure. This tendency is confirmed in Rosso's painting of *Moses Defending the Daughters of Jethro*, of 1522. The forceful stylization of the male bodies is set in relief by harsh angular modelling and 93 cubelike treatment of the forms. In Jacopo da Pontormo's *Visitation*, the cylindrical volume of the central group (itself composed of rounded forms) contrasts with the severely flat surfaces and perfect angles of the setting. Daniele da Volterra pursued analogous experiments. His Virgin in the *Holy Family* in the Pannocchieschi Collection in Siena, foreshadows—at a distance of four centuries!—those gigantic figures which Pablo Picasso was painting in the 1920's.

A taste for the accentuation of volume is not peculiar to the Florentine painters. It can be met with in France in some of the works of the School of Fontainebleau, and later in a 100 work such as the anonymous *Portrait of a Woman*, in the Musée Granet at Aix-en-Provence. In this painting the oval of the pearl earring harmonizes with the oval of the face and the rounded shapes of the breasts. In Spain, similar examples may be found in the work of Luis 240 de Morales. His *Madonna and Child and Saints* (New York, Hispanic Society of America) is composed of a repetition of smooth and regular oval forms. A highly exaggerated treatment of

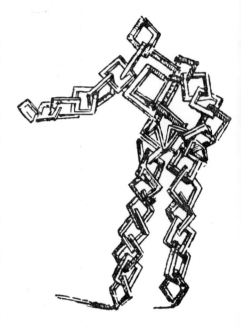

GIOVANNI BATTISTA BRACELLI
Fantastic Geometric Figure from
"Bizzarrie di varie figure"
Etching

ALBRECHT DÜRER
Saint Paul and Two Cubic Heads (drawing
Dresden, Staatliche Kunstsammlung

ROSSO FIORENTI
Moses Defending the Daughters of Jet
Florence, Uf

254   volume can be found in the Netherlands, exemplified here in the curious engraving of *Hercules* by Hendrick Goltzius. In Germany this insistent expression of volume was extensively developed by Albrecht Dürer.

The Dresden Library possesses a Dürer sketchbook containing illustrations for his treatise published in 1525, with the characteristic title *Instructions on the Mensuration of line, plane, and three dimensional bodies, by the use of the circle and rule.* These illustrations include a series of figures broken up into polyhedrons. Although it is true that these sketches constitute studio exercises rather than finished works of art, they nevertheless show how strong was the artist's interest in the geometry of the human body.

GIOVANNI BATTISTA CASTELLO
Madonna and Child
Genoa, Galleria di Palazzo Bianco

All these tentative explorations culminated in the work of Luca Cambiaso, whose cubic studies in pen and wash show him to be an authentic precursor of Cubism. His drawing of 103 a *Group of Cubic Figures* in the Uffizi has an affinity with the mannequins of Fernand Léger. In Genova, Cambiaso was the master of a whole cubist group which flourished at the end of the sixteenth and the beginning of the seventeenth centuries. One of his pupils was Giovanni Battista Castello, who painted the *Madonna and Child* in the Palazzo Bianco at Genoa. The perfectly rounded spheres which form the heads of these figures are only superficially disguised by their facial features. Giovanni Battista Bracelli, a later Genoese follower of Cam-102 biaso, created a series of etchings of fantastic geometric figures *(Bizzarrie di varie figure,* published in 1624), exactly the sort of thing brought back into fashion by the Surrealists. The impact of one man's ideas upon the creative thinking of another makes it conceivable that Federigo Zuccaro may have derived, to some extent, from Cambiaso—with whom he worked at the Court of Philip II of Spain in 1585—the concept of the *disegno interno*, which Zuccaro then expounded in his *Idea de' Pittori, Scultori ed Architetti* of 1607. Was it not in effect the "ideal" forms of eternal geometry which are beyond a purely sensory vision that Cambiaso was seeking to extract and define?

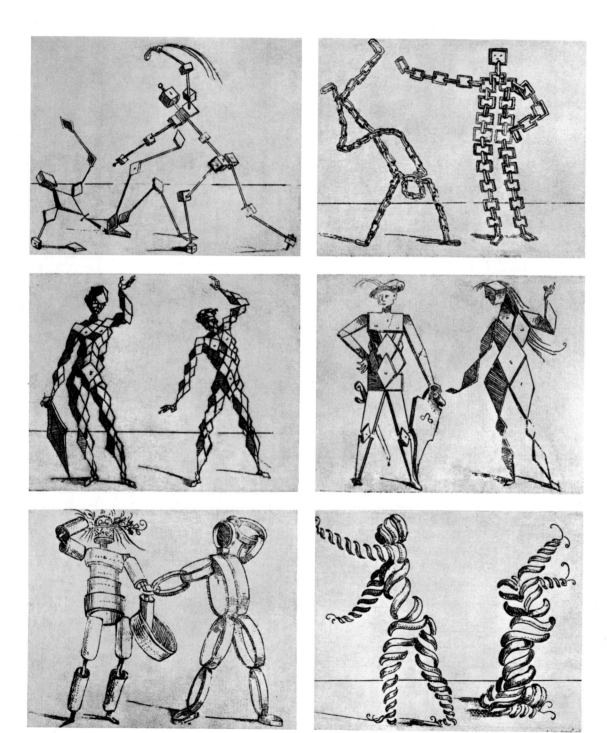

GIOVANNI BATTISTA BRACELLI
Fantastic Geometric Figures from "Bizzarrie di varie figure," 1624
Etchings

CAMBIASO
up of Cubic
es (drawing)
ence, Uffizi

The Poetry of Geometry

Even in their abstractions Mannerist painters retained a sense of the figurative. At the same time that they reduced the human body to geometrical diagrams, they frequently chose to represent geometrical objects with an extreme realism, an imaginary realism, but realism nevertheless.

An anonymous Italian engraver of the early sixteenth century, the monogramist ⵏ has left us a very few curious prints of *Stereographic Forms*. We are confronted in these works with a perfect example of the mysterious object which reveals the inner structure of things, while being itself an artificial construction. Thus is created an elusive example of the fantastically occult. Similarly Leonardo da Vinci in his drawings for Luca Pacioli's *De Divina Proportione* (1509) also created some fantastic geometrical objects which seem to have escaped from another world.

Another exceptional geometric achievement was that of Lorenz Stoer, a goldsmith and engraver who worked in Nuremberg and Augsburg during the second half of the sixteenth century. The eleven woodcuts contained in his slim treatise *Geometria et Perspectiva* (1567) are modestly presented as examples of perspective, but they are, in fact, veritable geometrical landscapes in which the vegetable world is replaced by disquieting helixes, and where polyhedrons and globes in unsteady equilibrium substitute for the human figure.

Like Lorenz Stoer, Wenzel Jamnitzer was a goldsmith and engraver at Nuremberg. His *Perspectiva corporum regularium* (1563 and 1568) offers us a wide choice of delectable dodecahedrons, octohedrons, hollow cones, cones in relief, pyramids, etc. While Stoer's prints evoke landscapes, the composition of some of Jamnitzer's prints are more reminiscent of geometrical still lifes.

These works are very far from being merely studio exercises or scientific illustrations. The artists of the sixteenth century undoubtedly had a lively admiration for these beautiful,

MONOGRAMMIST ⵏ
Stereographic Forms
Engravings

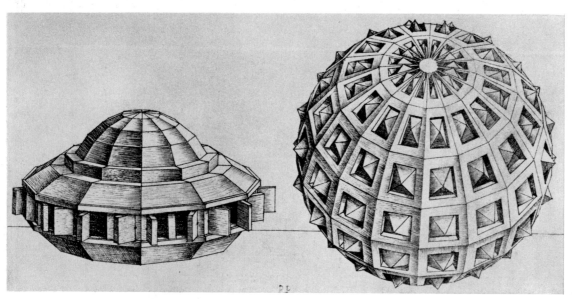

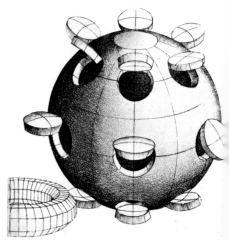

LORENZ STOER
Geometric
Landscapes from
"Geometria et
Perspectiva," 1567
Woodcuts

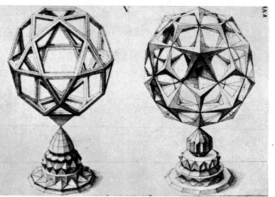

precise forms. A great number of paintings—*Portrait of Luca Pacioli and a Young Man* signed and dated Jaco. Bar. 1495 (Naples, Museo di Capodimonte), Hans Holbein the Younger's *Portrait of Nikolaus Kratzer* (Paris, Louvre) and his *Ambassadors* (London, National Gallery)— present strictly geometrical objects treated with loving care. A striking example of the use of geometrical objects is found in the painting in the Prado, attributed to Lelio Orsi, of the *Allegory of Christ and the Church*. By a strange geometric expressionism, Christ's agonies, symbolized by the Cross, are multiplied a thousand fold. This veritable forest of crosses is the ultimate poetic expression of the geometrical fantasy of Mannerism.

Attributed to LELIO O
Allegory of Christ and the Chu
Madrid, Pr

FATO PRAEVENTVS F· MAZZOLI·   PARME
NSIS   ABSOLVERE· NEQVIVIT

PARMIGIANINO
Prophet (detail from the Madonna
of the Long Neck)
Florence, Uffizi

Elongation of the Figure

So completely conscious of style for its own sake, and having complete mastery over his design, the Mannerist artist could not resist playing with that design. He treated lines as a musician might treat a musical theme, varying them and modelling them according to purely aesthetic preoccupations, without concerning himself unduly with the realities they were supposed to represent. The result was a great liberty in the rendering of form.

The best known example of the Mannerist play with form—one which is often considered to epitomize the Mannerist movement—is the elongation of the human figure. Parmigianino is commonly accepted as the artist who introduced this new fashion, the prototype of which is considered to be his *Madonna of the Long Neck,* of which we reproduce here only the detail of the prophet. The *Madonna of the Long Neck* was painted about 1535, but examples of elongation are to be found already in the late fifteenth century, in the works of some of those artists who were the precursors of Mannerism, such as Sandro Botticelli. Botticelli's 126 *Venus,* illustrated here, dates from about 1482. Thus in the case of elongation, as with many other features of the Mannerist style, Mannerism resumed, after the brief interval of the High Renaissance, tendencies already visible in the later fifteenth century.

The normal proportion of the European body is seven and a half times the length of the head. Yet Dürer, in his *Four Books of Human Proportion,* published in 1528 after his death, claimed that the ideal total height of the body is nine times that of the head. This proportion was repeated in many of the other treatises of the era, notably by Agnolo Firenzuola (1500—

PAULUS MOREELSE
Grotto of Venus (detail)
Leningrad, Hermitage

1550) in his celebrated dialogue *On the Beauty of Women*. So widespread was this tendency to elongation throughout all of Mannerist art, that it would be superfluous to list examples. We shall note only the striking proportions used in the paintings reproduced in these immediate pages: Paulus Moreelse, *Grotto of Venus*, 10 heads; Bartholomeus Spranger, *Hermaphroditus and the Nymph Salmacis*, 9 heads; Cornelis Engelbrechtsz, *Saint Helen and the Emperor Constantine*, 10½ heads, Hans von Aachen, *Bacchus, Ceres and Amor*, 9 heads.

Elongation of the human figure was a most pronounced feature of Mannerist expression. It is precisely this feature which produced the elegant effects so characteristic of the works of Parmigianino, Angelo Bronzino, and the School of Fontainebleau. Moreover, elongation and the resulting dematerialization of the body played an important role in the development of the mystical religious art of painters such as El Greco.

BARTHOLOMEUS SPRANGER
Hermaphroditus and the Nymph Salma◀
(detail)
Vienna, Kunsthistorisches Museum

CORNELIS ENGELBRECHTSZ
Saint Helen and the Emperor Constantin◀
(detail)
Munich, Alte Pinakothek

110

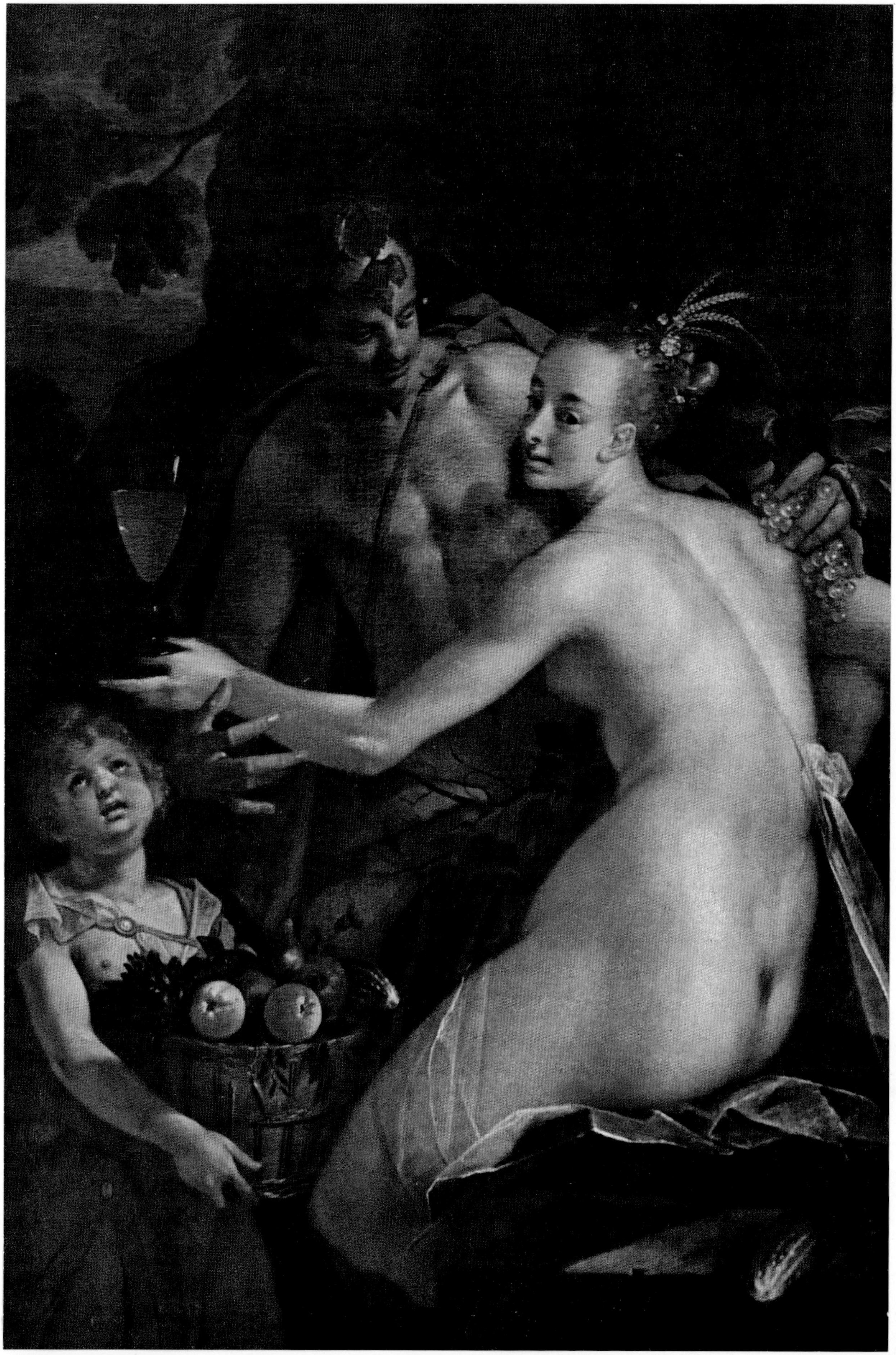

S VON AACHEN
hus, Ceres and Amor
a, Kunsthistorisches Museum

ANGELO BRONZINO
The Annunciation (detail of the Madonna)
Florence, Palazzo Vecchio

Distortion and Play of Perspective

The elongation of the human figure is only one aspect of the general predilection for distortion in Mannerist art which often tended to produce strange and disturbing effects.

The elongation of the Madonna in Angelo Bronzino's *Annunciation* creates an expressive elegance. But were it not for the elaborate arrangement of the drapery, which leaves us in doubt as to where the body ends and the legs begin, the effect would be quite monstrous. In Jacopo da Pontormo's drawing of a *Seated Nude,* all the details of the disproportion are visible, and the result is indeed disquieting.

In following these trends, Mannerism occasionally produced truly acromegalic images. Pellegrino Tibaldi's frescoes of the *Story of Ulysses,* in the Palazzo Poggi in Bologna, achieve strangely disturbing effects of proportion. The expressive power of such distortion is illustrated

JACOPO DA PONTORMO
Seated Nude (drawing)
Florence, Uffizi

here in Tibaldi's drawing of *The Holy Family*, in which a traditionally tranquil scene takes on an infernal quality.

Bronzino, Pontormo, and Tibaldi were all superb draughtsmen, so there can be no question of mere clumsiness. Their exaggerations resulted rather from a technical virtuosity in which distortion was used as a visual and artistic experiment in problems of optics and perspective. Parmigianino, as a young man, painted a *Self-Portrait* seen in a convex mirror, which makes his hand appear disproportionately large. These preoccupations with distorting perspective were sometimes pushed so far as to render the image unrecognizable. Eventually they led to esoteric picture-puzzles, where the painting or drawing viewed from the front in normal perspective appears as a confused tangle of lines. But when the same picture is viewed laterally, at the required angle and distance, it is easily possible to distinguish inscriptions, portraits, or small landscapes.

The master of the anamorphic rebus was Erhard Schön, a disciple of Dürer in Germany. One of his puzzle-engravings, dated 1535, at first glance resembles a rather incoherent landscape, but when viewed at a sharp angle to the surface, it resolves itself to the eye as four portraits: Charles v, Ferdinand i, Paul iii, and François i. His picture-puzzle reproduced here car-

116

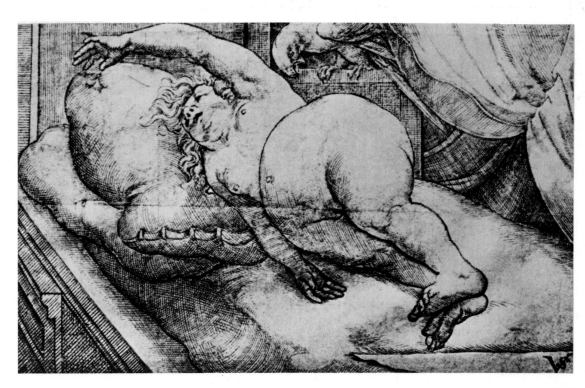

115

115 ries the title *Hinaus, du alter Tor!* ("Get out, you old fool!"), and the reader may be left to discover its secret on his own.

These exercises, which may seem rather childish to us, were tremendously popular at the time (see Jurgis Baltrušaitis: *Anamorphoses ou perspectives curieuses*, Paris, 1955). Even monarchs commissioned anamorphic portraits of themselves. The National Portrait Gallery in London, for example, possesses an anamorphic portrait of Edward VI dated 1546, and we know from Padre Accolti's treatise, *Lo inganno degl'occhi (The deception of the eyes)* that Cosimo II de' Medici had himself painted in this manner. A considerable number of learned works—Daniele Barbaro's *Pratica di perspettiva* (1559), Salomon de Caus's *Perspective* (1614), François Nicéron's *Perspective curieuse* (1638), etc.—included serious dissertations upon the phenomenon of anamorphosis. This "prospettiva segreta" or "secret perspective," as Barbaro called it, satisfied the Mannerist penchant for ambiguity and double meaning.

Among the various forms of distortion practiced by Mannerist artists we may include 115 the effects of foreshortening. The *Reclining Woman* by Virgel Solis, the engraving of *David and Goliath* by an artist of the School of Fontainebleau, and the series of engravings after Cornelis Cornelisz van Haarlem are just a few examples to illustrate the startling effects which could be obtained with this device. All these works, in their studied and self-conscious use of foreshortening, clearly attest to the strong preoccupation of Mannerist artists with distortion and the play of perspective.

The Serpentine Line and Mannerist Movement

Giovanni Paolo Lomazzo, in his *Trattato della Pittura* (1584), records a somewhat sibylline utterance attributed to Michelangelo, and then plunges in to a long dissertation on the *linea serpentina* or serpentine line. On the strength of this passage in Lomazzo, Michelangelo has been considered to be the creator of the *linea serpentina*. However dubious such a categorical allocation, the fact is that Lomazzo and his generation of Mannerist artists revered the genius of Michelangelo, and therefore their having credited him with the creation of the serpentine line reveals the importance of this stylistic form for the Mannerist style.

A very important factor in the development of the taste for serpentine movement of form was the discovery in Rome in 1506 of the *Laocoön*. This Late Hellenistic sculpture, now in the Museo Vaticano at Rome, dates from the first century B. C. It made an extraordinary impression on the artists of the time, and especially on Michelangelo. It revealed a hitherto unknown aspect of antique art: the *Laocoön* did not exhibit the calm idealism of Classical Greek sculpture, but rather a dramatic expression of torment. In the writhing serpentine lines of its composition, the *Laocoön* also provided a stimulating example of the representation of movement in art.

EL GRECO
Laocoön and his Sons
*Washington D. C., National Gallery,
Kress Collection*

JEAN VISET
Acrobats
Etching

JOACHIM WTEWAEL
The Flood
Nuremberg, Germanisches Nationalmuseum

Underlying the Mannerist artist's use of the serpentine line was an intense preoccupation with the movement of the human body. Many Mannerist figures, with their limbs coiled like springs, are essentially studies of delayed motion. Their actual forms suggest and indeed demand a future form. We see them in a moment of dangerously unstable equilibrium, whence their disquieting effect. In this analytical preoccupation with movement there is a certain analogy with the Futurist artists of the twentieth century, although of course the results are very different.

118   One example of the influence of the *Laocoön* group, all the more striking because it actually depicts the story of *Laocoön and his Sons*, is the painting by El Greco in the National Gal-

JAN GOSSAERT MABUSE
Adam and Eve
Berlin, Charlottenburg Schloss

lery in Washington, D. C. The body of the son of Laocoön at the left, and the serpent he is gripping are both stretched taut like drawn bows. The old father, Laocoön, has either just fallen or is in the process of falling, and one feels that he will not remain in that same position for more than a fraction of a second further.

This representation of the "analysed moment" of an action reoccurs throughout Mannerist art. The engravings after Cornelis Cornelisz van Haarlem of *Icarus, Phaeton, Ixon,* and *Tantalus* portray specific poses of figures falling through space. Compositions such as Jean Viset's *Acrobats* or *The Flood* by Joachim Wtewael are based upon the repetition of serpentine forms and are made up entirely of poses and gestures which are about to be abandoned. These works are visions of the instantaneous on the point of a complete transformation, but the formal analysis of the figures is so consciously studied and elaborated by the Mannerist artist as to render their implied movement curiously static. And indeed in the Mannerist use of the serpentine composition, the expression of movement is always subordinate to the artistic experimentation with shapes. In the *Adam and Eve* by Jan Gossaert Mabuse, for example, the bodies of the two figures are twisted into an almost perfect circle, the lines of which are echoed in the precise coils of the serpent. In this weird composition it is most obvious that the artist's main preoccupation was an aesthetic play with form.

It is interesting to note that the use of the serpentine line was by no means restricted to the portrayal of the human body. It was used in many details of Mannerist painting, as for instance in the detail we reproduce here of Albrecht Dürer's *Madonna and Child,* and in the *Winter Landscape with Gipsies* by Gysbrecht Lytens (Vienna, Kunsthistorisches Museum), with its mass of frozen trunks and branches, the whole universe seems to twist and undulate.

117

119

120

11

123

Black Backgrounds

A figure represented against a uniformly dark surface assumes an especially marked relief. The use of black backgrounds in paintings, so common during the sixteenth century, is yet another manifestation of the prevailing concern with the clarity of line and contour.

Black backgrounds were used in particular by certain German painters, most notably
127 Lucas Cranach the Elder. His *Venus and Cupid* which we illustrate here is a typical example of a great number of such works by this artist. The black background, however, had already been used in a similar fashion by the foremost Italian precursor of Mannerism, Sandro Botti-
126 celli, whose *Venus* we confront with that of Cranach. Similar backgrounds were also used by Mannerist artists in the Netherlands and in France, as witnessed by the examples shown here

SCHOOL OF FONTAINEBLEAU
Jupiter and Nymph
New York, Wildenstein Gallery

124

LUCAS VAN LEYDEN
Allegory of Fortune *(detail)*
...rg, Musée des Beaux-Arts

SANDRO BOTTICELLI
Venus
Berlin, Former Staatliche Museen

LUCAS CRANACH THE ELDER
Venus and Cupid
Munich, Alte Pinakothek

NICHOLAS HILLIARD
Portrait of a Young Man (miniature)
London, Victoria and Albert Museum

125 of the *Allegory of Fortune* by Lucas van Leyden and the *Jupiter and Nymph* by a painter of the
124 School of Fontainebleau.

During the Mannerist period the dark, nocturnal setting was very much cultivated by groups of painters who specialized in night scenes, but the backgrounds we are discussing here are quite different. There is no effort to create the atmosphere of night, rather these flat black backgrounds are a kind of screen of nothingness, an abstraction against which the startling reality of form detaches itself. Mannerist painting had a strong taste for artificial backgrounds in general. The English miniaturist Nicolas Hilliard, for example, painted a *Portrait of a Young Man* against a background of flames. In this miniature portrait, intended for the sitter's beloved, the flames symbolize the ardor of the young man's passion.

Painted Frames

The concept of the artificial background is related to another Mannerist device: the painted frame.

In Italy during the fifteenth century Mantegna and his followers, the School of Ferrara, and the Venetian, Carlo Crevelli, had frequently surrounded their central subject with architectural or sculptural motifs, garlands of flowers, fruits, and vegetables.

During the sixteenth century this trend was greatly elaborated. In a painting such as *The Temptation of Saint Anthony* by Jan Gossaert Mabuse, the architectural elements, arranged symmetrically around the central subject, form a veritable frame. Similar framing

JAN GOSSAERT MABUSE
The Temptation of Saint Anthony
Kansas City, Nelson Gallery of Art

SCHOOL OF FONTAINEBLEAU
Nymph
Paris, Galerie Charpentier

devices are found in Mabuse's *Danaë* in the Alte Pinakothek, Munich, as well as in *The Trials of Job* by Bernard van Orley, and Gillis van Coninxloo's *Family of the Virgin*, both in the Musée d'Art Ancien in Brussels. A painter from Bruges, Lancelot Blondeel, developed this idea still further. He enclosed tiny, usually insignificant scenes within extremely complicated painted frames. These frames are by far the most interesting and poetic part of his works. By a typically Mannerist paradox, the frame became the picture. In France, the feigned frame enjoyed great vogue. The taste for elaborate decorative frames had been introduced by Rosso in the stucco surrounds of his frescoes at Fontainebleau. The great beauty of this decorative work in stucco inspired imitation in paint. Innumerable panels and canvases were painted with a proportionately small scene in the center, surrounded by architectural details, grotesques, fruits, flowers and vegetables, and decorative sculptures in the form of nymphs, fauns, and terminals. A characteristic example is the painting of a *Nymph*, reproduced here, by a master of the School of Fontainebleau who was obviously inspired by the stucco surrounds of a decorative frieze. Innumerable engravings were made after Rosso's frescoes and stucco ornamentation at Fontainebleau, particularly by René Boyvin and Fantuzzi. These engravings not only popularized his style in France, but also made it well known abroad. Hans Rottenhammer's *Venus and Minerva*, with its elaborate painted frame in imitation of stucco, is obviously inspired by Rosso's works at Fontainebleau.

In France, the style of the painted frame was developed in a highly personal manner by certain artists. Among the most beautiful examples should be cited the works of François Dubois the Elder. As can be seen from the painting illustrated here, his frames are filled with curious details executed with loving care, and yet they never appear crowded or overworked.

The painted frame continued to enjoy tremendous popularity in the late sixteenth and seventeenth centuries, especially in Flanders. Joris Hoefnagel, Jan Bruegel the Elder and the Wierix family surrounded modest figures of Madonnas, saints, and Gospel scenes with delicious wreaths of flowers, birds, and insects. This fashion, however precious and charming, finally began to cloy, but many fine examples can be found which are both original in design and exquisite in execution.

132

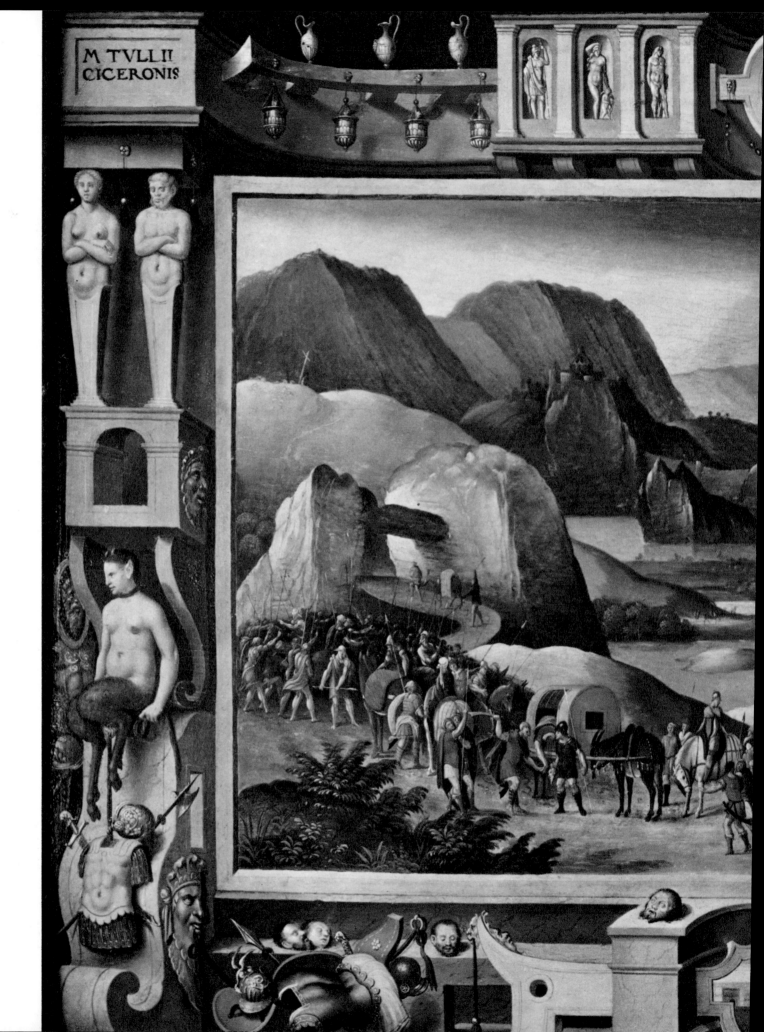

INDIGNVS
INTERITVS

FRANÇOIS DUBOIS
THE ELDER
The Murder
of Cicero
*Geneva, Collection
of Mme de Budé*

133

Fascination of the Night
Illumination of Darkness

Mannerism is the style of variety and contradiction: its penchant for obscurity is almost as marked as its penchant for extreme clarity.

Night held an extraordinary fascination for Mannerist poets and artists. "O notte, o dolce tempo, benchè nero...,, ["O night, o sweet time, tho' black..."], exclaimed Michelangelo, who was the creator of a marvellous statue of *Night*. "O notte, a me più chiara e più beata" ["O night, for me more clear and blissful"], sang Gaspara Stampa. Ronsard wrote a *Hymn to the Night*, and many of his works contain charming nocturnal thoughts: "Just like a traveller who, at nightfall, / Wandering in a wood where no moonbeam penetrates, / loses himself at every turning..."

> »Tout ainsi qu'un passant qui, parmi la nuit brune,
> Errant dedans un bois sans ayde de la lune,
> S'esgare en mille lieux...«

Sir Philip Sidney sang the praises of the night as a sure refuge for the unhappy:

> »O night, the ease of care, the pledge of pleasure,
> Desire's best mean, harvest of hearts affected,
> The seat of peace, the throne which is erected
> Of human life to be the quiet measure,
> Be victor still of Phoebus' golden treasure...«

Honoré de Bueil Racan, even while cursing the night, described it in most poetic terms: "The eternal torches which move round the world / pierce the waves' clear black with their long rays, / And stretch so bright and lovely to the gaze / That it seems the sky lies in the waters' heart."

> »Les flambeaux éternels qui font le tour du monde
> Percent à long rayons le noir cristal de l'onde,
> Et sont vus au travers si luisants et si beaux
> Qu'il semble que le ciel soit dans le fond des eaux.«

In painting, night scenes appear to have originated in the Netherlands with Geertgen tot Sint Jans. His *Nativity* in the National Gallery in London is lit solely by the radiant body of the Infant Jesus and the whiteness of an angel hovering in the sky. Another picture in the National Gallery in London, *The Marriage of Saint Catherine*, by a pupil of Geertgen's, is a clumsy but charming attempt at a nocturnal landscape lit by the illumination of a Gothic window. Examples of night painting are also found in Italy during the fifteenth century and perhaps owe something to the influence of northern art.

During the Mannerist period of the sixteenth and early seventeenth centuries night painting was widely developed, and given the Mannerist genius for variety and imagination

this type of scene took many forms, from the realistic to the utterly fantastic. The problem of nocturnalism in paintings is of course to illuminate the night. A solution particularly favored by Mannerist artists was that of a conflagration. We here reproduce three beautiful and strik-
136 ing examples of the night illuminated by fire: *The Burning of Troy* by Abraham Bloemaert,
137 Orazio Grevenbroeck's *Rape of Persephone,* and Jacob Isaacsz van Swanenburgh's *Pluto in the*
138 *Underworld.* Hieronymus Bosch also used this device, notably in his *Last Judgment* (Vienna, Kunsthistorisches Museum) and *The Garden of Delights* (Madrid, Prado). Pieter Bruegel the Younger had such a reputation for these blazing scenes that he came to be known as Hell Bruegel.

An analogous device was that of fireworks displays, torchlight parades, and the whole scope of festival illumination. Among the notable practitioners of this technique was An-
139 toine Caron de Beauvais. His curious scene of the *Death of Semeles* is lighted by the flames of her pyre and torches borne upon the backs of elephants.

135

The artist who brought the painting of night scenes to its supreme height was the Italian, Michelangelo da Caravaggio, who worked in the late sixteenth and opening years of the seventeenth centuries. The obscurity of the dark setting of his paintings were penetrated by a strong contrast of light which intensely illuminated his figures in a realistic fashion. Works by Caravaggio, such as the paintings of the life of Saint Matthew in the Contarelli Chapel in San Luigi dei Francesi in Rome, or *The Seven Acts of Mercy* in the Chiesa del Monte della Misericordia in Naples, had a tremendous influence. Among his followers were not only Italians but also a host of northerners who were studying and working in Rome and Naples. Illustrated in this volume are works by two followers of Caravaggio: *The Resurrection* by a French follower who worked in Rome, known as Cecco del Caravaggio, and *The Denial of Peter* by an unknown follower. Indeed it was the northern followers of Caravaggio who developed the particularly realistic aspects of his work, and specializing in scenes lighted by a torch or single candle,

88

142

ABRAHAM BLOEMAERT
The Burning of Troy
Frankfurt, Städelsches Kunstinstitut

made of night painting a special genre. One of these Caravaggisti, as the followers of Caravaggio are called, the Dutch painter Gerrit Honthorst, was known in Italy as Gherardo delle
Notti (literally, Gerrit of the Nights) for his many paintings of night scenes.

Finally we come to nature's illumination of the night: moonlight. It seems that Giorgione
painted moonlight scenes, but unfortunately none remain. Moonlight was the lighting always
used by Albrecht Altdorfer in his nocturnal landscapes. The French Mannerist painter known

JACOB ISAACSZ VAN SWANENBURGH
Pluto in the Underworld
Amsterdam, Rijksmuseum

138

ANTOINE CARON DE BEAUVAIS
The Death of Semele
Paris, Jean Ehrenmann Collection 135

as Monsù Desiderio specialized in fantastic nocturnal landscapes, which were often illuminated with moonlight. We here reproduce his *Fantastic Cityscape* eerily lighted by a cloud-covered moon. In the early seventeenth century, artists such as Adam Elsheimer and Paul Bril painted a number of very beautiful moonlight landscapes. Later the Dutch painter, Aert van der Neer, made a specialty of this type of landscape, thus creating a genre which achieved tremendous success among pre-Romantic artists.

Atmospheric Effects

With the moonlight scene we approach a still further refinement of Mannerist painting: the depiction of atmospheric effects. Rose and green twilights were developed by Nikolaus Manuel Deutsch and Albrecht Altdorfer. Glowing rose amber twilights were used by Niccolò dell'Abbate, as can be seen here in the color detail of his *Rape of Persephone*. Even richer and warmer crepuscular lights were a regular feature of the paintings of the Ferrarese masters, Dosso Dossi and Ippolito Scarsellino. Using murky green clouded skies, Lelio Orsi exploited the effects of a threatening storm, as in his *Way to Emmaus*. Among the Venetians, storm effects were treated by Giorgione in his *Tempest* (Venice, Accademia), and by Tintoretto, most outstandingly in his *Removal of the Body of Saint Mark* (Venice, Accademia), a scene which takes place in a fantastic rain storm. But perhaps the most expressive and stirring Mannerist evocation of the effects of a stormy sky is El Greco's *View of Toledo*.

Among the many variations in the depiction of the light effects of the atmosphere is the rendering of soft and hazy contours or surfaces, known as *sfumato*. The creator of *sfumato* was Leonardo da Vinci, and his influence is easily recognizable in the works of his followers, such as Sodoma. *Sfumato* was particularly developed as an expressive device by Correggio and above all Domenico Beccafumi. As employed by Mannerist artists, *sfumato* was an artificial, cerebral atmospheric effect, used less for the portrayal of natural light phenomena than, for example, the evocative surface treatment of the female body. Correggio was celebrated for his *sfumato* treatment of the nude. His works such as the beautiful *Danaë* in the Galleria Borghese in Rome had great influence on other artists. The pale half lights which bathe the tender, vibrant body of Venus in Ippolito Scarsellino's *Venus and Cupid* owe much to Correggio's use of *sfumato*.

IPPOLITO SCARSELLINO
Venus and Amor
Parma, Galleria Nazionale

RECO
of Toledo
id, Collection of the Condesa de Oñate

The Mannerist Use of Space

It has often been claimed that the Mannerist handling of space, in contrast with the spatial clarity of the High Renaissance, represents a regression toward the spatial incoherence of Medieval painting. This judgment is certainly not without some foundation. It is true, for example, that the many Mannerist paintings in which figures are placed against a uniformly black background have an affinity with the use of flat gold backgrounds in Medieval altarpieces. It is also true that the extreme clarity of outline, which is one of the principal characteristics of the Mannerist style, is in some respects an affirmation of the objects and figures themselves as opposed to the space containing them.

Too frequently, however, discussion of the so-called Mannerist negation of space is rendered sterile by prior acceptance of the premises of a most gratuitous historical philosophy. A whole series of critics have based their views on the theory of Oswald Spengler, which claims that for the High Renaissance, as for every dynamic culture (what Spengler calls a Faustian culture), space is the basic reality inside which objects and figures range themselves in an orderly fashion. In Mannerism, on the other hand, as in all cultures where the sense of reality has become dulled, images achieve an ascendancy over space. Space begins to lose its homogeneity and is sometimes even entirely abolished. These sweeping theories do not take

FOLLOWER OF MICHELANGELO
DA CARAVAGGIO
The Denial of Peter
Florence, Galleria Corsini

account of the facts. Mannerism in no way renounced the Renaissance conquest of perspective and the representation of three-dimensional space. The Mannerist artist was simply less bound by these rules and concepts. In the realm of space as in other aspects of style Mannerism expounded variation and nuance. For the Mannerist artist the representation of three-dimensional space was no longer an absolute as it had been for Raphael; it was just one artistic means among others to be used in the rendering of images. Rather than the abolition of space, we are confronted in Mannerism with a more complete mastery over the use of space, a freeing of space through plays of perspective or the creation of atmospheric effects.

Indeed, Mannerist painting had a special fondness for the juxtaposition of several distinct spaces within a single picture. In *The Denial of Peter,* by a follower of Caravaggio, several actions, separated by sudden ruptures of perspective or lighting, seem to be unfolding independently as in a dream. Space divides itself into isolated but continuous zones, and recedes into private compartments formed by openings and recesses. Further examples of this type 87 of composition are reproduced here in *The Marriage at Cana* by Ludger Tom Ring the Younger 120 and *The Flood* by Joachim Wtewael.

A similar treatment of space is seen in many of the panoramic scenes painted by Joachim Patinir, Niccolò dell'Abbate, and Maerten van Heemskerck. In these landscapes it is impossible to visually absorb all the different parts of the picture at the same time. Two such panoramic details are reproduced here: one from Niccolò dell'Abbate's *Mythological Scene* (London, National Gallery), and one from Heemskerck's *Rape of Helen* (Baltimore, The Walters Art Gallery). These artists, following a technique familiar to Chinese landscape painters, composed their landscapes as if viewed simultaneously from slightly different points of view, whence the fascinating richness and complexity of these scenes. The observer does not see everything at first glance, but rather he is invited to wander through these landscapes, to follow a particular path, to discover a hiding place.

Although primitive artists had also made use of the juxtaposition of completely distinct spaces and the multiple viewpoint, there is no question of primitivism when these devices are employed by Mannerist artists. On the contrary, these Mannerist works are extremely sophisticated in conception, combining in a contrary fashion the unity and multiplicity of space.

Two further ways in which the Mannerist painter exploited space are really two totally opposite conceptions: in one, relatively shallow space is crammed with an incredible accumulation of figures, objects and details; in the other, a deep space is created and is left almost completely empty.

Claude Deruet's *Rape of the Sabines* is a good example of accumulation. Many other examples of such crowded space can be found in the works of Hieronymus Bosch, or in the overladen tables, kitchens, and market-stalls painted by Pieter Aertsen and Joachim Beuckelaer. But the paramount example of the Mannerist penchant for accumulation and crowded space is, of course, Tintoretto's monumental canvas of *Paradise*, in the Sala del Gran Consiglio of the Palazzo Ducale in Venice, which swarms with every order of celestial being.

The use of bare and empty space can be seen here in the *Denial of Peter* by a follower of Caravaggio, and the scene of *Workers in a Wine Cellar* by Jean de Gourmont. This mode of empty space was particularly exploited by certain still life painters. Most remarkable among them was Juan Sanchez Cotan, a detail of whose stark and beautiful *Still Life with Melon* (San Diego, Fine Arts Gallery) is reproduced in this volume. This same sparseness of object in relation to surrounding space is also well illustrated here in the economical *Still Life with a Basket of Glasses* by Sebastian Stosskopf.

Accumulation and emptiness, these two extreme approaches to the utilization of space —like the opposite and yet related manias of claustrophobia and agoraphobia—reveal a pressing preoccupation with space. They symbolize too the dualism of simplicity and multiplicity, stripping bare and complication, which is also found in the literature of the age.

Rabelais, for example, was a compulsive compiler of comical lists, interminable cascades of words thrown out at random one after the other. In Chapters 26 and 28 of the Third Book of his *Gargantua and Pantagruel* the litany of "ball-bags" yields a total of 337 varieties; Chapter 38 lists 208 varieties of "fools;" Chapters 30, 31 and 32 give a comprehensive anatomical description of King Lent. Some of Rabelais' enumerations could be illustrated with Mannerist paintings. His list of Gargantuan games (Book One, Chapter 22) recalls Pieter Bruegel the Elder's painting of *Children's Games*, in the Kunsthistorisches Museum in Vienna. The fabulous menu of Manduce (Fourth Book, Chapters 59 and 60) might well be evoked by the still lifes of Pieter Aertsen or Joachim Beuckelaer. For such a confrontation the reader should compare the extract from the menu of Manduce and the related painting on pages 12 to 15.

These verbal accumulations, paralleling the accumulation of forms in painted images, continued in literature into the early seventeenth century. Tabarin's *Etrennes universelles pour*

JEAN DE GOURMONT
Workmen in a Wine Cellar
Frankfurt, Städelsches Kunstinstitut

l'an mil six cent vingt-et-un (Gifts unlimited for New Year's 1621) anticipates by three centuries the macaronic lists in Jacques Prévert's *Paroles*. In his book, Tabarin details the imaginary gifts, ranging from apples of the Hesperides to cod-lice, which he intends to present to each guild in the country.

The artistic exploitation of emptiness, bareness, and simplicity as seen in the works of Jean de Gourmont and Juan Sanchez Cotan, also had its literary equivalent. This can be found in the bald sonnets of Maurice Scève and Louis Labbé.

Mannerist Color

Mannerist painters have the reputation of being clever draughtsmen but poor colorists. In the case of certain individuals, or certain schools or generations of Mannerist painters this judgment is not wholly unfounded. It certainly applies to some Italian Mannerists of the later sixteenth century. For example, the frescoes of Giorgio Vasari and his pupils in the Palazzo Vecchio in Florence, or the frescoes by Federigo Zuccaro in the Cathedral of Florence, suffer greatly from a coloring which is insipid and gaudy at the same time. A number of painters of the Schools of Utrecht, Haarlem, and Prague of the later sixteenth century were also rather poor colorists. Having seen a black and white reproduction of a work by Joachim Wtewael, Cornelis Cornelisz van Haarlem, Hans von Aachen, or Josef Heintz, for example, it is often disappointing to see the original canvas for the first time: the rather uninspired color adds nothing to the accomplished elegance of the design.

It is, however, quite false to suggest that all Mannerist painters were mediocre colorists. In color as in design, Mannerist painting is characterized in general by its technical virtuosity, its boldness, imagination, and constant quest for new solutions. Perhaps the reason for the disrepute of the Mannerists' ability as colorists lies in the fact that they rarely allowed color to achieve independent play on its own account, as did the great colorists such as Titian and Rubens. This is not to say that color was necessarily subordinate to design or that Mannerist painting was simply colored drawing, but rather that color, together with design and theme, formed a component part of a total effect.

Mannerist artists took great care in the selection of their colors as well as in the application of them, often giving to their paintings the charm of an encrusted jewel. In Jan
22 Bruegel the Elder's *Still Life with Wreath of Flowers* the purity of the red, white, and blue flowers seen against the warmth of the golden plate and the flat blackness of the background is arresting in its exquisiteness.

The Mannerist search for the new and the rare led inevitably to the use of colors and color schemes considered ugly and therefore avoided up to that time. Just as our contemporary music, in search of renewal, employs tones which would have appalled Bach or Mozart, so the Mannerists used a whole range of exquisitely cold and acid colors, bright pinks, intense blues,
151 raw greens, and metallic yellows. The *Venus, Cupid, Time and Folly* by Angelo Bronzino witnesses the precious beauty that can be made to emanate from a combination of intense blues and pinks set off by a touch of acid green.

The clarity of hue in Bronzino's painting enhances its likeness to an enamel relief, but in the Mannerist handling of color there can also be found many examples of a rich gradation
150 of shade and texture. In the detail of Maerten van Heemskerck's *Entombment*, which we here confront with the painting by Bronzino, can be seen a fine variation of tone within each field of color. In his painting of the fabrics, furs, jewels, and flesh Heemskerck displays great virtuosity in creating the widest variety of reflections and mats.

Often Mannerist painting combines the taste for rare colors with a virtuosity of contrasts and gradations: the result is an arresting beauty and richness. This can be seen in the *Allegory of*
59 *Peace* by an anonymous master of the School of Fontainebleau. The porcelain whiteness of the figure is seen against the distant landscape of a cold turquoise, while her robes are a blending of yellow, orange and red contrasted with a rich purple. To augment the chromatic richness of this coloring the highlights and reflections of her purple skirt are rendered in yellow.

Mannerist artists were also capable of achieving evocative effects with a range of very subdued colors, such as the muted brownish gray of the flesh tones of the figure shown in the

152 detail of Niccolò dell'Abbate's *Rape of Persephone*. Similarly restrained, but equally effective is the murky green of Lelio Orsi's sky in *The Way to Emmaus*.

155 Among the new color effects exploited by the Mannerists should be noted the use of extremely pallid tones. This is very obvious in the case of the porcelain whiteness of flesh tones 59 as seen in the *Allegory of Peace* of the School of Fontainebleau. But pallid tones were also 154 exploited by El Greco to different ends. The mystical atmosphere of his *Saint Sebastian*, for example, depends greatly on the heavy use of a cold bluish white.

Because of their mastery of color, Mannerist painters were often able to arrive at a bold 156 chromatic solution with very limited means. In the *Portrait of a Woman* by Adriaen van Cronenburg the soberness of design and concept is played up by a few arresting accents of pure 157 red. In the *Baptism of Christ* by Jan van Scorel and the *Burning of Troy* attributed to Jacques 158 Callot the landscapes are rendered by fine gradation of the tonality of a single hue, and the whole chromatic composition is in each case set off with a very few touches of red. The 243 *Weather Witches* by Hans Baldung Grien is an excellent example of the Mannerist virtuosity in the handling of a variety of tones within a single hue: the color of this painting is entirely composed of subtle variations of earth tones.

The Mannerist researches in color often led to strange chromatic harmonies. Jacopo da Pon-93 tormo's *Visitation* plays upon the juxtaposition of close variations of acid greens contrasted with an equally fine range of pallid pinks and yellows. A harmony of faint, almost washed 177 out colors accented by one bright hue is seen in Joachim Beuckelaer's admirable *Still Life* in which the earthen ware, the pewter, the greenish gray towel and the orange red beams correspond, with very slight variations of tone, to the feathers, cucumbers and cabbages, the meat, and the oranges and lemons.

The play of color seen in Mannerist painting demanded resources of the most delicate sophistication in the artist. For many years of our history, however, these overpowering subtle and knowledgeable stridencies and dissonances of Mannerist coloring were considered to be gross lapses of taste. It is only quite recently that our contemporary interest in dissonance has enabled us to learn to understand and enjoy the chromatic creations of Mannerism.

The Themes
of Mannerist
Painting

Elegance

The extreme clarity of outline and preoccupation with the definition of contour, which as we have seen is one of the primary characteristics of the Mannerist style, is accompanied, in terms of inspiration, by a sensual delectation of the visible world. Mannerist art, however, is never an art of pure sensation. Man is both sense and intelligence, and Mannerism's overt intention

CORNELIS CORNELISZ VAN HAARLEM
The Three Fates
Engraving by Jan Muller

ANGELO BRONZIN
Portrait of Lucretia Panciatich
Florence, Uffi

is neither to sacrifice the senses to the intelligence nor the intelligence to the senses. Mannerism is as far from either a mystical or a classically rational vision of the universe as it is from a vision of pure sense impression. One can easily accuse Mannerist art of diametrically opposed faults, say that it is boringly realistic or that it is lost in its own dream world, that it lapses into a crude lasciviousness or represents an over-restrained idealism. Basically, however, such contradictory accusations succeed in proving only that it is the most complete art imaginable, an art in which man renounces none of his possibilities.

Mannerist sensuality always contains a certain element of calculation. The primary aspect of this partnership between the sensual and the cerebral in Mannerist art is elegance. Elegance is beauty refined by some conscious intention. The intention may be that disdainful 163 haughtiness which characterizes the portraits of Angelo Bronzino or, without going as far as disdain, it may be a certain withdrawal in relation to the vulgarities of life, a slightly distant tone which one encounters in a great number of works of this era. On the other hand, the intention may be simply a deliberate avoidance of ugliness. For a Mannerist artist such as 162 Cornelis Cornelisz van Haarlem, even an ominous subject like *The Three Fates* could be endowed with an elegance of attitude and gesture which renders it a pleasure to the mind and eye. Myths, allegories, and religious scenes were often, first and foremost, a pretext for the 166 conscious display of beauty, or more precisely, grace. Is not the *Amor and Psyche* of Jacopo Zucchi above all an essay in grace and elegance? This same tendency is to be found in the literature of the period. In the writings of Ronsard, Luis de Gongora, and Giovanni Battista Marini the search for the elegant turn of phrase is given more importance than the subject itself.

SCHOOL OF FONTAINEBLEAU
Venus Bewailing the Death of Adonis

ANTOINE CARON DE BEAUVAIS
The Funeral of Amor
Paris, Louvre

Preciosity

Mannerist elegance can often slip into over-refinement and affectation. A work such as Jacopo Zucchi's *Amor and Psyche* is almost too pretty. The elegantly poised Psyche, her nude body encircled by an exquisite girdle of pearls, the carefully arranged flowers, and the little dog are all just a bit too systematically delicate.

In the work of an Italian painter such as Zucchi this preciosity of concept is still tempered by the innate Italian deference to a classical sense of restraint and monumentality. In the works of certain northern artists, however, this tendency to preciosity is given full rein. A mythological scene such as *Venus Bewailing the Death of Adonis* by a master of the School of Fontainebleau seems to be enacted by a preciously delicate courtier and a pretty young princess. The sham grief of Venus is attended by wispily clad ladies in waiting. Similar in conception are the *Dancing Nymphs* by another artist of the School of Fontainebleau. Over-refinement characterized court life in France during the latter part of the sixteenth century. This atmosphere is directly reflected in the works of Antoine Caron de Beauvais. His scene of *The Funeral of Amor*, so delicately and carefully rendered, underscores the preciosity of the subject, probably based on one of the court ballets.

164

165

Miniature painting was a most suitable medium for this preciosity. In Nicholas Hilliard's miniature *Portrait of a Young Dandy*, the foppishly dressed young man languishes by a tree, delicately patterned over by the leaves and blooms of a rose bush.

169

It is perfectly permissible not to like this "mannered" style, but it would be absurd to dismiss it entirely as an approach to art. These simpering affectations do not lack a certain

charm if one accepts them for what they are, that is to say light-hearted and ephemeral games. At the time they provided a final sophistication in taste, and introduced a fresh nuance into European aesthetics. Let us not forget that some very great cultures—that of Japan during the Heian period, for instance—were based on preciosity, and some of the noblest writers of the sixteenth century, Shakespeare included, cannot be properly appreciated if one does not understand this spirit of preciosity.

Mannerist preciosity did not even spare religious art. Affectations analogous to those 82 of secular painting can be found, for example, in the sweet Madonnas of Federigo Barocci and his school, the laughing angels of the master of the "Paraizo" of Lisbon, or in the languishing poses and gestures of the saints of Jacques Bellange.

A whole school of German poetry of the early seventeenth century—Friedrich von Spee,

NICHOLAS HILLIARD
Portrait of a Young Dandy (miniature)
London, Victoria and Albert Museum

Komm mein Herz, komm mein Schatz,
Komm mein grüner Freudenplatz...
Komm mein liebstes Angesicht...
Komm mein Röslein, meine Blume...
Komm mein Himmel, meine Welt
Komm mein Bräutigam, komm mein Kuß...
Komm mein Jesus, meine Freude.
(Angelus Silesius)

Angelus Silesius, Paul Gerhardt—specialized in religious Mannerism. Spee wrote pious pastoral poems and some of his love-songs to Jesus ("I no longer belong to myself, I am thine, I admit my defeat... I can neither speak nor sing..., strength drains away from me, desire will overwhelm me") were of a perturbing equivocalness. Angelus Silesius (Johann Scheffler) was no less passionate: "Come my heart, come my treasure, / Come green land of my joy! / Come, my adored countenance... / Come my rose, come my flower... / Come my sky, my universe... / Come my betrothed, my embrace, / Come, my Jesus, my joy!"

Johann Klaj composed deliciously sugary Christmas lullabies in which "little" angels ("Engelein") gambol around the "little" Jesus ("Jesulein"). One may be exasperated by such **finicking**, and yet a few of these poems, such as *Christ's Little Lullaby* by Paul Gerhardt (found **here on page 78**) are in their way little masterpieces.

Rare Pose and Studied Gesture

Related to the penchant for elegance and preciosity was the Mannerist love of the rare pose and studied gesture. The figure of the good thief from Domenico Beccafumi's *Christ in Limbo*, the executioner in the *Beheading of John the Baptist* by an anonymous Dutch painter, or the

172 figures of *Venus and Cupid* in the engraving after Bartholomeus Spranger, are all quite far from being natural figures. They are posing in the literal sense of the word.

   Mannerist artists adored poses and never wearied of inventing new ones. If one studies,

175 for example, the series of goddesses engraved by Jacques Ducerceau, which are ultimately based upon designs by Rosso Fiorentino, one sees that the artist has made a deliberate effort to vary the poses as much as possible. This quest for new attitudes resulted frequently in extraordinary contortions. This is the case in the *Ascension of Christ*, in Berlin, by an

173 anonymous Dutch painter, or the *Ceres and Vulcan* by a master of the School of Fontainebleau.

DUTCH ARTIST OF ABOUT 1520
Ascension of Christ (detail)
Berlin, Former Staatliche Museen

DOMENICO BECCAFU
The Good Th
(Detail from Christ in Lim
Siena, Pinacoteca Nazion

DUTCH ARTIST OF ABOUT 15
The Beheading of John the Bapt
Berlin, Former Staatliche Muse

BARTHOLOMEUS SP
Venus at her Toilet
Engraving by Sadele

INSIGNIS GALEA ATOS INSIGNIS GORGON PALAS

JACQUES ANDROUET DUCERCEAU
Minerva
Copy of an engraving by Caraglio after a
drawing by Rosso Fiorentino
Engraving

VIRGEL SOLIS
Aurora
Engraving

It may be worth emphasizing at this point the close interplay between style and theme which is perhaps the principal law of artistic creation and which is very evident in Mannerist art. The style of the serpentine line suits perfectly the Mannerist taste for attitudinizing and reciprocally, Mannerist attitudes give rise to the serpentine composition. In the same way we have already noted that the stylistic insistence upon outline and definition of contour serves the concept of elegance, and elegance demands this clarity. Styles and themes aid each other mutually and each achieves its aim through the action of the other.

These rare attitudes sought by Mannerist artists were not of course in limitless supply. One can see, for instance, that Virgel Solis in his engraving of *Aurora* used the identical pose of the *Minerva* in Ducerceau's engraving, which itself was ultimately based on a design by Rosso previously engraved by Caraglio. It was through such borrowings that the typical Mannerist attitudes emerged and solidified.

In the same way, there exist families of Mannerist faces. A particularly frequent face, usually female, bears an expression which hovers between disgust and stupidity and verges on caricature. Such a face is often seen in the works of Bartholomeus Spranger. The best example III among his works reproduced here is the face of Amor in Spranger's painting of *Bacchus, Ceres and Amor*, in Vienna. This affectation is the result of a blending of distortion as a process and expressionism as an idea. Thus here again we find the profound unity of style and theme in Mannerism.

JACQUES ANDROUET DUCERCEAU
Neptis, Juno, Ceres, Opis
Copies of engravings by Caraglio
after drawings by Rosso Fiorentino
Engravings

NEPTIS AEQVOREAS INTER CELLEBERRIMA MATRES

ET SOROR ET CONIVNX IOVIS EST SATVRNIA IVNO.

ALMA CERES DOCVIT SEGETVM SPEM CREDERE SVL CIS

OPIS SATVRNI CONIVNX MATERQVE DEORVM

175

The Love of All Things Good and Beautiful

The Mannerist era was dominated by the ethics of sensuality. Never had Horace's dictum *Carpe diem* ("Enjoy the present day") been more often or more ardently repeated. As Joachim du Bellay re-expressed it, in admirable verse, one's first concern must be with life: "Let us live.../ The day is extinguished each evening and is relit each morning,/ And the seasons repeat their customary course: / But when man has lost this gentle light, / Death makes him sleep an eternal night. / He is truly mad who, exchanging the assurance / Of present good for a dubious hope, / Has always to deny his own desire."

Such advice is not simply an invitation to indulge in the delights of love. Even a libertine like Théophile de Viau proclaimed that the object of pleasure should be the entire universe: "One should," he said "have passionate feelings not only ... toward beautiful women, but also toward all kinds of beautiful things."

"Vivons...
Le jour s'esteint au soir, et au matin reluit,
Et les saisons refont leur course coustumière:
Mais quand l'homme a perdu ceste doulce lumi
La mort luy fait dormir une éternelle nuict.
Celuy vrayement est fol, qui changeant l'asseur
Du bien qui est present, en douteuse espérance,
Veult toujours contredire à son propre désir."
(Joachim du Bellay)

SEBASTIAN STOSSKOPF
Still Life with a Basket of Glasses
Strasbourg, Musée des Beaux-Arts

JOACHIM BEUCKELAER
Still Life
Antwerp, Museum van Schone Kunsten

Some of the most curious examples of Mannerist literature are devoted to litanies of the visible world. Around 1530, Italian poets liked to compose short humorous pieces, often fairly vulgar—so-called *capitoli*—in praise of the most diverse objects. There are *capitoli* by Angelo Bronzino on the paint-brush and the radish, by Agnolo Firenzuola on the sausage, by Francesco Maria Molza on the fig, by Giovanni della Casa on the oven, by Benedetto Varchi on hard-boiled eggs. Francesco Berni, a celebrated author in his time, specialized in this minor form and wrote *capitoli* in praise of chards, peaches, eels and gudgeons: "O saintly, lofty and glorious gudgeons... / O boneless fish, o saintly fish, / Soft, sweet, delicious..."

CLARA PEETERS
Still Life with Tart and Olives
Madrid, Prado

"O santi, eccelsi e gloriosi ghiozzi...
O pesci senza lische, o pesci santi,
dolci, gentili, deliziosi... (Francesco Berni)

Foodstuffs held an honored place in these litanies of good and beautiful things. In the same spirit Rabelais in *Pantagruel* drew up a list of the prodigious number of dishes which the Gastrolaters offered their divinity; and these interminable lists are, through sheer repetition and the accumulation of countless varieties of food, as poetic as they are appetizing (see pages 13 to 15).

Luis de Gòngora, in a *Letrilla* of 1581, sketched with his pen a charming still life "of little cakes, of fresh loaves..., of chestnuts and of acorns." And Girard de Saint-Amant, the most sensual of poets (his verses have titles such as: *Pleasure, Debauchery, The Cabarets, The*

Cheese, The Vine, Cider, Guzzling, The Gluttons...), dedicated to a melon a poem whose lines almost melt in one's mouth (see page 16). And Ronsard sang the leafy joys of the salad.

This gastronomic literature is amply illustrated by the still lifes of the Mannerist painters: mounds of foodstuffs by Pieter Aertsen and Joachim Beuckelaer, Juan Sanchez Cotan's humble but marvellous fruits and vegetables, and throughout the first half of the seventeenth century, the deliciously precise pictures by such artists as Osias Beert, Clara Peeters, Peter Binoit, and Pieter Claesz. This is by no means a purely realist art. One might call it rather a surrealism of the universe around us. We do not use the word surrealism gratuitously: when Salvador Dali painted his *Bread-basket*, he surely had in mind the loaves depicted by Pieter Claesz and other Mannerist painters of still lifes. Sanchez Cotan's *Melons*, the cardoon in the still life by Juan van der Hamen, or Clara Peeters' olives and tart are no longer the modest items from the grocer's and fruiterer's trestle with which one was familiar; or rather they are the same, but apprehended in a privileged moment and—if we may be forgiven this well-worn phrase—

17
178
179

LUDOVICUS FINSONIUS
Still Life with Flute Player
Oxford, Ashmolean Museum

"*A salad let us gather and prepare...*
Seek diligently the tufted lamb's lettuce,
The slender-leafed pasqueflower,
I shall gather the moss's companion,
The tender-rooted liverwort,
And the bud of the flowering currant bush...
We shall wash the herbs heaped in our hands
In the sacred flow of my lovely fountain; ...
Sprinkle them with rose-hued vinegar,
And coat their surface with an oil of Provence...
(Ronsard)

seen in the light of eternity. These succulent victuals do not simply appeal to the pleasures of eating; each olive, each fruit, each fragment of bread recalls to us what an extraordinary adventure it is to live in this universe.

Foodstuffs were just one pretext among others to secure a profound and direct contact with the totality of existence. Any object at all was capable of evoking this same revelation: the perfectly proportioned *Musical Instruments* by Evaristo Baschenis, *a Basket of Glasses* by Sebastian Stoskopff, or the flowers and jewels of Jan Bruegel the Elder's *Still Life with a Wreath of Flowers*.

We shall examine in a later chapter Mannerism's encyclopedic curiosity about everything that lives or grows: the entire animal, vegetable and mineral kingdom. It is difficult to distinguish the science from the poetry in this abounding curiosity. Each is mingled inextricably with the other in a commonly shared amazement at a universe which is present in its entirety in each of its details.

181

Adoration of the Female Body

Among the objects of the universe, there was one supremely privileged object which Mannerism never tired of depicting: the female body.

Other cultures in other epochs were, of course, greatly inspired by the female body, but not even the pagan cultures of ancient times or the voluptuous eighteenth century were ever so consistently, so single-mindedly engrossed in the theme as was Mannerism—almost to the point of mania. Allegory, mythology, history, the Bible, the martyrdom of the saints all provided the Mannerist with the opportunity of stripping woman bare. Venus, Diana, the Muses, Eve, Bathsheba, Judith, the chaste Susanna and Lucretia, Saint Catherine on the wheel, Mary Magdalen in her desert, the Virtues, the Liberal Arts, even personifications of the Church itself were often only pretexts for exploiting one and the same theme: a woman's body.

SCHOOL OF FONTAINEBLEAU
Water Deities (detail)
New York, Wildenstein Gallery

POPP
The Three Grace
Florence, Uffiz

VINCENT SELLAER
Susanna and the Elders (detail)
Antwerp, Zuttere Collection

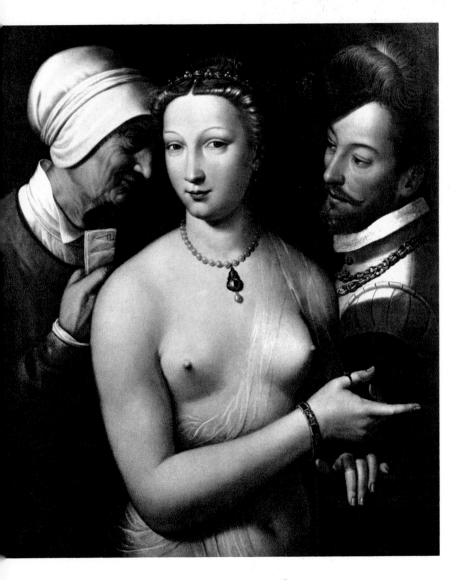

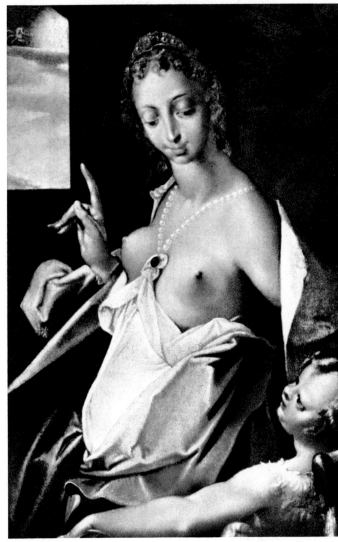

The French, especially, both painters and poets, seemed possessed by a positive obsession for the female body. Clément Marot wrote a poem in honor of the *Lovely Breast* (see page 41) which served as a model for a whole series of poetic eulogies of the female body: Jean de Vauzelle's *The Hair*; Maurice Scève's *The Brow, The Eyebrow* and *The Throat*; Albert le Grand's *The Ear*; Antoine Héroet's *The Eye* and Mellin de Saint-Gelais's poem on the same theme; Eustorg de Beaulieu's appreciations of *The Nose, The Cheek, The Tongue* and *The Teeth*; Victor Brodeau's *The Mouth*; Claude Chappuy's *The Hand*; Gilles d'Aurigny's *The Fingernail*; Bonaventure Des Périers' *The Navel*; Jacques Le Lieur's *The Thigh*; Lancelot Carle's *The Knee*; François Sagon's *The Foot*. An anonymous versifier permitted himself to eulogize the "bien suprême" (the phrase by which a woman's sex was delicately alluded to at the time), and Eustorg de Beaulieu—though a priest—ventured on such descriptions in even more intimate detail.

Ronsard was the most eloquent of all these devotees of the female sex. In his poem *The Bath of Callirée*, he regrets his inability to imitate Coeneus and turn himself into a woman so that he can spy on his beautiful mistress as she takes her bath. At night he dreamed of "This body, this belly, and this bosom / Colored like a finely-worked ivory, / In which I beheld twin apples, / Rising and falling in this watery prison / As do the waves which play around their

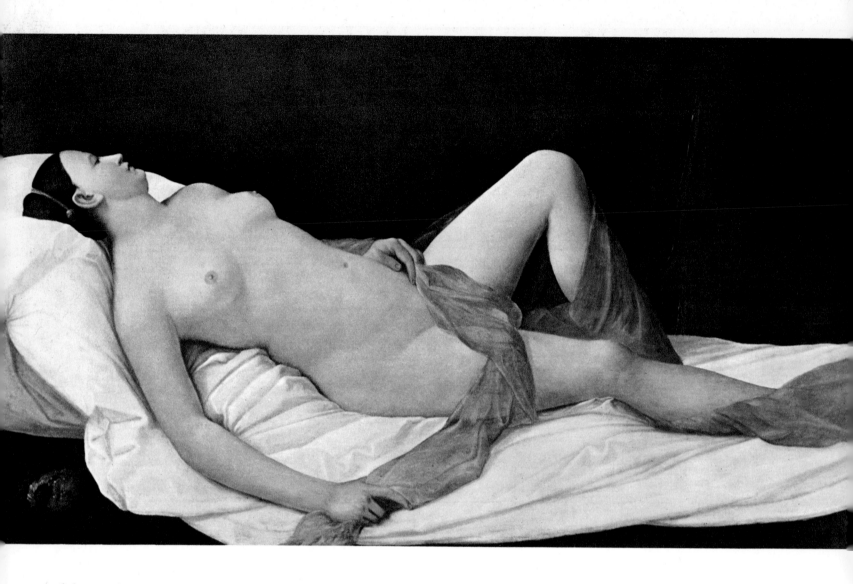

globes ..." *(Fantasy to His Lady).* And in his *Elegy to Janet, Painter to the King,* Ronsard detailed amorously those charms of his mistress which he would wish to find reproduced in her
portrait, not forgetting her most secret charms ... Ronsard's Janet (probably to be identified with
François Clouet who became painter to King François I in 1541), and his fellow painters at the
French court of Fontainebleau, had no need of these encouragements. Their whole art con-
39 sisted principally of a series of variations on the nude female body, painted for its own sake,
40 as being the most beautiful object which the earth had to offer.

The French, however, were only the most impassioned and devoted zealots of a cult
which had succeeded in dominating the whole of Europe. Italian writers composed treatises
on feminine beauty: Agnolo Firenzuola's *On the Beauty of Women,* Francesco Luigino da
Udine's *The Book of the Beautiful Woman.* Painters of every nationality, except of course
183 the Spaniards, turned out infinite variations of *The Judgment of Paris, The Three Graces* and
Venus before a Mirror, all themes which allowed the viewer to perceive at first glance the full
treasures of a body seen simultaneously from the front, from the back and sideways.

In the later sixteenth century this cult of the female body was held somewhat in check in
the visual arts by the prudery of the Counter-Reformation. But since it is less dangerous to say
than to show, it continued to flourish in literature through the early seventeenth century. It is
particularly marked in the works of the Italian poet Giovanni Battista Marini and the German

VENETIAN ARTIST
OF THE 16th CENTURY
Sleeping Venus
Florence, Conte Contini Collection

"*Un peu plus bas, en miroir arrondi,*
Tout potelé, grasselet, rebondi,
Comme celuy de Vénus, pein son ventre;
Pein son nombril ainsi qu'un petit centre,
Le fond duquel paraisse plus vermeil
Qu'un bel oeillet favori du Soleil.
Qu'attends-tu plusè portray moy l'autre cho.
Qui est si belle, et que dire je n'ose,
Et dont l'espoir impatient me poind;
Mais je te pry, ne me l'ombrage point,
Si ce n'estoit d'un voile fait de soye
Clair et subtil, à fin qu'on l'entre-voye."

(Ronsard

186

A little lower down, round like a mirror,
All dimpled, plump and curved,
Like that of Venus paint her belly;
Paint her navel like a tiny center,
Its recess seeming rosier
Than a carnation favored by the Sun.
What do you await portray me that other thing
So beautiful, I dare not mention,
Tho' impatient desire for it weighs upon me;
But I beg you do not conceal it,
Unless, perhaps with a silken veil
So fine and thin that one may see through it."
(Elegy to Janet, Painter to the King)

lyrical writers. Some of Marini's short poems such as *The Breast of his Lady* or *The Sparse Tuft on the Waves* could well take their place among the earlier French eulogies of the female body, as could indeed the anonymous German lyric, signed C. H., from a collection compiled by Benjamin Neukirch: "In our paradise are apples of love / Softer than the fruit which Eve desired to eat... / A table covered with a satin cloth, / A perfect ivory next to which gold is tarnished... / A snow that is alive...."

The word "cult" which we have used for this adoration of the female body is not exaggerated: a genuine religion was in the making. As an example, one may quote the extraordinary sonnet, in the *Amours de Théophile* of Marc de Papillon de Lasphrise (Théophile de Viau), in which the poet applies to the woman he loves the gestures and terms of the liturgy: "When the happy day comes that I shall sacrifice / My body upon your Altar consecrated by holy Desire..."

The same tone of adoration is to be found in a poem by David Schirmer in which he describes his emotions while leaning over his sleeping mistress: "Here sleeps my paradise, bestrewn with roses, / And her breast, my torment, gently heaves; / An amber perfume rises from her lovely bosom; / Here my paradise lies at rest in the green meadow."

But however exalted this cult may have been, there was nothing Platonic about it. The Mannerist era did not profess any excessive respect for love. Even quite apart from openly

erotic poetry such as Aretino's *Sonnets luxurieux*, Ronsard's *Livret de folastries*, Thomas Carew's *Rapture*, and certain poems from the collection compiled by Benjamin Neukirch, almost the whole of Mannerist literature envisages love in its most sensual aspect. Jacopo Sannazaro's *Arcadia*, Ariosto's *Orlando Furioso*, Tasso's *Jerusalem Delivered*, Edmund Spenser's *Faerie Queene*, Giovanni Battista Marini's *Adonis* are all filled with the thrill of desire. The woman of Mannerism is not the Lady of the Medieval courtly romance. She is always either a seductress or a quarry. On the one hand she can be an enchantress such as Homer's Calypso, Ariosto's Alcine, Tasso's Armide, or a woman of pleasure fleecing some old fogy or a young fop, or yet again a goddess shamelessly parading her charms before Paris. On the other hand, she can be a nymph fleeing from the faun, Diana caught unawares by the hunter, the Sabine women carried off by force, the chaste Susanna spied on by the Elders, Lucretia dishonored, Ariosto's beautiful Angelica exposed to the monster (and to men), or Ariosto's other heroine, Isabella, in the hands of the bandits, or Tasso's Sophronia half naked at the stake. In painting as in literature, Mannerist eroticism hesitated between prostitution and rape, and it was often quite difficult to distinguish one from the other, so complaisant the pursued nymphs, so flirtatious the Susannas and Lucretias. Giovanni Battista Marini, in his *Galleria* (1620), standing before such a painting of Lucretia proposed the following little homily: "Lady, antiquity has erred in calling you virtuous; for though you now pierce this bosom soiled by an obscene love, yet still you did not fail to take an illegitimate pleasure then. If you wished to be praised by us, you should have killed yourself before, not after."

185
36
95
184

Perversion

As can be seen, Mannerist eroticism slipped readily into perversion. But what is perversion but a sexuality in which the intellect intervenes? In this we find exemplified the particular character of Mannerist sensuality, that is, not a pure sensuality but a sensuality mingled with the complications of reflection.

A very general and primary characteristic of erotic perversion in Mannerist art is *voyeurism*. Mannerist painters were particularly fond of subjects like Acteon surprising Diana and her nymphs, David watching Bathsheba, the Elders spying upon Susanna. Often artists and writers expressed these same ideas without the aid of Biblical or mythological subjects. Marc de Papillon de Lasphrise (Théophile de Viau) in his *Amours de Théophile* watched his half naked fair one "through a cunningly concealed opening...." We have already noted that Ronsard in his *Bath of Callirée* dreamed of transforming himself into a woman so that he might

HEINRICH ALDEGREVER
Bath House Scene
Engraving by Virgel Solis

JAN VAN HEMESSEN
Brothel Scene
Berlin, Former Staatliche Museen

witness with impunity his mistress taking her bath. This theme of the bath—a typically voyeuristic theme—recurs constantly throughout Mannerist painting. Sometimes the *voyeur* is depicted in the picture, as in the scenes of *Susanna and the Elders.* More often, however, the *voyeur* is the beholder himself: at least the artist would seem to be persuading him to play this role. Indeed the Mannerist style, with its accent on visual clarity and meticulous illustration, obligingly offers the beholder all the details he could possibly desire.

184

The sixteenth century storyteller Matteo Bandello describes, in one of his stories, a scene which is a pure striptease. A deceived lover forces his mistress to stretch out on a bed designed for lying-in-state, and then disrobes her little by little in front of his assembled friends: "... the Lady was covered only with a single, flimsy shift which did not succeed in concealing fully any of the parts of her delicate and supple body. Pompeio lifted the hem of this shift and drew it back a little, revealing two slim little feet of a dazzling whiteness, with tiny, well-shaped toes ending in pearly nails; he soon drew the garment back farther, revealing almost the whole of her thighs... Then Pompeio, after concealing with a corner of the garment what lay between her thighs, revealed her bosom, a delicious sight for the spectators... Everyone gazed

BAR·SPRANGERS·ANT·FECIT·

with delight at this white, firm bosom, with its two round, hard breasts which would have seemed made of alabaster were it not that the Lady's trembling lent to them a gentle fluctuation most charming to see" (*Novelle*, I, 3).

186 Many pictures of the epoch, for example the *Sleeping Woman* by a Venetian artist of the sixteenth century in the collection of the Conte Contini, might well be an illustration of the final stage of the little sport just described.

Baths and striptease bring us to prostitution. Flemish, Dutch, and German painters produced innumerable representations of the Prodigal Son in the company of prostitutes and of 190 lustful old men caressing young girls. An artist of Antwerp, Jan van Hemessen, specialized 185 in brothel scenes. The theme of the procuress recurred frequently in the works of the School of Fontainebleau. Ronsard, in his *Elégies*, advised the bashful lover to go the Ile de la Cité, visit the establishment of "Jeanne la grise" and there, picking out the girl who most resembled his beloved, forget the eyes of the one on the body of the other. A sonnet by Girard de Saint-Amant was devoted to the brothel ("Enter the brothel with a grave demeanor..."). But the master commentator on prostitution was Aretino, and the bawd was an essential character in the sixteenth century Italian theater.

193 Prostitution is not in itself a perversion. What is perverse is to take a special pleasure in the atmosphere of prostitution and in the degradation of sexuality which prostitution implies. It may be objected that sixteenth century man was simpler and more brutal, and saw nothing more in these paintings and verses than a gross Rabelaisian naughtiness. In many cases this view is certainly to be doubted. The lecherous old men are often too obviously ignoble, and the joy of the bawds often too obscene, for this to be simply a question of easy-going gaiety. A painting in Bordeaux attributed to Giulio Cesare Procaccini could represent *Susanna and the Elders*, but seems more specifically to depict a young woman being sold. There is nothing Rabelaisian about the expression of desperation on the face of this young girl. The element of perversity—that is to say, the delectation in evil recognized as such—is unmistakable.

Another aspect of Mannerist perversion is the taste for diversity. The plenitude of beauty is wearisome and Mannerism prefers variations and rarities. It is the unripe fruit which is particularly appreciated. Ronsard *(Ode* xv) states this in straightforward terms: "L'âge non meur, mais verdelet encore, / Est l'âge seul qui me dévore / Le cœur d'impatience atteint..." ["Age that is not ripe, but still tinged with green, / Is the only age which devours / My heart overwhelmed with impatience..."] Aretino writes in his *Ragionamenti* that "the Venetians have very special tastes; they desire buttocks, breasts and firm flesh, from fifteen or sixteen years old to twenty at the most." Such also is often the taste of the painters. For example, the *Bathing* 192 *Nymphs* in Parmigianino's frescoes of the legend of Diana and Acteon at Fontanellato are 127 quite adolescent, and Lucas Cranach the Elder's women are nearly always of slightly prenubile age.

On the other hand, old women are of equal interest to the perverse imagination. Un-296 questionably, the hideous *Naked Witch* in the drawing by Nikolaus Manuel Deutsch and the 258 *Aged Nymph* engraved by René Boyvin after Rosso Fiorentino spring primarily from an aesthetic perversity, expressionism. But it is permissible to think that these drawings and engravings, like the descriptions written by Ronsard and Edmund Spenser (see page 297), also contain a certain erotic curiosity. Brantôme, in any case, devoted an entire dissertation in the *Vies des Dames galantes* to the love affairs of old women, in which he assures the reader that it is possible to find as much, or more, pleasure with them as with younger women.

After the variation of age, we have that of race. Hieronymus Bosch and Cornelis Cornelisz van Haarlem liked to contrast white and black female nudes. A verse of Camões celebrated the beautiful captive Barbara, either a Negress or a mulatto, "whose brown color so dear to love... would be envied by the snow." A poem by Giovanni Battista Marini was dedicated to a black slave: "You are black but you are beautiful...; ivory and pearl grow dull and dim compared with your body's ebony...."

Yet another method of varying the usual nude was to exotically adorn her with jewels and other finery. This type of erotic trapping was particularly favored by Nikolaus Manuel Deutsch. In his *Judgment of Paris*, for instance, Minerva is crowned with five ostrich feathers and her nude body adorned with a bowed sash. Lucas Cranach the Elder achieved most titillating effects with this device. He reduced the clothing of his many Venuses to a fashionable red hat, or to a few pieces of jewelry as in his *Venus and Cupid* reproduced in this volume. These various adornments, be they transparent veils or jewelry, add spice to the nudity which they accentuate through the provocation inherent in patently inadequate clothing. A particularly frequent procedure was to clothe the woman in a costume which is perfectly decent apart from the fact that it leaves the breasts bare. A striking example of this is seen in the painting of *Lot and his Daughters* by Frans Floris.

But the most radical variation of the erotic object was of course homosexuality. In place of a normal woman, the artist did not substitute a very young girl or an ancient crone, but preferred to feature a boy of more or less effeminate appearance. In imitation of the Ancients, in a search for unusual sensations, from an overdeveloped taste for elegance and affectation, or for any number of other reasons, the sixteenth century—at least among the ruling classes— was profoundly attracted by the idea of homosexualism. During that epoch, Italy was the pederast's paradise. Matteo Bandello, one of the most reliable guides to contemporary morals, narrates the story of a certain Porcellio who (in Bandello's euphemistic terminology) "loved young goat's flesh more than any other food...." He became so gravely ill that his wife feared he was in danger of death and, wishing him to have the opportunity of confessing his sins, called upon an old and saintly monk, to whom she revealed her husband's vice. The monk questioned the sick man and asked him gently if he had never committed the "sin against nature." The latter replied indignantly: "You are asking me a strange question, Padre; to what are you referring? Never in my life have I committed the sin against nature." The monk was contrite when he heard this statement and went to reprimand the spouse for what he took to have been a calumny; but she persuaded him that she had not lied and he therefore returned to the sick man's bedside. On this occasion he made his questions more explicit. Upon which, Porcellio replied in an amused tone of voice and shaking his head: "Oh, oh, Reverend Padre, you were not adept in questioning me. To amuse myself with young boys is more natural to me than it is natural for a man to eat and drink, and yet you asked me if I had sinned against nature! Come, come, Padre, you just don't known a dainty morsel when you see it." (*Novelle*, I, 6.)

No less edifying is Francesco Maria Molza's *Story of Ridolfo of Florence*. Ridolfo liked boys; however, heeding his parents' remonstrations, he agreed to wed an attractive young girl whose particular charm for him was that she had a fairly masculine appearance. But he soon reverted to his old habits, this time with his page. His exasperated wife decided to revenge herself and, in order to punish him by appropriating the object of his sinful activities, she became the mistress of the page. Ridolfo discovered them *in flagrante delicto* and, pederast though he was, he became so jealous of his wife that he prepared to kill her. Faced with death,

she had the brilliant idea of covering her face by pulling up her skirts under pretext of avoiding the sight of the incipient death-blow; this action revealed to her husband "the parts which she knew pleased him so greatly." Ridolfo, enchanted by this spectacle, regretted immediately his wrath which had threatened to cost him this treasure, and reconciled himself with his wife; "and all three lived happily together for a long time thereafter, although no one knew rightly which of the two was more completely Ridolfo's wife."

These tales give an adequate idea of the moral atmosphere prevailing in Italy during the Mannerist era. Pederasty was not simply a common practice but an openly admitted activity. One of Francesco Berni's *capitoli* is entitled *On a Young Boy*, and the author here explains what he would do if someone gave him a nice young boy, as Maecenas had presented a young boy to Virgil. Leonardo's emotional existence was dominated by masculine friendship, he frequented the company of adolescents of dubious morals and even chose one of these companions, Jacopo Saltarelli, to be his model in painting the child Jesus. Although Benvenuto Cellini never admitted any homosexual tendencies, his autobiography contains several extremely equivocal anecdotes. One day, for instance, invited to an artist's party to which each guest was required to bring a "crow" (courtesan), he had himself accompanied by a young boy, Diego, whom he had dressed up as a girl. The guests vied in complimenting him on the beauty of the supposed young girl, and Diego was the belle of the ball. One feels that Cellini tells this story with a degree of enthusiasm which is rather suspect, and insists rather more than necessary on the boy's success. In fact, he seems as proud of Diego as if the boy had been his mistress (*La Vita* I, 30).

According to Giorgio Vasari, Giovanni Antonio Bazzi, Il Sodoma, always had around him "young boys and adolescents, for whom he displayed an extraordinary liking," whence his name of Sodoma, an appellation in which he gloried. And Michelangelo, at the age of fifty-seven, became smitten with a young Roman noble, Tommaso de' Cavalieri, who provided the inspiration for some of Michelangelo's most beautiful sonnets (see pages 294 and 295). Some of these poems are sheer cries of frustrated desire, all the more moving for the fact that they owe nothing whatsoever to the then fashionable Anacreontic verse form, and if in his last poems the passion seems to have become sublimated into a Platonic affection, we are still confronted with a most strange love.

Homosexuality was no less fashionable in England. Christopher Marlowe, in his plays and poems, mentions it frequently without attaching the least stigma to it. His *Edward II* includes a scene of passionate love between the king and his favorite, Piers Gaveston; the opening scene of *Dido, Queen of Carthage* shows Jupiter "dandling Ganymede upon his knee;" in *Hero and Leander* he gratuitously adds an openly homosexual episode—the love of Neptune for Leander—which formed no part of the original Greek legend. And as we all know Shakespeare's amorous *Sonnets* are dedicated to a man, the mysterious Mr. W. H. It is perhaps an interesting subject for reflection that the two greatest lyrical poets of the Mannerist epoch—Michelangelo and Shakespeare—should have derived inspiration for their most beautiful verses from what appear to have been homosexual attachments.

Countless sixteenth century paintings reveal the influence of homosexual inclinations. The ambiguous expressions and the equivocal features of the personages of Leonardo's paintings have been much studied. Sodoma's works are also redolent of overt homosexualism. His

FRANS FLORIS
Lot and his Daughters
Stuttgart, Staatsgalerie

295   equivocal young Isaac in *The Sacrifice of Abraham*, set up in the Cathedral of Pisa for the edification of the faithful, is a prototype of the minion. The figures in Mannerist paintings are at times so curiously ambiguous that it is difficult to identify the personages of the picture.
194   Such is the case with Bartholomeus Spranger's *Hercules and Omphale Disguised*.

    Despite Henri III and his foppish courtiers, French sixteenth century art appears to have been little concerned with such perversions. The Frenchmen of this epoch were so enamoured of womankind that, if they interested themselves in homosexuality at all, it was always female homosexuality! Brantôme, who devotes a few pages of his first Discourse in the *Vies des Dames galantes* to Lesbianism, gives it as his opinion that this vice is far less repugnant than its masculine equivalent. Pontus de Tyard, bishop of Chalon-sur-Saône, stretched complaisance so far as to write an *Elegy for a Lady Enamoured of Another Lady:*

200

"Hélas! beauté d'amour, te choisiray-je aux hommes!
Ha, non: je cognois trop le siècle auquel nous sommes.
L'homme aime la beauté et de l'honneur se rit,
Plus la beauté lui plait, plustot l'honneur perit.
Ainsi du seul honneur cherement curieuse
Libre je desdaignois toute flamme amoureuse,
Quand de ma liberté Amour trop offencé
Un aguet me tendit subtilement pensé.
...Il fait ardoir un feu
Hélas qui me croira!—de si nouvelle flamme
Que femme il m'enamoure, hélas! d'une autre femme."

"Alas! beauty of Love, should I find you freely among men! /Ah, no: I knew too well the times in which we live. / Man loves beauty and mocks honor, / The more beauty pleases him, so much the more does honor perish. / Thus, dearly curious about honor alone, / I freely disdained every amorous flame, / But Love, too offended by my freedom, / Proffered me a cunningly-conceived taper. / ...Which ignited a fire / —Who will believe me, alas!—with so new a flame / That it makes me, a woman, enamoured, alas!, of another woman."

One may perhaps find an echo of these reveries of Gomorrha in the anonymous painting in the Louvre of two young women, naked and portrayed at half-length in a bathtub, the fingers of one gently clasping a nipple of the other. This is generally considered to be an allegory on the royal pregnancy of Gabrielle d'Estrées, the mistress of Henri IV. But a painting often expresses something entirely different from its official subject, and consciously or unconsciously the artist has presented us with a vivid image of Lesbos.

Finally we come to the supreme sin, the violation of humanity's first taboo: incest. It is a theme which is by no means uncommon in the sixteenth century theater. In Sperone Speroni's play *Canace* (1546), Macareo and Canace, brother and sister, become lovers, have a child, kill it, and then kill themselves. One of the masterpieces of the Elizabethan theater, John Ford's *'Tis Pity she's a Whore*, has incest as its central theme. In the very first scene, Giovanni defends eloquently his love for his sister Annabella:

"Shall a peevish sound,
A customary form, from man to man,
Of brother and of sister, be a bar
'Twixt my perpetual happiness and me?
Say that we had one father, say one womb
(Curse to my joys!) gave both us life and birth;
Are we not therefore each to other bound
So much the more by nature? By the links
Of blood, of reason? Nay, if you will have't,
Even of religion, to be ever one,
One soul, one flesh, one love, one heart, one all?"

The declaration of mutual passion in Act Two, Scene One, is comparable in its passionate intensity to the famous balcony scene in *Romeo and Juliet*.

It is not so easy to present the theme of incest in painting, simply because it is difficult to indicate in a picture that a man and woman are related, let alone brother and sister. The artist is limited to easily recognizable themes. One theme which is not in itself incestuous but which permits the introduction of an equivocal image is that of Perra offering her breast to her father, Cimon, condemned to starve to death in prison, a subject known as Roman Charity. But the incestuous subject *par excellence* was that of *Lot and his Daughters*. This theme was popular all over Europe in the Mannerist epoch, and especially among northern artists. It was treated notably by Lucas van Leyden, Jan Matsys, Joachim Patinir, Lucas Cranach the Elder, and Bartholomeus Spranger. The two paintings of this subject reproduced here, by Frans Floris and Joachim Wtewael, underscore most emphatically the incestuous eroticism of the Biblical story. The sudden and widespread interest in this particular passage of the Bible is quite extraordinary, and provides a final proof of the Mannerist taste for perversion.

FLEMISH ARTIST of about 162
The Feast of Herod (deta)
Madrid, Prad

Sadism

In a certain sense, erotic perversity is always sadistic. The voyeur, the lover of "variations", considers the other person not as a living being but as an object to be observed or collected or used for amusement. An earlier chapter of this book discussed the female body considered as the most beautiful object in the world: it is not by chance that the word "object" springs immediately to one's mind when one looks at a nude depicted by a Mannerist artist. Mannerist sensuality is a latent sadism and often results in a manifest sadism.

Certainly the artist was scarcely able to close his eyes to the cruelty surrounding him during the sixteenth century: there has rarely been a more thoroughly and atrociously cruel epoch. Compilations such as the *Acts and Monuments of these latter and perilous days* (1563) by John Foxe, or the *Theatrum crudelitatum haereticorum nostri temporis* (1587) by Richard Vestegan are catalogues of the appalling torments by means of which both Catholics and Protestants attempted to insure the triumph of their particular brand of Christianity. Judges

such as Henry Boguet, chief justice of Burgundy, or Martin del Rio, one of the magistrates of the Duke of Alba's notorious "council of blood," composed what can only be described as brochures of torture, designed for the guidance of their colleagues who were dealing with cases of sorcery. The background history of the time abounds with horrible anecdotes: the Grand Duke Cosimo de' Medici brought back to Florence his political enemies, when they had been captured by the Spaniards, so that he might torture them at leisure; Muzio Colonna paid six hundred ducats for the person of Amico d'Ascole, so that he might have the satisfaction of personally cutting his throat; Henri III forced his sister Margot to witness, throughout an entire day, the agonies of her lover, d'Aubiac, who had been hung by his feet from a gibbet outside the princess' window.

Thus it could be argued that the cruelty shown in sixteenth century literature and art merely reflects the very real cruelty of the epoch, and constitutes a testimony to the manners and morals of the time rather than a gratuitously perverse reverie. This is doubtless true of a work of protest such as Agrippa d'Aubigné's violently satirical poem *Les Tragiques*, and it is at least partially true of a realist work of fiction such as Johann Jakob Christoffel von Grimmelshausen's *Simplicissimus*; but it is no longer true in the case of works of pure imagination —stories or dramas—in which the cruelty clearly represents a deliberate pursuit of strong, rare emotions.

Many Italian storytellers of the epoch resort to sadism as a simple method of inciting the reader's interest. In Matteo Bandello's *Tale of Pandora*, a husband forces his wife to strangle her lover with her own hands. Anton Francesco Grazzini, called "Il Lasca" (1503–1583), was a notable precursor of our own century's *humour noir* or "sick humor." His stories *The Student's Vengeance* and *A Brother's Vengeance* recount in a light-hearted vein some practical tricks, the victims of which emerge horribly mutilated, beard and eyebrows singed, streaming with blood. But in his *Tale of Sergio* Grazzini abandons his tone of pleasantry and achieves the ultimate in sheer horror. In this tale, Currado, prince of Fiesole, surprises his young wife with Sergio, his son by a previous marriage. On the spot, he has their eyes torn out, their tongues cut off, and their hands and feet chopped off, and leaves them in this state upon the bed that had witnessed their love. "The poor unhappy lovers, without tongues, eyes, feet or hands, their life blood gradually ebbing from seven separate wounds, were close to death. Yet, when they heard Currado pronounce his final words, then heard his retreating footsteps and the closing of the door, they felt for each other, clasped each other with their bleeding stumps and, with their mouths united, their bodies pressed as tightly together as possible, awaited death in suffering." (*Cene*, II, 5.)

Another Italian writer, Giambattista Cinzio Giraldi (1504–1573), achieved fame for the scenes of atrocious cruelty with which he larded his dramas. His efforts, however, pale in comparison with the wave of sadism which swamped the English theatre during that century. In Shakespeare's *Titus Andronicus*, two brothers rape a virtuous young woman, Lavinia, then cut off her tongue and hands to prevent her from revealing the crime, but Lavinia, using a staff of which she holds one end between her teeth while manipulating the other end with her feet, writes in the sand the names of her aggressors. Her father, to avenge her, cuts the two young men's throats and bakes their heads in a pie which he persuades their mother, ignorant of its true ingredients, to eat at a banquet. The final curtain falls on a description of the torments which "that damn'd Moor" Aaron is to undergo: "Set him breast-deep in earth," is the command, "and famish him; There let him stand, and rave, and cry for food...." Most of these horrors, however, take place off-stage. Christopher Marlowe is less delicate, and presents his

NIKOLAUS MANUEL DEUTSCH
The Martyrdom of the
Ten Thousand (detail)
Öffentliche Kunstsammlung

207

horrors before the eyes of the audience. In *Tamburlaine the Great*, we see Bajazeth, Emperor of the Turks, dragged in a cage behind his conqueror. Tamburlaine, banqueting with his followers, amuses himself by taunting the captive Emperor. As the wretched man slowly dies of hunger and thirst, Tamburlaine listens with pleasure to his curses and occasionally proffers him a scrap of meat impaled on the tip of his sword. To escape his torments and put an end to his shame, Bajazeth brains himself against his cage. His wife, seeing him dead, does likewise. In the second part of the drama, Tamburlaine appears, whip in hand, riding in a chariot drawn by two vanquished kings, bits clamped in their mouths. When they are exhausted, they are unharnessed, hanged and replaced by two further royal captives. The protagonists of *The Jew of Malta*, Barabas and his slave Ithamore, are the very incarnation of that aspect of sensual vice which is extreme cruelty. In the end, however, virtue triumphs and Barabas, the victim of the torture he himself has devised, falls into a caldron of boiling water and dies screaming and cursing. Such diabolical scenes are common throughout the Elizabethan theater. In John Webster's *The White Devil*, for instance, the Duke of Brachiano is assassinated by means of a poison sprinkled in the helmet which an armorer fixes over his head. While he is suffering terrible agonies as the poison takes effect, his enemies, disguised as Capuchin monks, conjure up images of Hell, assuring him that he will soon be there. In Thomas Dekker and Philip Massinger's *Virgin-Martyr*, the audience witnesses the various tortures inflicted on the Christians.

ANTONIO TEMPESTA
Varieties of Martyrdom from
"Trattato degli istrumenti di martirio"
of Antonio Gallonio, Rome, 1591.
Engraving

MAERTEN VAN HEEMSKERCK
The Stoning of the Elders, from the
story of Susanna
Engraving by D. V. Coornhert

CORREGGIO
The Punishment of Juno (fresco)
Parma, Convento di San Paolo

Painting was no less sadistic. A favorite subject of the epoch, for instance, was *The*
207 *Martyrdom of the Ten Thousand*, which permitted the depiction of an orgy of torments. The
painting of this subject reproduced here, by Nikolaus Manuel Deutsch, is horrifying in its
gruesomeness: a copse of dead trees is strewn with bleeding bodies impaled by the spike-like
stumps. Alessandro Allori painted for the church of Santo Spirito in Florence an alley bor-
dered with crucified or impaled martyrs, which would have done honor to one of Octave
Mirbeau's menacing parks. The curious drawing by Maerten van Heemskerck of the stoning
of the two elders who had falsely accused Susanna of adultery is a sort of analytic study of
torture accompanied by a chorus of violence. This taste for torments did not display itself
solely in subjects of martyrdoms: Pieter Bruegel the Elder, for instance, made his painting of
Justice (from the series of the Four Cardinal Virtues) serve as the pretext for a detailed catalogue of tortures.

The obsession with torture became even more pronounced toward the end of the
sixteenth century. Under the influence of the Counter-Reformation the scenes of martyrdoms
multiplied in the churches. In Rome the Jesuits had their colleges and churches of their colleges decorated with the most gruesome scenes of Christian martyrdoms, in order to exalt the
courage of the young seminarists. In about 1585, Pomarancio (Niccolò Circignani) frescoed
the whole interior of the church of Santo Stefano Rotonda, the church of the college of the

S. AGATHA VIRGO
ET MARTYR

GIOVANNI STRADANO
The Martyrdom of Saint Agatha
Engraving

German Jesuits in Rome, with some thirty scenes of martyrdom: the most hideous atrocities were depicted with a ferocious tranquility.

In 1591, there appeared in Rome a treatise on the instruments and methods of torture used by the Pagans against the Christians. This was the *Trattato degli istrumenti di martirio e delle varie manieri martoriare*, written by the Oratorian, Father Antonio Gallonio. This strange work was illustrated with forty-six engravings by Antonio Tempesta, in which the martyrs are depicted crucified, sawn asunder, crushed, burned, hanged, roasted alive, or torn with pincers, and all this debauchery of the imagination is presented with calm analysis. The explanatory captions for the one plate of this treatise which we illustrate here are as follows:

"A. Martyr suspended by both feet, with a great stone attached to the neck.

B. Sometimes, the Holy Martyrs, after being smeared with honey, were tied to stakes driven into the ground, and thus exposed to the rays of the sun to be tortured by the stings of bees and the bites of flying insects.

C. Martyr suspended by one foot; one of the legs is bent double at the knee and maintained in this position by an iron band, the other being weighted with a heavy lump of iron."

The element of sexual perversity in sadism appears fully when the victim is a woman. Sadism is an extreme form of rape and, at the same time, a hypocritical manner of representing rape. But Mannerist eroticism was particularly fascinated by the idea of rape. In *Orlando Furioso*, for example, the protagonist, Angelica, is perpetually in danger of being raped, by Sacripanto, by Renaldo, by an ancient hermit, and by Roger who, after delivering her from the sea-monster, cannot resist the temptation offered by this beautiful naked body. Another heroine of the epic, Isabella, only escapes Orderic in order to fall into the hands of brigands who intend to sell her into slavery in the Sudan.

When young women are so closely pursued in the great poetic epics, one can imagine their fate in more frivolous stories. One of Aretino's tales in his *Ragionamenti*, "The Gallant's Revenge," recounts the story of a young man who revenges himself on a disdainful beauty

AN UNKNOWN PORTUGUESE MASTER
OF THE EARLY 16th CENTURY
Scene of Hell (detail)
Lisbon, *Museo Nacional de Arte Antigua*

by waylaying her, having her raped by forty peasants, then tossed in a blanket, whipped and finally hunted naked through the countryside.

The bound woman was a frequent theme in Mannerist painting: the classical subject of *Perseus and Andromeda*, for example, abounds in the sixteenth and early seventeenth centuries. The fettered limbs of Andromeda allowed the artist to show her nude body most vulnerably and passively exposed. Giorgio Vasari's painting of this subject in the Studiolo of Francesco I in the Palazzo Vecchio in Florence is a precious und studied rendering of this essentially erotic scene. The theme of the bound female is also found in the literature of the time. Ariosto, in the tenth Canto of *Orlando Furioso*, describes at length the predicament of Angelica exposed naked on a rock. In the second Canto of Tasso's *Jerusalem Delivered*, Sophronia, tied to the stake, is described succulently for the benefit of the reader: "Already her raiment and her chaste mantle have been torn from her, and rude hands are gripping her dainty arms..."

It is true that sadism appears frequently in Italian art in the late sixteenth century, but this was under the influence of the Counter-Reformation. Because of the Italian deference to the classical tradition and the more healthy sensuousness of the southern character, however, this theme of erotic cruelty—the woman bound or suspended—did not traditionally produce in Italian art the pathological horrors found in the works of many northern artists. Indeed this theme was capable of evoking, in the hands of Italian artists, charming erotic conceits. The

209 *Juno Chastised* by Correggio, which is found in one of the grisaille lunettes of his frescoes in the Convento di San Paolo at Parma, is a delightful provocative detail. Juno is a very young girl with long flowing hair and a deliciously modelled little body. The subject comes from Book XV of the *Iliad*, where Jupiter reminds Juno of having chastised her by hanging her from the sky, her hands bound together, and a golden anvil fastened to her feet to make the punishment more severe. How very different is the effect of this little figure by Correggio from a

211 detail like the three women suspended by their knees in the *Scene of Hell*, by a Portuguese master of the early sixteenth century.

The erotic cruelty of Mannerism is perhaps most clearly revealed in the martyrdom of female saints. Under pious pretext the saints are presented in the most suggestive attitudes: nude or at least with part of their clothing torn away or slipping off, fastened to a cross or a stake while they are flagellated, burned or otherwise mutilated and tormented. The gruesome *Martyrdom of Saint Agatha*, about to have her breasts torn off was one of the more popular

210 scenes of female martyrdom. The engraving of this subject, illustrated here, by Giovanni Stradano, is not a rare, selected example, it is instead most typical.

That this cruelty was mixed with a strong erotic intention may be proven somewhat by the subsequent evolution of the scenes of female martyrdom. The gruesome scenes of martyrdom so very common in the late sixteenth century were, as has been stated, largely influenced by the spirit of the Counter-Reformation. The gruesome facts certainly did not wholly disappear in the rendering of such scenes in the mid-seventeenth century, but the Baroque art of this more confident era of the Catholic Restoration tried to seduce the spectator rather than exalt him by fright. In the scenes of female martyrdoms by a Baroque artist such as Francesco Furini, the elaborate and detailed rendering of the means of torture has been deleted from his

214 representation. In Furini's *Young Female Martyr*, reproduced here, the cruelty is only suggested by the almost invisible arrow which pierces her throat and the column and rope which suggest that she is bound. But Furini's martyrdom is quite frankly a pretext for the display of sensuality. In this heavy and refined eroticism Furini is only developing an element inherited from Mannerist art.

GIORGIO VASARI
Perseus and Andromeda
Florence, Palazzo Vecchio, Studiolo

Melancholy

There is a very direct relationship between sensuality and melancholy. The beauty of things is ephemeral, and to take joy in them is to condemn oneself surely to eventual regret. To express the dilemma in more immediate terms: to consummate pleasure is to kill it, and so another new pleasure must be sought. This brings in its train inevitable complication and even perversion, and there eventually comes a day when only the impossible can provide satisfaction, strong passions give place to a "wave of passion," to "desire" lacking a precise object. Thus we have what one now calls *mal du siècle,* Romantic spleen, Existentialist despair...

The Mannerist epoch, sensual and perverse, had much in common with the eighteenth century, which showed similar signs of melancholic obsession. A premonition is provided by Jacopo Sannazaro in his *Arcadia,* written in 1480 but not published until 1501, where we can find effusions of hyper-sensitivity which would not disgrace a pre-Romantic hero: "There is no music or song," declares an unhappy lover, "but that brings a flood of tears to my eyes in reminding me of those happy days... Yet I shall spare you the details of these woes of mine, stating simply that all is displeasing to me. There is no festival or jollity which could possibly give me a sense of pleasure, let alone diminish my torments, to which the gods, if they listen to my prayers, will put an end by granting me a speedy death."

Already there was a search for solitude, the night, desolate vistas. In Sannazaro's words: "Like the bird which fears the rays of the sun, I seek, alas, dark and shady places, while the

day lights up the rest of the earth. For me, the most serene days are those which are full of shade; flower-filled meadows are for me no more than thorny heaths; and when the sun shows itself to mankind, it appears to me obscured always by a dense cloud."

Giovanni della Casa, the author of the famous treatise on good manners, *Il Galateo*, and a great poet, wrote a sonnet on the loneliness of winter forests (see page 10). Philip Sidney celebrated the "delightful solitude" of the woods. Andreas Gryphius dedicated one of his most beautiful poems to solitude. In France, Girard de Saint-Amant composed, in 1619, an ode entitled *La Solitude*:

"O que j'aime la solitude!
Que ces lieux sacrés à la nuit,
Eloignés du monde et du bruit,
Plaisent à mon inquiétude!"

["How dearly I love solitude! / How greatly these places, sacred to the night / And far from the world's bustle, / Please my anxious mind."] This ode had an enormous success in its time and was widely imitated, in particular by Théophile de Viau *(La Solitude)* and by Vion Dalibray *(Horreur du désert)*.

A melancholic manner and appearance became fashionable. Giorgio Vasari, in his *Lives*, constantly emphasizes the melancholic nature of many of the painters of his epoch — Piero di Cosimo, Jacopo da Pontormo, Michelangelo, Francesco Salviati, Daniele da Volterra, Rosso Fiorentino…. Probably in another era these same artists would not have demonstrated so clearly their humors, and their biographer would not have emphasized this trait so heavily. But in the sixteenth century, as in the Romantic nineteenth century, to be unhappy was in

style. Already in 1494, Marsilio Ficino, in his *De vita triplice*, associated melancholy with poetic creation. Men born under the sign of Saturn, he writes, "rarely have ordinary characters and destinies. They are beings separate from the others, gods or ruffians, happy or profoundly miserable." It was considered flattering to be easily distinguished from the crowd, even if only by ill fortune. Ronsard declared that he was "timid, suspicious, sad and melancholic." Some pages of Camões could almost be extracts from (or parodies of) the commencing chapter of Chateaubriand's romantic episode *René*:

"When, escaped from the maternal prison, I saw daylight, at once the fatal influence of the stars dominated me. They refused to me the freedom which was my right. A thousand times destiny has shown me the better path and, despite myself, I have chosen the worse. And that my torments might be commensurate with my age, when as a tiny baby I opened my eyes gently, the fates decreed that immediately a sightless child (Love) should wound me. My childish tears already had the bitterness of recollections of love and the wails which burst from me as I lay in my cradle might have been taken to be sighs of unhappiness." (Camões, *Canzones*, XI.)

Such disillusion and world-weariness were by no means rare at that time in Portugal, the land of the *saudade*; in 1601, Francisco Rodrigues Lôbo published a pastoral novel which bore the characteristic title *O Desenganado* (The Disenchanted).

The Elizabethan theater brought the melancholic personality into focus. The prototype is, of course, Hamlet, but the "melancholy Dane" is far from representing an isolated case. There are also Jaques — the "melancholy Jaques" of *As You Like It*, the misanthropic Duke in John Marston's *The Malcontent*, the melancholic Lovel in Ben Jonson's *The New Inn*, the sad Hippolito in Thomas Dekker's *The Honest Whore*, and many more besides.

Sad objects—moonlight, ruins, winter, solitude—and unhappiness itself became a new source of pleasure. During the first decades of the seventeenth century, Milton was able, apparently without shocking his readers, to contrast, in the diptych of *L'Allegro* and *Il Penseroso*, the pleasures of gaiety and those of melancholy. And the very fact of having reserved melancholy for the final statement seems to indicate on which side the poet's sympathies lay: "Hence, vain deluding joys, / The brood of Folly without father bred," he commences the poem, and goes on to state unequivocally "Hail divinest melancholy."

But Mannerist melancholy was not simply a fashionable attitude adopted by sophisticates in search of new sensations. One can find in the sixteenth century and early seventeenth century literary passages which betray a real sense of despair and whose sincerity cannot be doubted: "I pursue an unattainable ideal" (Camões, *Sonnet* XLVIII); "Anguish which nourishes thee and fills thee full of fear..." (Giovanni della Casa); "My soul, like to a ship in a black storm, / Is driven I know not whither" (John Webster, *The White Devil*, v. 6); "I drag with me a prison from which I cannot escape" (Théophile de Viau, *Elégie*); "Despair, I invoke thee from the depths of my distress" (Tristan l'Hermite, *Le Désespoir*).

All the themes of melancholy so dear to Mannerist literature are to be rediscovered in the painting of the epoch. The literary quest for solitude finds its artistic counterpart in the development of landscape painting. Although the foreground of sixteenth century landscapes is still frequently filled with human figures, these figures no longer invade the scene itself, and the middle ground and background offer a wealth of solitary retreats for meditation: sunken pathways, shady copses, mountain sides dotted with caverns. This atmosphere of sadness is compounded by nocturnal settings, moonlight effects, and the evocative use of ruins in these landscapes.

DOMENICO BECCAFUMI
Head of a Woman (detail
from Christ in Limbo)
Siena, Pinacoteca Nazionale

The melancholy of the sixteenth century produced some works which heartily justify our comparisons with the Romantic period. The dreamy quality which pervades the print of *"The Dreamer"* by an artist of the School of Marcantonio Raimondi might well cause it to pass for a Romantic vignette of the early nineteenth century.

Prints depicting the *Allegory of Melancholy*, such as that by Virgel Solis, abounded in the sixteenth century. In this allegorical representation of melancholy, however, there remains a certain contradiction between the essentially Medieval concept of the "humors," and so specifically modern a concept as melancholy. These prints are interesting commentaries on the fashion of melancholy, but with the exception of Albrecht Dürer's engraving of *Melancholia* they are rarely profoundly melancholic works.

The genuine anguish of Mannerism must be sought in works other than those which illustrate specifically the allegory of melancholy. An interesting example is the strange engraving by Jacob de Gheyn II, dated 1613. This work, so strongly evocative of desolation and solitude, most probably depicts some allegory, but for want of a more erudite title *"The Lonely* 217 *Old Man"* seems most appropriate. One may also mention here the tormented face of Hans 216 Baldung Grien's *Saturn,* the desperate expressions of the damned in Michelangelo's *Last Judgment* in the Sistine Chapel, or the infinitely sad faces of the personages in Domenico Beccafumi's *Christ in Limbo,* of which we here reproduce a detail. Equally indicative of Mannerist anguish and melancholy is the inner-directed or distant gaze to be seen in some of the portraits by Parmigianino and Angelo Bronzino. With these images modern sensibility was born.

Excessive sensibility, refuge in solitude, love of sadness, the melancholic pose—here are surely all the seeds of Romanticism. The more one studies Mannerism, the more it seems certain that Mannerism and Romanticism are two separate passages of one single movement. It is extraordinary that this evidence has for so long been obscured from us by the confusing dogmas of cultural history.

219

The Inspiration of the Dream

"I can escape despair only through imagination," wrote Camões in one of his *Canzones*. The imagination is the habitual companion of melancholy; anyone dissatisfied with this world, or bored with this world, has a natural tendency to demand from the imagination other worlds, not necessarily better ones, but at least worlds that are different from our own.

The magic entrance to those other worlds is the dream. The Mannerists, fascinated as they were by the night, sensitive and melancholic, could not fail to be interested by dreams, night's supreme gift, an inexhaustible source of new sensations, a perfect escape from daily existence.

There is no doubt whatsoever that sixteenth century man dreamed a great deal. Jacopo Sannazaro put into his *Arcadia* one of the first "modern" dreams ever to be recorded, a dream

GIULIO ROMANO
Roman Prison
Engraving by Giorgio Ghisi

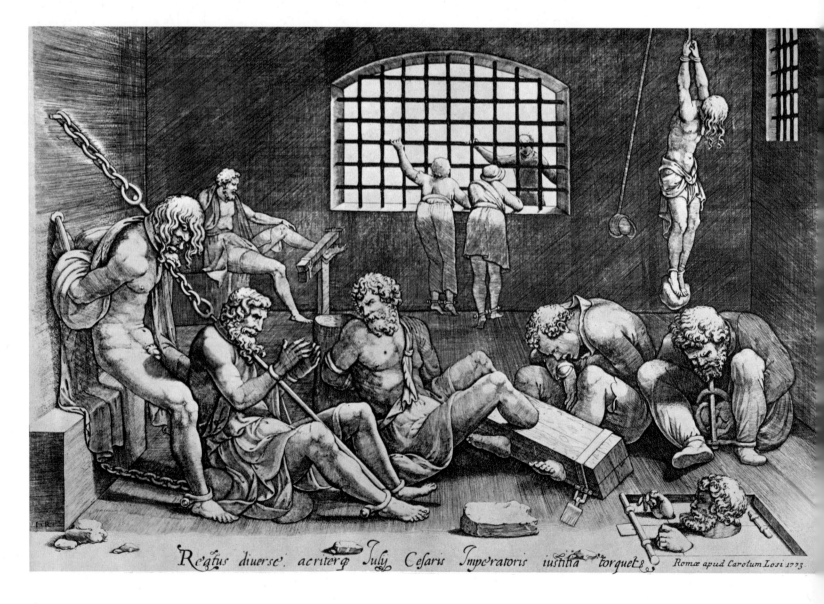

220

free of symbolic preoccupations and medieval prophecies, a dream of pure imagery:

"I know not whether it was a result of all I had seen during the day; I passed from a long reverie into a deep sleep, during which I felt myself affected by keen pains and varying emotions. It seemed to me that, far from the woods and the other shepherds, I found myself in an unknown wilderness, surrounded by abandoned tombs, without perceiving anything which I recognized. I wished to cry out, but my voice died in my throat; making futile efforts to escape, my weakness kept me rooted to the spot. It seemed to me that I listened to a Siren seated on a rock and I wept bitterly, while a wave from the sea washed over me, taking my breath away so that I almost choked to death."

SEDET ÆTERNVM
QVE SEDEBIT ÎFOELIX

222

LUCA PENNI
"Raphael's Dream"
Engraving by Giorgio Ghisi

223

Albrecht Dürer has left us the transcription of one of his dreams, which he also illustrated by a hastily executed watercolor (see pages 300 and 301). Jerome Cardan (1501–1576), the great mathematician and philosopher, in the thirty-seventh chapter of his memoirs, *The Book of my Life*, records a particularly curious waking dream from his childhood:

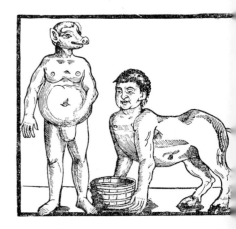

"…I used to vision, as it were, divers images which seemed to consist of very small bronze rings such as vests composed of chain mail—although up to that time I had not yet seen a linked cuirass. These images arose from the lower right-hand corner of the bed, and, moving upward in a semicircle, gently descended on the left and straightway disappeared. They were images of castles, of hours, of animals, of horses with riders, of plants and trees, of musical instruments, and of theaters; there were images of men of divers costumes and varied dress; images of trumpeters, even, with their trumpets as it were, ready to play, but no voice or sound was heard. Besides these visions, I beheld soldiers, swarming peoples, fields, and shapes like unto bodies which even to this day I recall with aversion. There were groves, forests, and other phantoms which I no longer remember; at times I could see a veritable chaos of innumerable objects rushing dizzily along in a mass, without confusion among themselves, yet with ter-rific speed… Even flowers of many a variety, and four-footed creatures, and divers birds ap-peared in my visions, but in all this exquisitely fashioned pageant there was no color: as I have said, they appeared to be of bronze."

Ronsard's work contains several dreams (particularly in the *Bocage Royal* and the *Elégies*), as does that of Joachim du Bellay (*Songe*), and Edmund Spenser (*The Faerie Queene*), while Shakespeare's plays are filled with narrations and enactments of dreams. In the tenth canto of his *Adonis*, Giovanni Battista Marini describes at length an "isle of dreams," surrounded by a dead sea, and René Descartes has left us the account of a strange dream of fantastic architecture.

Artists too were fascinated by the dream as a potential theme for their compositions. The painting of *"The Dream"* attributed to Dosso Dossi in the Gemäldegalerie in Dresden is a work which evokes not only the whole quiet atmosphere of sleep and dreams, but also their bizarre and fantastic imagery. The handsome engraving of the *Sleeping Mars* by Jacob de Gheyn III, with the dark shadows about the figure and upon his face and closed eyes, and the simple falling lines of his weighty robe suggest the heaviness of profound sleep.

205
221

Some works, like the engraving by Marcantonio Raimondi called *The Dream of Two Young Girls*, were representations of a particular dream. With a rather naïve literalness such works represented both the dream and the dreamer. The engraving known as *Raphael's Dream* was engraved by Giorgio Ghisi after a drawing by Luca Penni who was himself inspired by a sketch by Raphael. This work would seem to be far more advanced in terms of its approach to the representation of a dream, in-as-much as it does not show the dreamer himself. But the fact is that rather than representing an actual dream of Raphael's, the engraving illustrates Canto IV of the *Aeneid*, in which the poet, led by the Sibyl, descends into the grotto of Averne. Although this is not an actual representation of a dream of Raphael's, it is no less clearly the product of a dream-inspired imagination. The deliberately false perspective, the storm-tossed sea peopled with monsters, the strange ruined amphitheater at the top of the mountain, and the dense forest at the left of the scene are all typical and authentic elements of a dream work, with its perfectly gratuitous nature and its natural incoherence. Indeed the true oneiric in-spiration of Mannerism should be sought in just such works and not in those which represent a specific dream. The imagination fed by dreams can most readily be found in such fantastic creations as Bosch's *Garden of Delights*, *Charon Crossing the Styx* by Jacob van Swanenburgh, Callot's *Temptation of Saint Anthony*, or the haunted towns painted by Monsù Desiderio.

222
291
286
135

UNKNOWN MASTER
Congenital Monsters
Woodcuts

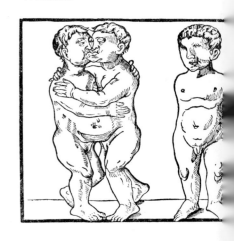

224

Monsters and Giants

Mannerism made extensive use of fantastic images: most common was the monster. The literature of the epoch (Ariosto, Tasso, Rabelais, Ronsard, Spenser, etc.) is filled with dragons, harpies, hydras, gorgons, sphinxes, giants and dwarfs. We know that monsters were a favorite theme for the Mannerist painters of the North: works of Hieronymus Bosch, Jan Mandyn, Pieter Bruegel the Elder and the Younger, Jacob van Swanenburgh, and Marten de

ARENT VAN BOLTEN
Monsters (drawing)
London, British Museum

AGOSTINO VENEZIANO
Dragon and Butterfly
Engraving
London, The Warburg Institute

Vos abound in fantastic creatures. We here reproduce a leaf from an album in the British
225 Museum by the Dutch draughtsman, Arent van Bolten, which is filled with the most bizarre
and grotesque monsters. The Italians too were intrigued by this same theme. The engraving
225 of a *Dragon and Butterfly* by Agostino Veneziano, a pupil of Marcantonio Raimondi, is no
less fantastic than the creatures of Arent van Bolten. The decorative frescoes and stuccoed
grotesques of the School of Raphael, particularly those by Giovanni da Udine and Aenea Vico,
are rampant with strange monsters. The subject of monsters was given a pseudo-scientific
treatment by the Neapolitan Giambattista della Porta in his treatise on physiognomy, *De
347 Humana Physiognomia* (1586), in which he expounded the theory of zoomorphism and found
analogies between the features of men and animals.

The giant was the favored monster of monumental decoration in Italy. The sculptor
Bartolommeo Ammanati (1511–1592) filled the gardens of the Orsini Villa at Bomarzo with
stone giants and other monsters, and Giulio Romano, in the Palazzo del Té, at Mantua, frescoed an entire room with the story of the *Fall of the Titans*. When standing within this relatively small room the effect of these enormous monsters as they are crushed by the falling
architecture is an overpowering experience of the bizarre imagery of Mannerism.

ANTOINE CARON DE BEAUVAIS
The Emperor Augustus and the
Tiburtine Sibyl (detail
Paris, Louvre

GIULIO ROMANO
The Fall of the Titans (fresco)
Mantua, Palazzo del Té, Sala dei Giganti

Ambiguity and Double Meaning

Another characteristic of Mannerist art which is perhaps of oneiric inspiration is that of ambiguity. In dreams, people and things are never exactly what they seem; they are either in contradiction with themselves, being one thing and its very opposite simultaneously; or, if they do achieve a moment of precise definition, it is only in order to change just as abruptly and become something else. A simple example is the monster which is at once man and beast, quadruped and serpent. But Mannerism made use of all sorts of subtler ambiguities.

The *trompe-l'œil*, so common in the fresco decoration of the sixteenth century, was clearly an intended ambiguity: false doors with painted personages about to enter the room, false balconies painted with convincingly real figures can be seen in the decorations of many palaces and villas of the time.

The Mannerist period was equally fond of myths of transformation. The *Metamorphoses* of Ovid was tremendously popular, and such a constant source of inspiration for artists that it would be a tedious task to list the many representations of Proteus, Daphne, Circe and Hermaphrodite. The Mannerist epoch also loved masquerade. There are innumerable engravings or sketches for masked ballets by René Boyvin (after Rosso), Giorgio Vasari, Antoine Caron de Beauvais, Jacques Callot, Stefano della Bella and others. Equally cherished were those pseudo-humans, automatons. In 1509, for the entry of Louis XII into Milan, Leonardo da Vinci constructed a mechanical lion which approached the king and greeted him. Francesco I de' Medici and the Emperor Rudolf II both collected automatons.

In Mannerist art one often meets an equivocal image which can be called the statue-human figure. This curious concept can even be found in the literature of the time: in Ariosto's *Orlando Furioso*, Roger, seeing Angelica on her rock, "thought almost that it was a statue of alabaster or some precious marble." The artists of the School of Fontainebleau particularly developed this type of ambiguity. In the *Emperor Augustus and the Tiburtine Sybil* by Antoine Caron de Beauvais, for example, it is impossible to say whether the figure surmounting the fountain is a woman or a statue.

Double meaning was sometimes taken so far as to constitute a conundrum. This is the case with the anamorphoses of Erhard Schön, which have already been discussed, and above all with the still life objects transformed into allegorical portraits by Giuseppe Arcimboldo and his school.

Arcimboldo was for eleven years the favorite painter of that very strange monarch Rudolph II at his court in Prague. He specialized in metaphorical figures. His *Allegory of Water* is composed of fishes, octopus, crabs, crayfish, starfish, eels, frogs, turtles, etc. and adorned with a string of pearls, while his figure of *Earth* was composed of various mammals. His allegories of the seasons were treated in the same way. We here reproduce his *Allegory of Summer*, who is dressed in a coat of wheat and whose head is made up of a great variety of fruits and vegetables of the full summer season.

Among the lesser known works attributed to Arcimboldo, one may mention the curious representation of the *Trojan Horse* which introduces a new type of metaphor. Here the Greek warriors who should be concealed inside the animal actually constitute its external shape.

227
230
231

GIUSEPPE ARCIMBOLD
Allegory of Wate
Vienna, Kunsthistorisches Museu

Arcimboldo had innumerable disciples and imitators whose work is often difficult to distinguish from his own. But a place apart must be given to the great Flemish landscape artist 232 Joos de Momper who has left us a series of the Four Seasons; his *Winter*, reproduced here, is one of the most ingenious and powerful of all Mannerist paintings with double meaning.

The anamorphic conundrums of Erhard Schön had their equivalent in the literature of the epoch, in books of picture-puzzles and riddles, such as the sort of amusing cabbala published in 1550 by Giovanni Battista Palatino, or the curious work by Tabourot des Accords, *Les Bigarrures* (1572). This later work was a compilation of charades, riddles, acrostics, and anastrophic verses, "composed," states the author, "to amuse himself, and then to amuse some other person, and so all others as well."

The work of Arcimboldo already represents a new level of achievement, being the modest equivalent in painting of concettism in poetry. With concettism, as in Arcimboldo's paintings, the chief concern is to avoid expressing things directly. Luis de Góngora, for example, wishing to say that a lady can no longer remove from her finger a ring that has grown too tight, wrote a most complicated verse which may be interpreted as: "A diamond, brilliant emulator of my constancy [the poet's love is as indestructible as the diamond], it, too, im-

GIUSEPPE ARCIMBOLDO
The Trojan Horse
Lucca, Pinacoteca Nazionale

prisoned in gold ['it too': like the poet himself, ensnared in the net of his mistress' blonde tresses] was likewise the prison [could not be removed] of the articulated mother-of-pearl [the finger]."

An extreme example such as this evidently verges on the ridiculous. Nevertheless, when one thinks of it, these methods are precisely those used by modern poets such as Stephane Mallarmé, Paul Valéry, Rainer Maria Rilke and T. S. Eliot. It would not be difficult to extract from the works of these writers passages of equally super-refined preciosity; but the converse is also true, and one can find in the writings of the great Mannerist concettists — Góngora, John Donne, Giovanni Battista Marini, Étienne Durand—advance echoes of the *Cimetière marin* or the *Waste Land*.

"*Prisión del nácar era articulado*
de mi firmeza un émulo luciente,
un diamante ingeniosamente
en oro también él aprisionado."
(Góngora)

232

Allegory and Symbol

In keeping with the love of ambiguity and double meaning, the inspiration of the dream, and the use of fantastic imagery Mannerist artists were passionately devoted to allegory and symbol.

This is seen first of all in their love of subjects from classical mythology. Indeed classical mythology is largely based upon an allegorical and symbolic system: Venus is love, Mars is war, Aeolus the wind and so forth. And one should remember too in judging and looking at Mannerist mythological works that, although this symbolic language seems to us a pompous cliché, these were fresh images for the sixteenth century, filled with poetic possibilities. The Mannerist taste for allegory was by no means limited to the gods and demi-gods of antiquity. Mannerist artists and writers also relied upon the complicated Medieval allegories. With erudition and imagination they elaborated both the Antique and Medieval allegories and symbols. In still other instances they invented their own.

The allegorical subject matter of much Mannerist painting was often extremely erudite and obscure. This is above all true for the decorations executed for the princely palaces and villas in the later sixteenth century. Very often the subject matter of these works was the creation of a scholar or literary figure. Thus the complicated allegories of the frescoes by Federigo and Taddeo Zuccaro in the Palazzo Farnese at Caprarola were devised by the humanist scholar Annibale Caro. In these frescoes mythology, history, and tradition are blended into a eulogy of the Farnese family. Without great study these frescoes would remain meaningless for us today. It is even true that they might have been so for the large public in the sixteenth

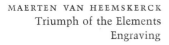
MAERTEN VAN HEEMSKERCK
Triumph of the Elements
Engraving

233

century. But we must remember that such works were specifically created for a closed, aristocratic circle to whom they were not only perfectly understandable but greatly enjoyed for their erudition and allegorical expression. This taste was not limited to the Italian courts of the time. The same obscurity of subject matter is prevalent in the work of the School of Fontainebleau of the second half of the century. The strange allegories of Antoine Caron de Beauvais, like his *Funeral of Amor*, may seem inexplicable and ridiculous to us but one must bear in mind that such works reflected the ballets and ceremonies so common at the court of the later Valois kings, and thus they were executed in a language understood by their select audience.

The taste for allegory in the Mannerist period, however, was widespread and by no means limited to the princely courts. Certain allegories were understood by all. Engraved prints were a medium directed to a large public, and in the sixteenth century allegorical prints abounded. The Flemish, Netherlandish and German engravers—Maerten van Heemskerck, Virgel Solis, Hendrick Goltzius, Jan Muller and others—have left us a great number of allegorical engravings. These were often not only single sheets but whole series of allegories of the humors of the planets, the virtues, the vices, the liberal arts, the continents, or the nations of Europe, or yet again the seasons, the elements, or the senses.

The enormous popularity of symbolism is witnessed by the proliferation of emblem books or books of allegorical devices such as Andrea Alciati's *Emblematum liber* (Augsburg, 1531), the *Dialogo dell'Imprese...* by Paolo Giovio (Rome, 1555), *Imprese...* by B. Pittoni (Venice, 1562), *Iconologia* by Cesare Ripa (Rome, 1593), or the *Amorum Emblemata* by Otto van Veen (Antwerp, 1609). These works and a great many others like them were known

MAERTEN VAN HEEMSKERCK
Allegory of Nature
Engraving

ETIENNE DELAUNE
Allegorical Scene
Engraving

ETIENNE DELAUNE
Allegorical Scene
Engraving

throughout Europe, translated and published in many languages. They had a tremendous influence on the literature and art of the period.

By the mid-sixteenth century the fashion for symbolism had become sufficiently widespread to provoke mockery. Bernardo Bibbiena, in his *Calandria* (Act II, Scene III), pokes fun at this mania for allegory, and Aretino in his *Ragionamenti* sketches a burlesque portrait of a lover who sought to express the hope of his passion through the symbolism of a color: "One of these idle fellows suddenly thought up a solemn whim one day... To show that he lived only in the hope of winning the lady of his thoughts, and intending that she might guess the reason for his actions and deign to make him happy, he dressed himself all in green. Green were his cap, his cape, his doublet and hose, his scabbard, the tip of the scabbard and its handle, his belt, shirt and boots, even his hair and beard (for I believe that he also dyed them green), the plume of his cap and its clasp, his aglets and his cloak, all were green... He ate only green things, cucumbers, gourds, melons, purées of green herbs, cabbages, lettuces, borage, fresh almonds, and chick-peas. So that wine might seem green to him, he drank it from a green crystal goblet. If he ate something prepared in a gelatin, he contented himself with sucking the green laurel leaves embedded in the gelatin. He had his bread soaked in rosemary macerated in oil, so that it should be tinged green, and he sat on a bench specially painted green. He slept in a green bed and spoke of nothing but herbs, meadows, gardens and springtime... When he wrote to his lady love, he would write on sheets of green paper, and I believe that when he went to stool his droppings were green..."

A great many Mannerist images are almost undecipherable for us today. This is the case, for example, with the series of *Allegorical Scenes* by Etienne Delaune. Divorced from the allegory which united these images they are extraordinarily incongruous and our dominant impression is one of strangeness and mystery. We see them as a beautiful and curious collection of pure images. Most assuredly such was not the conscious intention of the artist. Our ignorance, however, enables us to appreciate how great was the margin of aesthetic existence which the artist has bestowed upon his images independent of the ideas they represent.

We can thus see that the Mannerist taste for allegory was enormous nourishment to the artistic imagination. Just as many religious subjects, such as the story of Susanna or Bathsheba, provided the artists with the desired opportunity of depicting the sumptuous beauties of the female body, so Mannerist allegory provided a pretext for the creation of rare images.

The possibilities inherent in this symbolic language of Mannerism are nowhere more apparent than in the work of Maerten van Heemskerck. Heemskerck engraved many allegorical triumphs, such as *The Triumph of War*, *The Triumph of Death*, or *The Triumph of the Elements* which we reproduce here. In this print the Elements, Fire, Earth, Air and Water, each bearing her own attributes, are seated upon a triumphal car which bears a globe. The car is driven by Time, and drawn by two winged horses bearing the symbols of the Sun and Moon. In such a work each detail, each attribute has a specific meaning, but the images are so rich they compel recognition in their own right. Even more imaginative is Heemskerck's admirable print of the *Allegory of Nature*. The juxtaposition of the seven-breasted Goddess, Nature, who suckles a baby, with the floating globe studded with instruments, seems a Surrealist fantasy. Very beautiful in its dramatic turbulence is the image created by Hendrick Goltzius in his *Allegory of the Two Poles*.

In his large painting of *Momus Finding Fault with the Work of the Gods*, Heemskerck was dealing with an extremely obscure mythological anecdote, which as was often the case required an inscription to make it at all intelligible. The lack of tradition for the representation

236

of this theme of Momus, fault-finding personified, gave reign to the artist's creativity. The allegorical content and the world of dreams seem to blend in this composition of multiple elements and disconnected setting. This example may perhaps explain why so many Mannerist dreams are symbolic or allegorical, such as the dream of the allegory of the Ganges in the fourth canto of Camões' *Lusiades*, or the dream of the allegory of Promise in Ronsard's *Elégie* XXI. These dreams may appear to us today as fabricated and artificial, but during the sixteenth century, at a time when the dream had not yet found its own language and allegory had not yet become dry rhetoric, they combined together usefully in expressing new forms of the imagination.

MAERTEN VAN HEEMSKERCK
Momus Finding Fault with the Work of the Gods
Berlin, Former Staatliche Museen

NOCTE SATVS, GENITORE ORBVS, SVM NOMINE MOMVS,
INVIDIÆ, QVE COMES, SINGVLA CARPO LVBENS.
FINGI HOMINEM CAVSOR CLATHRATO PECTORE, APERTIS
SENSIBVS, OCCVLTVM VT NIL SPECVS ILLE TEGAT.

HENDRICK GOLTZIUS
Allegory of the Two Poles
Engraving by Jan Muller

Occultism

The melancholic spirit, the dream-fed imagination, the love of double meaning, allegory and symbol were complemented by the strong belief in magic, astrology, alchemy, and sorcery. Magic is the materialization of imaginative processes; astrology and alchemy are symbolism become practical; hermetic philosophy heralds the world of double meaning; and in a more general sense occult power is the realization of the melancholic's individualistic reveries. The Mannerist era was the golden age of occultism. It was the epoch of Nostradamus, Cornelius Agrippa, Paracelsus, Guillaume Postel, Tycho Brahé, Jacob Boehme, and the Rosicrucians. Pope Leo x, Queen Catherine de' Medici, Duke Francesco i of Florence, King Henri iii of France, the Emperor Rudolph ii all pursued studies of astrology and alchemy. Some of the greatest writers of the century were convinced occultists: Ronsard believed firmly in the existence of intermediary spirits, the "Daimons," which peopled the universe; Rémy Belleau composed a long alchemistic poem entitled *Les Amours et nouveaux Echanges des Pierres précieuses* (see page 19); Rabelais, under the name of the "Great Haly Habenragel," was the author of a *Pronostication générale* for the decade commencing in the year 1532; Cyrano de Bergerac was interested in the Cabbala. Renowned artists such as Parmigianino and Domenico Beccafumi were alchemists. A series of words which achieved currency during the sixteenth century, "influence," "ascendancy," "disastrous," "ill-starred," etc., all derived from astrological terminology.

Expressions of occultism were no less frequent in the visual arts. Representations of astrologers, alchemists, magicians and sorcerers abounded. The influence of astrology may even be seen in religious art. In the *Madonna and Child and Saints*, by the pious Luis de Morales, one sees in the upper right hand corner a horoscope of the Infant Jesus. This was by no means an isolated and personal fantasy on the part of the painter. Jerome Cardan, for instance, had also made up a horoscope of the Infant Jesus and pronounced that he was born under the conjunction of Jupiter and the Sun! Many works which appear to us today to lack specific intention probably possessed an alchemical significance originally. This is almost certainly the case with a curious painting by Jan Mabuse in Vierhonten. In this work one sees the bodies of Hermaphrodite and the Nymph Salmacis unite into one single body. This scene can possibly be explained by the fact that Hermaphrodite was the alchemists' symbol of Sulphur and Mercury after conjunction.

But it was sorcery, above all, that exerted upon the imagination an extraordinary fascination mingled with horror. The persecution of so-called witches and sorcerers—the extent of which may be judged by studying such manuals of law and punishment as Jacobus Sprenger's *Malleus Maleficarum*—is proof enough of the importance accorded this problem by the authorities of the period. Only a few rebellious minds permitted themselves to doubt the reality of sorcery. Even such a figure as Ronsard apparently gave full credence to the worst legends. His *Ode xvi* is an invective against a witch: "Dweller in solitary places, / And in the horror of graveyards / Which you love to haunt, / At the sound of the spells that you mumble, / The bodies of the dead rise / From their lonely tombs. / You are dreaded in the villages: / All, fearing your sorcery / Close their houses to you, / Trembling with fear lest you

ostesse des lieux solitaires,
par l'horreur des cimetières
tu hantes le plus,
son des vers que tu murmures,
corps des morts tu des-emmures
leurs tombeaux reclus.
es la frayeur du village:
acun craignant ton sorcelage
ferme sa maison,
mblant de peur que tu ne taches
boeufs, ses moutons et ses vaches
jus de ta poison..."
onsard, Ode xvi)

240

239

should blight / Their oxen, sheep and cows / With the juice of your poison..." And he goes on to deplore the fact that a too lenient justice should have been content, in punishing misdeeds meriting death, merely to have the wretched woman whipped through the town!

Charles de Sigogne, in his *Stance satirique contre l'olivâtre Perrette*, shows himself no less superstitious or excited: "...At any hour one may find you, your shaven head / Covered by the skin of some strange beast, / Astride your broomstick, flying over Paris, / Entering the clock-towers, knocking on every door, / Hovering closely behind every churlish monk, / Beating out your mock music on pots and pans. / Often, to exercise your sorcerer's art, / You go, changed into wolf, to a hamlet's crossroads, / And there cruelly devour not only children but grown men, / Heedless of their cries and pleas; / Then, your belly full and jaws adrip with blood, / You strip off your magic skin and resume your real shape..."

Persecutions and imprecations would have been pointless if black magic and Satanism had not in fact exercised an extraordinary fascination over the minds of people in those times. No one of course boasted of having taken part in witches' sabbaths or black masses. But Benvenuto Cellini, for example, claimed to have conjured up the dead, at night, amid the ruins of the Coliseum, with the aid of a Sicilian priest possessing magical powers. They went through the whole gamut of a magical ceremony, magic circle, rare perfumes, foul potions, talismans—nothing was lacking, and the operation appears to have been entirely successful. Cellini desired to obtain the love of a certain Angelica: "The demons kept their word," wrote the sculptor, "and Angelica was in my arms exactly one month later, just as they had promised" (*La Vita*, III, 64).

Such practises were quite usual. Sannazaro, in his *Arcadia* (Prose Nine), enumerates a whole host of weird talismans: the root of the thistle, when it resembles the opposite sex, guarantees success in love; the heart of a mole, swallowed while it is still beating, or the eye of an East Indian turtle placed on the tongue permits one to predict the future; a particular stone found in the crop of a white cock will ensure victory in athletic competitions; another kind of stone, if it falls from the sky at the moment when the moon begins to wane, is favorable to amorous enterprises; a third type, wrapped according to a formula in a special herb, makes the bearer invisible; a hunter need only attach to his arm a tooth from the right-hand side of a hyena's jaw to be sure of never missing his aim; the tongue of that same animal, carried in the shoe, under the instep, prevents dogs from barking, while the whiskers of its muzzle together with a little skin from its genitals make a man irresistible to shepherdesses. In the same work (Prose Ten) are to be found descriptions of the incantations necessary for attracting or repelling love.

If one is to believe Aretino, Roman courtesans collected the umbilical cords of new-born children and various fragments of corpses (hair, skull, flanks, teeth, eyes) from which they fashioned love-philters. They even ventured into graveyards to gather up pieces of skin and rotting flesh which, when mixed with menstrual flux, was supposed to work wonders with a recalcitrant lover. Matteo Bandello, in one of his stories, mentions the case of a young man "who filled his room with skulls and bones, like a graveyard, so as to gain the favors of his beloved." And the sculptor Silvio Cosino de Fiesole flayed the skin off a hanged man and had made from it a jacket which when worn averted bad luck.

The theme of sorcery with its oneiric, nocturnal and erotic overtones fascinated the 244 Mannerist painters. The Ferrarese painter Dosso Dossi painted many very beautiful canvases of sorceresses in their magical kingdoms. The temptress Circe, surrounded by her animal friends, is the subject of his painting in the National Gallery in Washington. The rich, dense landscape setting is typical of Dosso's scenes of sorceresses. Nothing of the horrible consequences of her magic is depicted in the canvas; like the enchantress Circe herself Dosso's rendering of this theme charms by its beauty. But it is just this beauty and the unreal calm of this strange forest gathering which give the scene an aura of the occult. We hardly need the clue of the magic circle in the open book in order to sense the occult power of this woman and her beasts.

Among the northern artists, Hans Baldung Grien found one of his main sources of inspiration in the theme of sorcery, as in his painting of the *Weather Witches* exercising their magic upon the atmosphere. Northern artists were especially interested in rendering the horrible and frightening aspects of witches. Nikolaus Manuel Deutsch's drawing of an old *Naked Witch* is a veritable conjuration of ugliness. Hans Baldung Grien has left us many drawings of terribly macabre scenes of witchery. This taste continued in the north into the seventeenth century, Jacob de Gheyn II gives us a frightening array of macabre details in his scene of *The Witches' Kitchen*, in which we see poisonous fungi, a bat nailed to the floor, a disembowelled corpse, a rotting head, and bones being gnawed by rats.

JACOB DE GHEYN II
The Witches' Kitchen (drawing)
Oxford, Ashmolean Museum

DOSSO DOSSI
Circe and her Companions
Washington D. C., National Gallery

The Terrifying Image

The abominable images of sorcery lead us into the world of the horrible, the terrifying and the macabre. These images clearly derive from melancholic fantasies, from monsters and from weird dreams, in fact from the whole repertory of occultism, but there is also an element of sensualism about them. As in the case of sadistic instincts, they correspond to a need to experience new sensations and if necessary by the most disagreeable means.

Mannerist literature is rich in horrors. Ariosto, in the fifteenth canto of *Orlando Furioso*, describes a fearsome giant who "slaughters travellers, flays them, tears their flesh and sometimes eats them alive... He sucks the substance from their brains, drinks their blood, and gnaws the flesh clean from the bones which he scatters through the countryside, while the flayed skins he places around his cavern as trophies." The region surrounding the monster's dwelling is strewn with fleshless corpses, and the ditches run with blood.

Ronsard may possibly have remembered this passage when he described the cavern of the giant Amycus in his *Hymn of Pollux and Castor:* "Under a slab of rock is his cavernous dwelling, / Into which the Sun's bright rays never enter. / Before his cave there rises a stink of garbage: / Of carcasses of decomposing, rotting corpses: / Down there is the bone of a leg, there the bone of an arm, / All bleaching haphazardly in great heaps. / From the topmost summit of these hideous portals, / Hang the lifeless heads of slaughtered strangers / Which he has lined up, as if for a parade, / Stringing them on long glazed threads, and distilling the blood / Which drips, o horror!, through the cruel gashes / Of the slashed heads, from their spurting brains..."

No less fearsome is the Palace of Death in Giovanni Battista Marini's *Massacre of the Innocents:* "The outside walls are splashed with blood, and at their base lie severed heads and lopped-off limbs... Inside, the walls are hung with a multitude of cruel objects: wheels, chains, gibbets, pikes, millstones, spikes, axes and bloodstained knives... The vile habitation is surrounded by woodland in which dismal trees throw out sinister shadows; each plant is a sickness, each flower a poison; the winds are sighs, and the water freshly shed tears...."

In Giambattista Cinzio Giraldi's drama *Selena*, a princess holds her husband's skull in her hands throughout a whole act. Antonio Decio presents mutilated corpses on the stage. The macabre is, of course, an essential element of the Elizabethan theater, but the graveyard scene in *Hamlet* is mild in comparison with the horrors elaborated in some of the other English dramas of the same epoch. In Thomas Preston's *Cambyse*, we are shown a severed head with the flayed skin folded back against the ears (the stage directions explain that this effect can be obtained by means of a false skin). In John Webster's *Duchess of Amalfi*, in the dark one of the Duchess's brothers presents her a hand, but the hand she clasps is the severed arm of a corpse. *The Revenger's Tragedy* by Cyril Tourneur is even more horrible, if that is possible. A degenerate and depraved duke has poisoned the lovely Gloriana because she refused to satisfy his lusts; Vendice, Gloriana's betrothed, plots a strange revenge. By assuming the part of a pander to the old duke's lusts, he succeeds in bringing to him a pretty girl for his delectation but the "pretty girl" is nothing more than a dummy surmounted by the skull of

"*Il a, sous un rocher, pour sa maison, un antre,*
Où jamais du Soleil la belle clarté n'entre.
Devant son antre put une odeur de voiries,
De carcasses de morts relantes et pourries:
Ici l'os d'une jambe, et là celuy d'un bras
Blanchissent pesle-mesle à grands monceaux à
Tout au haut du sommet de ses hideuses portes,
Des estrangers occis pendent les testes mortes,
Que pour une parade il accroche de rang
A long filets glacez, distillantes de sang,
Qui repandent, horreur! par les playes cruelles
Du test froissé de coups, leurs gluantes cervelle.
(*Ronsard*)"

Nolim existimes ma
tricem hoc loco suum si-
tum seruare: sed aliquā-
tulum in latus conuer-
sam fuisse, ad vasorum
quæ ad ipsam pertinent
commodiorem explica-
tionem.

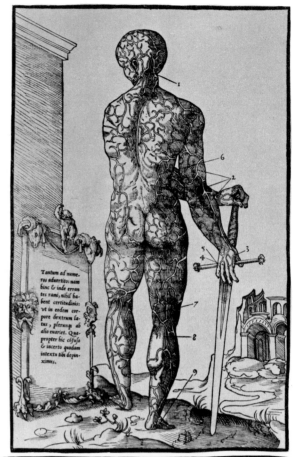

Tantum ad nume-
ros aduertito: nam
hinc & inde erran-
tes rami, nihil ha-
bent certitudinis:
vt in eodem cor-
pore dextrum la-
tus, plerunq; ab
alio euariet. Qua-
propter hic cõfuso
& incerto quodam
intextu tibi depin-
ximus.

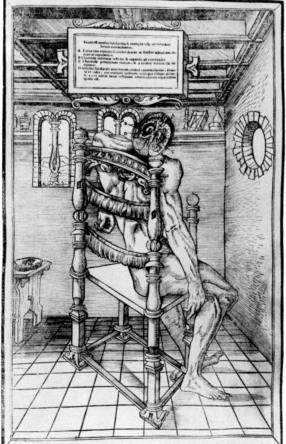

Exuta est cerebri soliditatis, & reiecta vsq; ad vertebras
horum conuolutiones.

A. Locus quo ventriculi cerebri dexter ac sinister astinũ; em ou-
runt ac copulantur.
B Choroidis insolescere refecto & expansio ad ventriculos.
C Choroidis prominẽtiam elatam, & à cerebri ventriculis re-
motam.
D Solidæ substantiæ anterioris cerebri ventriculorum, sequẽ-
tia est sedes, per medium splenem venis æq; obliquis ducit-
it est talum facit reliquum ventriculum capacitatem
spatia est.

Superior iecoris
lobusinuersus hic in-
telligatur, vt mani-
festiores sint portæ
& folliculi fellis in-
sertiones.

Anatomical engravings from
"De dissectione partium corporis"
of Charles Estienne, 1545

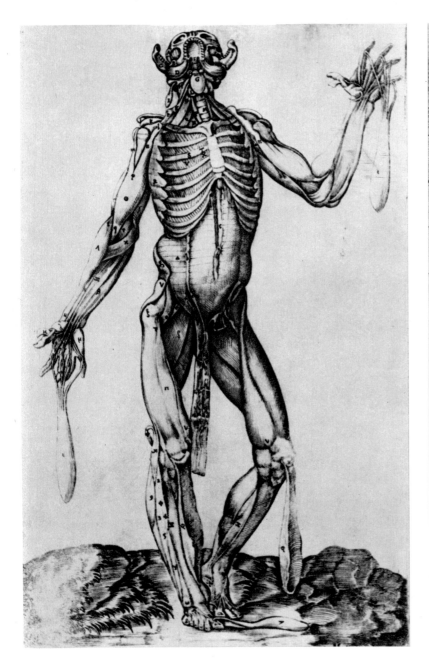
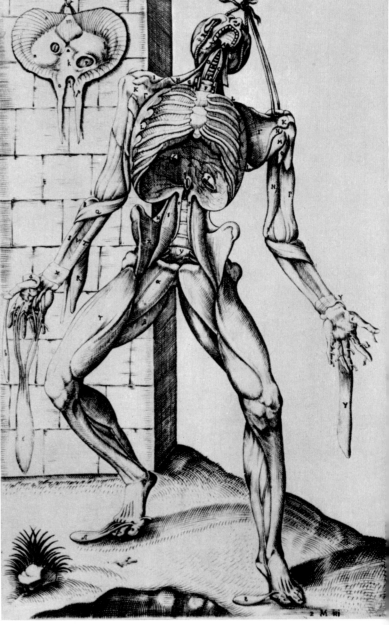

Gloriana draped with a veil and masked, the lips of the mask being poisoned. The old duke, in the semi-darkness, kisses these fleshless lips and dies slowly in dreadful agony, mocked by his enemy who proposes, among other charming ideas, to cut off his eyelids so that he shall not be able to avoid the mask's empty stare.

Macabre images are frequently to be encountered in Mannerist painting. We have already seen rotting limbs, entrails and scattered bones in the scenes of witchery. But the strange turn of the Mannerist mind was capable of making a realistically rendered severed head achieve the status of a decorative motif. In François Dubois the Elder's beautiful landscape with *The Murder of Cicero* just such unquieting details are placed upon the lower edge of the painted decorative frame. To make the presence of these little heads even more disturbing they are executed with a careful reality of detail and color. In the Mannerist period, subjects involving this motif of the severed head, such as *The Beheading of Saint John the Baptist*, *David and Goliath*, *Judith and Holophernes*, and *Perseus and Medusa*, enjoyed great favor.

132

Anatomical engravings from "Historia de la composicion del cuerpo homano" of Valverde, 1556

248

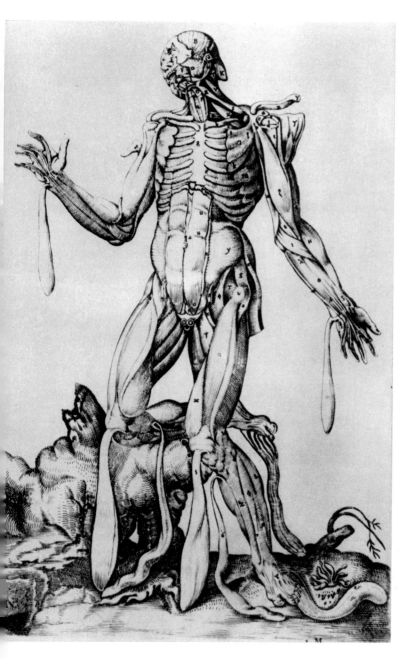

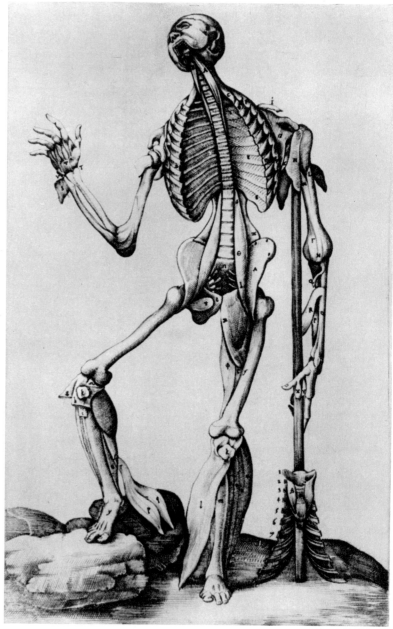

The isolated severed head formed in itself the subject of certain works: *The Head of Medusa, The Head of Saint John the Baptist on the Salver*. Often these heads with their livid hue, bared tendons, and veins spouting blood could resemble an exhibit from a chamber of horrors. The

251 *Head of Medusa* we illustrate here, by Victor Wolfvoet, is made particularly terrifying by the realistic rendering and vitality of the serpents who slither from her hair.

The fashion for macabre images was in large part linked to the development of anatomical research. Many painters, including Leonardo, Raphael, Michelangelo and Rosso, dissected corpses and, in view of the clandestine nature such operations necessarily assumed, they must frequently have found themselves in more or less macabre adventures. The influence of ana-

252 tomical studies is perfectly obvious, for instance, in a work like Jean Viset's *Dead Man*. But the plates which actually illustrated the sixteenth century treatises on anatomy in themselves count among some of the most interesting and curious productions of Mannerist art. The most celebrated of these plates are those designed by Jan Stefan Calcar for the *De humani*

HANS BALDUNG GRIEN
Death and a Maiden
Basel, Öffentliche Kunstsammlung

250

corporis fabrica by the great Flemish anatomist Andreas Vesalius, published in 1543. These illustrations were the object of innumerable copies and enjoyed an immense success throughout Europe for more than a hundred years. Calcar's anatomical plates, especially those of Book II, attain a tormented and fantastic kind of horror which has never been surpassed, even by Giorgio de Chirico or Salvador Dali. Two years after the appearance of Vesalius' work, the 247 *De dissectione partium corporis* by Charles Estienne was published in Paris. The illustrations of this treatise are extremely curious in their animation. This is explained by the fact that the plates were not made after original drawings, but rather the anatomical details were superimposed upon existing plates. Indeed some of these illustrations have almost the aspect of a *collage*. This addition to posturing and gesturing figures of organs stripped bare produces most curious images, for which many counterparts could be found in the work of Surrealist artists.

The animation of the figures in anatomical treatises was not completely an invention of the macabre Mannerist imagination. The animated skeleton was an image very commonly seen in the late Middle Ages in representations of the popular allegorical theme of the *Dance* 248 *of Death*. The engravings of Valverde's treatise, *Historia de la composicion del cuerpo humano,* 249 1556, illustrated here, show poses not unsimilar to the dancing skeletons from earlier prints of the *Dance of Death*. These engravings in Valverde's treatise, however, are far more complex in conception than the stark images of the Medieval skeletons. The Valverde plates are rife with a typically Mannerist ambiguity of intention. They illustrate scientific observations of the tendons and muscles of the human body. At the same time they are expressively animated, and for a final touch of the macabre, their hanging strips of flesh have gratuitously strange oval shapes.

251

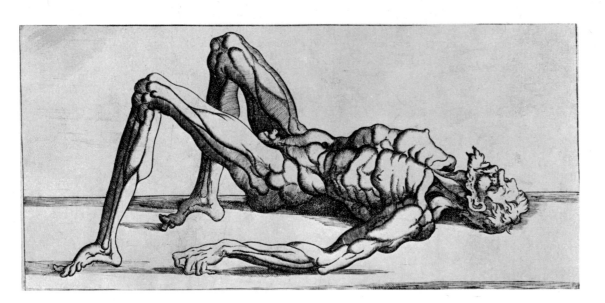

JEAN VISET
A Dead Man
Engraving by René Boyvin

The late Medieval theme of the *Dance of Death* was developed in still other ways by Mannerist artists. From the old series of the *Dance of Death,* artists such as Hans Baldung Grien made an independent subject of Death embracing Youth. In Baldung Grien's painting of *Death and the Maiden* the erotic and the macabre are blended into one hideous image. Very similar are these two quatrains from the *Sonnets de la Gélodacrye* by Jacques Grévin (1561): "These lovely curling tresses, piled splendidly / In a thousand different patterns, above your brow, / Will be no more in twenty or thirty years' time, / But will die, together with the coral of your two dead lips, / These two milky globes, these two protruding strawberries, / These two dimpled arms, and these beautiful fingers; / In the tomb only ashes will remain / Pressed heavily beneath massive stones..."

Another Medieval theme closely related to the *Dance of Death* was that of *Vanitas* and *Momenti Mori.* These themes became current again in the later sixteenth century under the influence of the Counter-Reformation, and Mannerist artists created frightening images to illustrate these ideas of the ephemeralness of our life on this earth. The poem by Jean-Baptiste Chassignet, *Scorn of life and consolation in the face of death* (see page 303) admirably expresses this concept. In Spain where the spirit of the Counter-Reformation continued in vigor longer than elsewhere in Europe, frightening representations of death in the Mannerist tradition were a specialty of the seventeenth century painter Juan de Valdès Leal. The terrifying detail of the decomposing corpse of a bishop, which we here confront with the poem by Chassignet, is from Valdès Leal's painting of *Finis gloria mundi.*

A particularly horrible image in Christian iconography is of course the crucifixion of Christ. The impact of its horror had become considerably diminished for the Western mind by sheer familiarity with the theme. Certain Mannerist artists, however, had the capacity to endow it once more with all its emotional force, most notably Matthias Grünewald in his famous Isenheim altarpiece (c. 1515), now in the museum at Colmar. More than a hundred years later, in 1633, the pious writer Auvray composed some verses on the crucifixion which could suitably be inscribed on the Isenheim altarpiece: "A massacred man hangs on this cross / His bloody flesh appears sewn to his bones, and his belly attached to the vertebrae of his back... / What still remains of his rended skin / pends in horrible flayed strips... / one sees within his large wounds, his veins, his tendons, nerves and arteries." (*Pourmenade de l'âme dévote,* pause v.)

250

302

"*Ces beaux cheveux crespez, qu'en mille et mil*
Tu trousses bravement sur le haut de ton front,
Dedans vingt ou trente ans au monde ne seront,
Mais avec le corail de tes deux lèvres mortes,
Ces deux mons cailletez, ces deux fraises retor
Ces deux bras potelez, et ces beaux doigts mou
Seulement au cercueil les cendres demourront
Encloses pesamment dessous les pierres fortes.
(*Jacques Grévin*)

Un homme massacré pendoit sur cette croix,
Sa peau sanglante estoit cousue avec ses os,
Et son ventre attaché aux vertèbres du dos...
Ce qui restait encore de sa chair détranchée
Pendoit horriblement par lambeaux écorchées
L'on voyoit au profond de ses larges ulcères
Ses veines, ses tendons, ses nerfs et ses artères.
(*Auvray*)

The Expressionism of Satire and Caricature

As we have repeatedly pointed out Mannerism was a style of diversity and contrast. The joyous aspect of the Mannerist spirit sought after beauty, expressing it in terms of extreme elegance, rarity or preciosity, while the melancholic aspect of the same spirit easily abandoned itself to the pursuit of the perverse and the coarse. With satirical and caricatural means, the Mannerist artist expressed the ugly, the ridiculous and the particular with the same zeal he gave to the expression of the beautiful, the sublime and the ideal.

We have already mentioned the success enjoyed during the sixteenth century by such treatises on good manners and social niceties as Count Baldessare Castiglione's *Libro del Cortegiano* (1528) and Giovanni della Casa's *Galateo* (1558). But in 1549 there appeared in Germany a satirical commentary in Latin verse by Friedrich Dedekind entitled *Grobianus*, which not only mocked the precepts of courtesy but in fact constituted a deliberate treatise of "bad manners." This work soon became famous, and was first translated into English in 1605. In 1739, Roger Bull dedicated his version of *Grobianus, or the Compleat Booby* to Jonathan Swift;

LUDGER TOM RING THE YOUNGER
Virgil and Meletus
Münster, Landesmuseum

253

HENDRICK GOLTZIU
Hercules
Engraving

Goltzius fecit et sculpt. A° 1589.

Fischer excu.

here are a few of the milder propositions: "*When Air imprison'd labours for a Vent, / That you shou'd belch, I give my free consent: / Nor belch to Halves—but of the Clangor proud, / Like some substantial Burgo-master, belch aloud... / To cut your Nails is neither meet nor right; / Long nails are ever grateful to the Sight; / The Hawks with pointed Talons seize their Prey, / What Bird by Kings is more admir'd than they? / Yet if you're bent upon it, while you dine, / Some interval to that grand Work assign. / If you your Knife not over-keen survey, / Fraught with the Pudding of a former Day; / These ills are soon remov'd—put off your Shoe, / Which for a Whetstone very well may do... / Do Lumps of Meat between thy Teeth inhere? / Remove them soon, my worthy Pioneer! / The Crocodile, tho' fam'd for wily Tricks, / When to his Jaws large Bits of Food affix, / Finds to his Cost the Grievance can't be stirr'd, / But by th' Assistance of a silly Bird;... / From you to Art be small Assistance ow'd, / Fingers and Hands hath Nature's self bestow'd; / Then or your Fingers or your Knife apply, / Nor on the Assistance of a Bird rely.*"

In 1517, one year after the appearance of Ariosto's *Orlando Furioso*, Teofilo Folengo published, under the pseudonym of Merlinus Coccaius, his *Baldus* and *Le Maccheronee*, mock epics in which the valiant knights become grotesque swashbucklers and Parnassus turns into a mountain of cheese and macaroni nourished by rivulets of sauce. This type of essentially burlesque literature, with its systematic playing down of heroic actions, generous sentiments and noble characters, enjoyed a great vogue in Italy. But the most illustrious satirical writer of the sixteenth century was a Frenchman: François Rabelais created a whole galaxy of immortal caricatures.

This same vein of satire and tendency to caricatural expression is evident in the visual arts, and neither the great men of the past nor mythological figures were spared deliberately grotesque portrayal. The fifteen busts of famous Florentines in the façade of the Palazzo Altoviti in Florence were commissioned by the Senator Baccio Valori in 1570, then owner of the palace. These representations of the great men of Florence are just too grotesque not to betray a conscious will to caricature in their expressionism. For the impression they create the palace became known as the "Palazzo dei Visacci" or "Palace of the Ugly Faces." This same satirical tone is often met with in paintings or engravings of the great sages or poets of ancient times. In the two portraits of ancient poets by Ludger Tom Ring the Younger, which we illustrate here, there is more than just a little fun-poking in this *Virgil* who carefully holds his spectacles in place, or the Greek tragic poet *Meletus* who wears a double braided beard. The grotesque exaggeration of the muscles in the engraving of *Hercules* by Hendrick Goltzius is certainly not a gratuitous miscalculation of the effect of such a rendering on the part of the artist. Rather, it is a deliberate mocking of the epopean strength of the mythological hero, an intent clearly indicated by the ridiculous expression of his face and eyes.

Among northern artists, less diffident to the classical tradition and traditionally given to realism, caricatural portrayal was very common and a whole set of caricatural types was developed, such as the lecherous old men in scenes of *Lot and his Daughters*, or representations of tavern scenes, or the greedy old crones in scenes of prostitution. At other times the realistic vein of northern art makes it difficult to distinguish caricature from a realistic expression divorced from satirical intent. In Martin van Heemskerck's *Saint Luke Painting the Madonna* it seems quite inadmissible to speak of a wilfully satirical interpretation of Saint Luke. Rather, what confronts us here is a pure expressionism achieved by the disturbing quality of realistically portrayed ugliness.

In the detail of *The Adoration of the Kings* by Hernando Yañez, which we illustrate here, there is indeed no caricature but instead the conscious study of the particular and different facial features of each figure. Leonardo's famous drawings from nature of caricatural types and his studies of facial expression had an enormous influence. It is possible that Hernando Yañez actually studied with Leonardo. In this work by Yañez we see this concern with the curious and individual facial features being developed in a characteristically Mannerist fashion towards expressionism and psychological sensibility.

One of the major victims of the Mannerist tendency to caricature was womankind. Adored above all else, she was also fated to be vilified most horribly. A frequent theme in sixteenth century epics is the sudden transformation of a radiantly beautiful young girl into a vile hag. In Ariosto's *Orlando Furioso* (Canto VII), thanks to his magic ring, Roger discovered the true features of the enchantress Alcide: "Her livid, leaden face was furrowed by wrinkles; only a few sparse white hairs remained on her head, and her last tooth had long since fallen from her gums..." And in Spenser's *Faerie Queene* (Book I, Canto VIII), the fair Duessa, once

HERNANDO YAÑEZ
Adoration of the Kings (detail)
Cuenca, Cathedral

MAERTEN VAN HEEMSKERCK
Saint Luke Painting the Madonna
Haarlem, Frans-Hals-Museum

stripped of her "royal robes" and "ornaments that richly were displaid," appeared in her true guise, a "loathly, wrinckled hag, ill favoured, old, whose secret filth good manners biddeth not be told."

The French poets of about 1600, such as Charles Timoléon de Sigogne, François Mainard, Théophile de Viau, among others, went further and did not hesitate to launch their barbs against real women. One may judge from this sonnet by Sigogne, directed against an aged coquette: "Your head resembles the grotesque figure decorating the neck of a lute, / Your eyes the single dots on two dice; your fingers a syrinx; / Your mottled hue elm-bark; / Your skin the reverse side of an ancient register; / Your drooping bosom a tramp's bundle; / Your erstwhile plumpness the branch of a tree; / Your long neck that of a camel; / Your arms the leads knitting together window-panes; / You have passed sixty years, you imitation slip-case for an oboe; / You have seen nine Popes reign and five Kings, / And you are still dressed in modern style! / Pack your bags, old woman, their contents are all worn out: / In Paris they shall use you as a lantern / If you can endure to have a torch thrust in your bottom."

"*Votre tête ressemble au Marmouzet d'un cistre,*
Vos yeux au point d'un dé; vos doigts un chalumeau;
Votre teint diapré l'écorce d'un ormeau;
Votre peau le revers d'un antique régistre;
Votre gorge pendante un bissac d'un bélitre;
Votre vieil embonpoint à celui d'un rameau;
Votre longue encolure à celle d'un chameau;

Votre bras à du plomb qui soutient une vitre;
Vous passez soixante ans, faux fourreau de haut-bois;
Vous avez vu régner neuf Papes et cinq Rois,
Et vous êtes encore vêtue à la moderne!
Troussez votre paquet, vieille, c'est trop vécu:
On vous fera servir à Paris de lanterne,
Si vous pouvez souffrir un flambeau dans le cul." (*Sigogne*)

These grotesque defamations of woman in literature had their visual counterparts in the gross housewives of Hans Sebald Beham, or works such as the horrible *Old Witch* by Nikolaus Manuel Deutsch and the engravings by René Boyvin of pathetically decrepit nymphs.

296

RENÉ BOYVIN
The Goddess Opis as an Old Hag
Engraving after Rosso Fiorentino

RENÉ BOYVIN
Aged Nymph
Engraving after Rosso Fiorentino

258

Curiosity and the Fascination of Natural History

Mannerism, this art with a spirit of diversity, was fascinated by the diversity of the natural world. New discoveries were being made in every field of the natural sciences and they did not fail to feed the imagination of the artists.

The curiosity of the Mannerist mind was exemplified by the investigations then being carried out in the field of natural history. During the sixteenth century, scholars such as Konrad Gesner, Carolus Clusius, Bernard Palissy and Thomas Moufet began to compile inventories of the world's animal, plant and rock life. This interest in natural history was by no means limited to a few specialists. Princes and wealthy merchants assembled collections of natural curiosities. Rudolph II had emissaries throughout Europe to buy rare specimens for his collection in Prague. It is true that the "Cabinet of Rarities" maintained by princes and monarchs certainly did not represent any effort at scientific cataloguing or selection. They were rather a conglomeration of objects, prized above all for their curiosity. It will be noted in the engraving of one of these little private museums illustrated here, that in addition to the collection of birds, mammals and reptiles, there is a collection of urns and vases, pieces of sculpture, books, and other objects. Despite the lack of systemization, and the naïveté and superstition which prompted this type of collecting, it clearly witnesses a surge of curiosity for the wonders of Earth. Philip II of Spain had a large collection of flowers and birds. The Fuggers in Nuremberg and the Medici in Florence had their own private aquariums and zoos. According to an English traveller, the menagerie of Duke Francesco I de' Medici contained five lions, three

JAN BRUEGEL THE ELDER
Allegory of Water (detail)
Paris, Hahn Collection

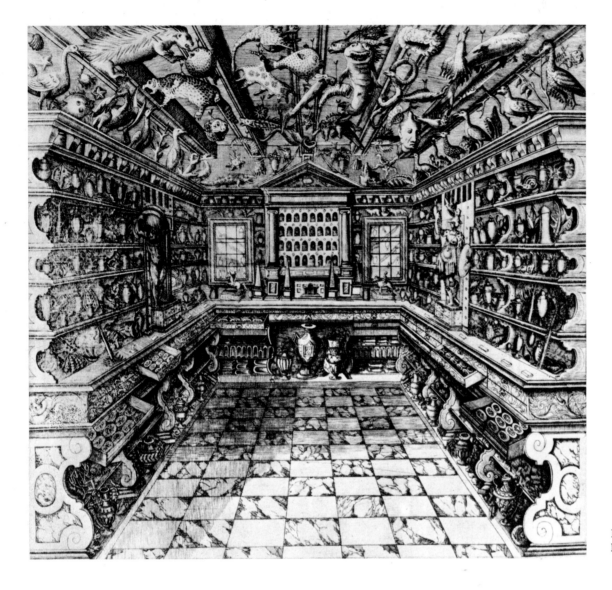

Rarities Cabinet
Engraving

tigers, wolves, eagles, bears, wild boars, a wild cat, a leopard, and even an Indian rat. On a much more modest scale, artists such as Sodoma and Rosso had their own little menageries. Benvenuto Cellini, in his *La vita* (I, 29), says that he used often to go walking alone along the seashore, amusing himself by "picking up pebbles and shells, all as singular as they were beautiful."

Some of the sixteenth century's most charming poems took for their subjects animals, plants and even minerals. In France, for example, Ronsard wrote poems on *The Marigold, The Pine-tree,* and *The Holly*, while Guillaume de Salluste du Bartas, in his *Première Sepmaine,* gives a day by day inventory of Creation. Rémy Belleau sang the praises of the Butterfly, Coral, the Oyster, the Snail, the Tortoise, the Glow-worm, and the Cherry; his *Amourous propositions and new comments concerning precious stones* of 1576 (see extract page 19), gives descriptions of the different gems, detailing their formation and color, and enumerating their magical powers.

Thus it is by no means coincidental if we encounter so many images of natural history in the visual arts of this epoch. Certainly representations of animals and plants abounded in Medieval art, but they were mainly used as symbols or as marginal decoration. But in the sixteenth century an artist of the stature of Albrecht Dürer was quite capable of devoting an

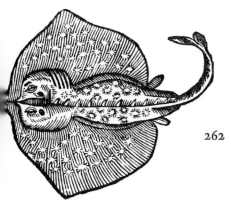

entire watercolor or engraving to a rabbit, a tuft of herbs, a bouquet of violets, a lobster, a walrus, or a rhinoceros. Virgel Solis engraved plates consisting wholly of various animals strangely interlocked with each other. At the court of Rudolph II in Prague much artistic energy was expended in the depiction of the wonders of natural history. One of the artists of Rudolph II's court, Joris Hoefnagel, was paid by his master one thousand gold crowns for his four volumes of engraved plates filled with birds, reptiles, small quadrupeds, fish, crustaceans, insects, fruits, and flowers. In these plates very diverse phenomena of nature, treated with great care in their details, are brought together in a *mise en page* as irrational as it is attractive and imaginative.

262

The many treatises on natural history written in the sixteenth century were illustrated with plates which often possess a real artistic value. Among the more important zoological works with significant illustrations was the *De Piscibus marinis* (1555) of Pierre Belon with illustrations by Georges Reverdy. Still other important publications were the vast *Historia animalium* of Konrad Gesner (published between 1551–1560) and the *Historia Naturalis* of the Bolognese doctor and naturalist, Ulisse Aldrovandi, parts of which were published from 1599 onward. These works were immensely rich in natural images and in a sense replaced the legendary bestiaries of the Middle Ages. The botanical studies of the period were equally

263

oodcut of Rayfish from
e reliquis animalibus
anguinibus" of Ulisse Aldrovandi

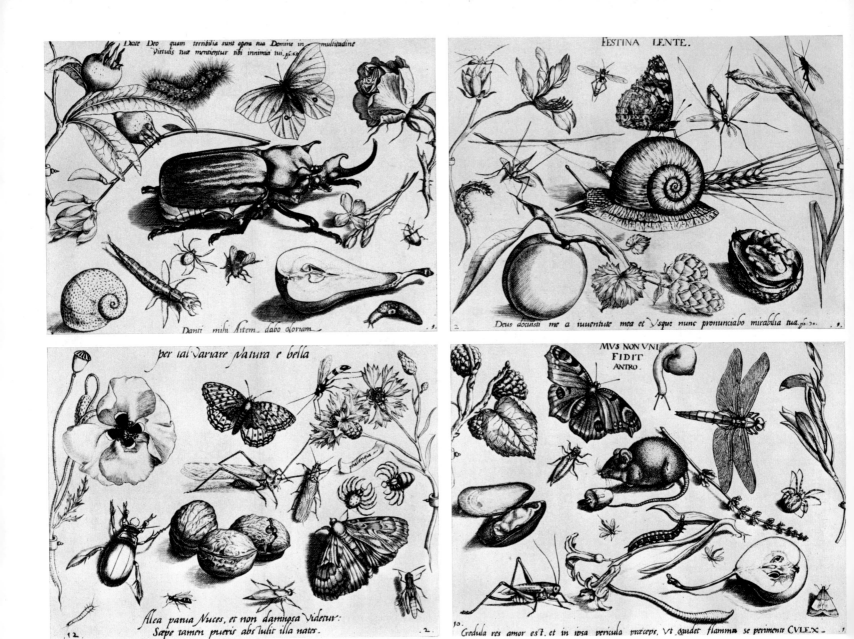

Dicite Deo quam terribilia sunt opera tua Domine in multitudine
Virtus tua mentientur tibi inimici tui. ps.63

FESTINA LENTE.

Danti mihi Artem dabo gloriam

Deus docuisti me a iuuentute mea et usque nunc pronunciabo mirabilia tua. ps.70

per tal variare Natura e bella

MVS NON VNI
FIDIT
ANTRO.

Alea parua Nuces, et non damnosa videtur:
Sæpe tamen pueris abstulit illa nates.

Credula res amor est, et in ipsa pericula præceps, Vt gaudet flamma se perimente CVLEX.

264numerous and richly illustrated. We here reproduce a plate by A. Sylvius from the *Plantarum seu stirpium historia* of Mathias de Lobel, published in Antwerp in 1576, which shows a delicately studied variety of flowers and thistles. Many of these studies, such as the *Geschichte der Pflanzen* (1554) of Rembert Dodonaeus, and the anonymous *Compendium de plantis omnibus* (1571) contain illustrations of considerable artistic value and a wealth of Mannerist images.

The inspirational value and the influence of these studies upon the artists of the period was tremendous. Among the Italian painters of the time Vasari cites Cristofano Gherardi as being greatly admired by his contemporaries for his paintings of plants, animals, birds, and fishes. Vasari also reports that Bachiacca executed for the office of Duke Cosimo de' Medici "all manner of birds and rare plants, divinely portrayed in oil." But of all the Italian artists 229 this new, rich imagery of nature was most fully exploited by Giuseppe Arcimboldo in his allegorical heads of the *Seasons* and the *Elements*. The precision and variety of the fish, water

JORIS HOEFNAGEL
Engravings from Album of Small
Animals, Insects, Fruits and Flowers

Woodcut of Fishes, Eel,
and Lobster from "De Mollibus
de Piscibus" of Ulisse Aldrovandi

reptiles and crustaceans in his *Allegory of Water* would individually serve most suitably as illustrations for a treatise of natural history. It should be mentioned that Arcimboldo worked for twenty-six years in Prague at the court of Rudolph II, where, as we have already noted, there was a great interest in the new discoveries of natural science. The case of Arcimboldo serves as an excellent example of the way in which information brought to light by the contemporary curiosity inspired the Mannerist artist, and in turn of the way in which the artist's own fantasy transformed these visual images into highly original and imaginative works of art.

Themes from natural history really triumphed in painting in the late sixteenth and earlier seventeenth century in the work of Jan Bruegel the Elder and his circle. Bruegel executed innumerable series of allegories of *The Four Seasons, The Five Senses, The Elements*, as well as paintings of *Noah's Ark* and the *Earthly Paradise*. These themes allowed him to present countless details of the animal and vegetable world executed with precision and realistic technique. Thus in his paintings of the *Allegory of Water* from the series of the *Four Elements* (we here

259 reproduce a detail of the painting of *Water* attributed to Jan Bruegel the Elder in the Hahn Collection) he presented everything living in or near the water, from the whale and the seal to the flying fish and the star-fish, from turtles to swans, ducks and seagulls, from carp and the familiar native trout to the moon-fish of the southern seas. In the same way his paintings of *Earth* are expositions of mammals and reptiles, and his representations of *Air* present a catalogue of birds, while the *Sense of Smell* is illustrated by an infinite variety of flowers. With Jan Bruegel the Elder as the nucleus, a whole constellation of artists specialized in these themes. His son Jan Bruegel the Younger and many other followers turned out innumerable replicas and variations of his allegorical series, which often makes attribution very difficult. Another artist whose works should be mentioned as strongly inspired by the new knowledge of natural history is Roland Jacobsz Savery. This artist produced many paintings of the *Earthly Paradise,* which are rich, dense landscapes teaming with every imaginable variety of animal. One of his paintings provides the best existing evidence of the now extinct dodo, a bird once indigenous to the Indian Ocean Island of Mauritius.

These works by Jan Bruegel the Elder and his school and those by Roland Jacobsz Savery so rich in images from natural history were still traditional paintings in being either still lifes or complete scenes of landscape and figures, often with allegorical or Biblical reference. But by the mid-seventeenth century, in the paintings of Jan van Kessel, the grandson of Jan

261 Bruegel the Elder, no such reference was needed. His painting of *Insects and Reptiles* illustrated here witnesses a more objective reality of conception than the earlier works of the Mannerist artists.

It must be seen that the interest of the Mannerist artists in the world of nature, though quite different from the efforts of the Encyclopedists two hundred years later, is still comparable in its catholicity to the encyclopedic mind of the eighteenth century. But the Mannerist artist's approach to this new knowledge was one of curiosity spurred by wonder.

A. SYLVIUS
Plants from "Plantarum seu stirpium historia" of Mathias de Lobel, 1576

FRANCESCO MAZZUOLI
The Diamond Mine
Florence, Palazzo Vecchio, Studiolo

TOMAS FEDRIANI F.

The Crafts and Mechanical Inventions

The encyclopedic tendency in the works of Jan Bruegel, which we have noted in his use of plants and beasts, is equally pronounced by his liking for tools and instruments invented by man. This is well illustrated by his series of the *Allegory of the Senses* in the Prado in Madrid. In the *Allegory of Touch,* on a table at the right of the picture are laid out a whole range of surgical instruments: probes, scissors, saws, cauteries, clips, and forceps of various shapes and sizes. In the center of the same painting is a winch with several pulleys. Similarly the *Allegory of Sight* presents a variety of optical and astronomical apparatus. In his *Allegory of Fire,* one of the paintings from a series of the *Four Elements,* in the Galleria Doria at Rome, Jan Bruegel not only shows the products of the forge, such as armour and cannon, but also the different stages in the firing and working of metal together with the appropriate tools.

This aesthetic interest in machines, inventions, and techniques of the various trades and professions was manifested throughout the sixteenth century. Many artists put their talents at the service of mechanics, and the sixteenth century treatises on mechanical inventions were well supplied with detailed illustrative plates. The *Theatrum instrumentorum et machinarum* of Jacques Besson (1578) contains sixty engravings by René Boyvin and Jacques Ducerceau. These artists were capable of endowing a pump or tower with all the grace and distinction of the style of the School of Fontainebleau. The plates of *Le Diverse ed artificiose macchine* of Agostino Ramelli (1588) show a variety of majestic machines from water towers and winches to engines of war such as battering-rams, assault towers and catapults. These complicated constructions with their giant gears have a surreal quality which certainly fascinated the Man-

269

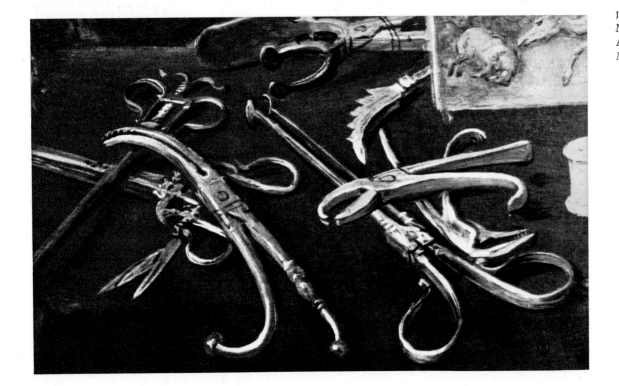

JAN BRUEGEL THE ELDER
Medical Instruments (detail from
Allegory of the Sense of Touch)
Madrid, Prado

ALESSANDRIO FEI
Goldsmiths' Workshop
Florence, Palazzo Vecchio, Studiolo

GIOVANNI STRADANO
Distillers' Workshop
Florence, Palazzo Vecchio, Studiolo

MIRABELLO CAVALORI
Fullers' Workshop
Florence, Palazzo Vecchio, Studiolo

nerist artist. Many of the complicated machines of torture in paintings of martyrdom, such as that of the *Martyrdom of Saint Catherine* by Lelio Orsi (Modena, Galleria Estense), can only be explained in the light of such fanciful inventions.

A similar interest in mechanical inventions and the crafts is manifested by the writers of the epoch. Ronsard, in his *Abrégé de l'art poétique* (1565), advises the poet to frequent craftsmen: "You shall, as often as possible, seek the company of artisans of every craft, such as those of Seamanship, Venery, and Falconry, and more especially the artisans of Iron, the Goldsmiths, Metal-founders, Farriers, Workers of Ores; and thence you shall derive many beautiful and lively comparisons together with the proper names of the tools to enrich your work and render it more agreeable and more perfect...." Rabelais recounts in *Gargantua* (Book 1, Chapter 24) that on rainy days Ponocrates sometimes took his pupil Gargantua on visits to the craftsmen's workshops: "Alternatively, they went either to see the drawing of metals or the casting of cannon, or paid visits to jewellers, goldsmiths, and cutters of precious stones; or to alchemists and coiners; or to tapestry-workers, weavers, velvet-workers, watchmakers, looking-glass makers, printers, musical instrument makers, dyers, and other craftsmen."

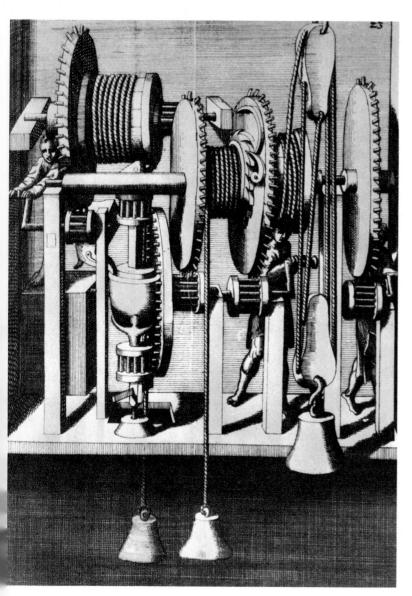

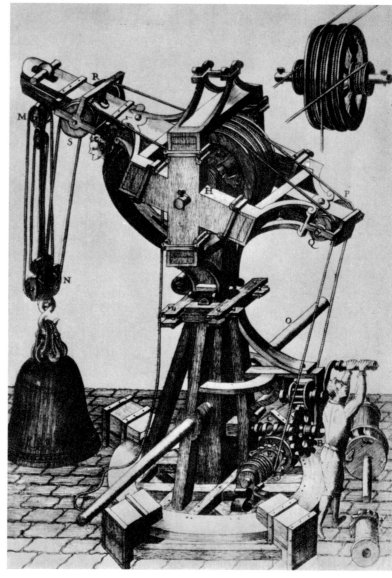

Engravings of Machines from "Le diverse e artificiose machine" of Agostino Ramelli, 1558

Such occupations on the part of the son of a monarch were by no means unusual in those times. In fact the princes of the sixteenth century were frequently skilled in some handicraft. Montaigne reports in his *Journal de voyage en Italie* that Duke Francesco I de' Medici was "himself a skillfull and diligent worker, able to counterfeit oriental stones and work crystal, for this Prince knows something of Alchemy and the mechanical Arts." Fynes Morison confirms Montaigne's information and tells us further that the Duke had discovered the secret of Chinese porcelain, that he had invented a method for smelting crystal, that he reared silk-worms, distilled liquors and worked at the forge. In an annex of the palace, Francesco I had in his employ artisans of all kinds with their own workshops, and he passed a great part of his time with these craftsmen, returning to work the moment his midday meal was completed. It was these interests and activities which served as the inspiration of the paintings of the crafts in the Studiolo of Francesco I in the Palazzo Vecchio at Florence, which include the *Distillers' Workshop* by Giovanni Stradano, the *Fullers' Workshop* by Mirabello Cavalori, the 267 *Goldsmiths' Workshop* by Alessandro Fei, the *Foundry* by Poppi, *The Invention of Gun-* 265 *powder* by Jacopo Coppi, and the working of a *Diamond Mine* by Francesco Mazzuoli.

Landscape and the Feeling for Nature

Among the wealth of new images and forms created by artists of the Mannerist period none is more significant for the development of Western culture than the birth of landscape painting. Whereas landscape had been the supreme expression of Chinese painting from the end of the T'ang Dynasty in the ninth century, European painting was dominated by the human figure until the sixteenth century. This difference in theme reflects a fundamentally different vision of the world and concept of life. In Western philosophy all revolved around man whereas the mind of the Orient sought to find for man a place in the universe. The appearance of the first European landscapists such as Joachim Patinir, Albrecht Altdorfer, Niccolò dell'Abbate and Pieter Bruegel the Elder was an extremely important cultural event. It marked a victory of the imagination and sensibilities over the basically rigid anthropomorphism of Western culture. Like the poetic interest in natural history the interest in landscape painting heralded the modern awareness of the reality of the universe.

The style of certain European landscapes of the sixteenth century often bears an affinity with Chinese painting. The drawing of a *Rocky Promontory* by Nikolaus Manuel Deutsch brings to mind the profiling of cliffs in Chinese landscapes. Likewise the formations in the landscape in the background of Albrecht Altdorfer's *Battle of Issus* are not unsimilar to the distant mountains depicted in Oriental works, and Altdorfer's landscape shows a striking resemblance to a painting of the *Grotto of the Immortals* by Tung Yüan, in the Museum of the Palace of Peking. The immensity of view seen in the panoramic compositions of the type illustrated here by the painting of Maerten van Heemskerck is close in its conception to Oriental scroll painting. To make these comparisons is not in any way to insist upon direct

JOACHIM PATINIR
Landscape (detail from the Temptation of Saint Anthony)
Madrid, Prado

NIKOLAUS MANUEL DEUTSCH
Rocky Promontory (drawing)
Basel, Öffentliche Kunstsammlung

influence of Oriental painting. Rather, these visual analogies are cited to underscore the fact of a new sensibility to nature in Western artistic expression in the sixteenth century.

It is of course true that landscape details and landscape settings can be found in earlier Western painting. Already in Medieval art one finds many such details, quite often executed with loving care, but it was only in the sixteenth century in the works of such artists as Joachim Patinir and Pieter Bruegel the Elder that the landscape itself began to dominate the whole conception of the work of art, and the mythological or religious scene contained in the landscape was relegated to secondary importance. Certain of the details of sixteenth century landscapes are indeed taken over from earlier Medieval forms. These strange isolated mountains or rocks to the left of the landscape background by Patinir which we reproduce here would seem to come from the ideographic rendering of mountains and hills in Medieval art. But Patinir has made of his whole landscape a sensitive and artistic recreation of nature. Likewise the strange sugar loaf mountain in El Greco's *Mount Sinai* seems to hark back to the ideographic hill-locks of Medieval painting, but El Greco has made of them a fantastic, nature inspired vision.

272

EL GRECO
Mount Sinai
Modena, Galleria Estense

The birth of landscape painting was far from being an isolated phenomenon, for this new feeling for nature appeared very plainly in the literature of the time. The fifteenth century was not yet over when Jacopo Sannazaro wrote, in the Preamble to his *Arcadia:*

"The lofty, densely foliaged trees with which simple nature, unaided by art, has covered the summit of the most fearful mountains, are generally more pleasing to the view than are those carefully nurtured and skillfully developed plants destined to ornament gardens. The ear is more enchanted by the warbling of birds flying in liberty in the woods than by the carefully studied song of birds enclosed in magnificent cages in the heart of towns."

This need for true nature, for nature untouched by man, was frequently expressed. Ronsard states in one of his elegies that he loves to steal away into woods, to lose himself in valleys, to conceal himself in some cavern. And in his *Amours de Marie,* he uses exalted terms to express the sacred delirium of communion with nature: « Je mourrois de plaisir voyant par ces bocages / Les arbres enlacez de lierres espars, / Et la verte lambruche errante en mille pars / Sur l'aubespin fleury près des roses sauvages...»

"I died from pleasure, seeing in these copses / The trees entwined with straggling ivy, / And the green wild-vine roaming everywhere / Over the flowering hawthorn close by the wild roses..." In these words we discover already in the sixteenth century an expression of a sensibility and emotional response to nature which is generally considered to be a creation of the Romantic movement of two hundred years later.

JACOB JACOBSZ VAN GEEL
Forest Landscape (detail)
Amsterdam, Rijksmuseum

273

As in the case of the inspiration from studies of natural history, the fantasy of the Mannerist artist desired to transform nature. Inspired by real nature he created ideal landscapes, landscapes truer than nature, so to speak, where water, trees and rocks are richer, more grandiose or more mysterious than in real life. In both literature and the visual arts of the time nature was most frequently described within an extraordinarily ideal context. The Island of the Blest in Tasso's *Jerusalem Delivered*, for example, is a place where the earth brings forth fruit in abundance, the climate is delicious, and the sea always calm. It was just this sort of setting which most fired the imagination of the painters. The favorite themes of the landscapists were just those which allowed for the richest possible portrayal of nature in all her beauty. The two recurrent themes were those of the *Earthly Paradise* or the idyllic glade in which nymphs disported themselves and the gods relaxed. Even without the aid of such idealistic subject matter the Mannerist artist sought to represent nature as grander and more fantastic than it appears. A
273 good example are the trees and forests of the Dutch landscapists of the earlier seventeenth
11   century. In the *Forest Landscape* by Jacob Jacobsz van Geel or the *Winter Landscape with Gipsies* by Gysbrecht Lytens, the massive denseness of gnarled trunks and twisted branches give to these forests an imagined energy and expressiveness which goes far beyond nature herself.

This desire to express the greatness and immensity of nature as well as her many curious and delectable details is, however, best seen in the panoramas created by the landscapists of the Mannerist period. These extensive views combine within a single picture all the various aspects of nature and thus constitute a sort of epitome of the universe. The panoramic land-
29   scape in the background of Albrecht Altdorfer's *Battle of Issus* dominates the actual battle scene in the foreground of the painting. It encompasses a whole town, hills, mountains, mountain chains and an island, as well as rivers, lakes and a distant ocean. Indeed the whole universe is evoked in the immensity of the sky, the variety of the clouds, and the glowing sun and moon (the latter not shown in the detail reproduced here). A similar magnitude of con-
276 ception is seen in the panoramic background of Maerten van Heemskerck's *Rape of Helen*. Temples, gardens and port-towns, ruins, bridges, rivers and castles, distant mountains and a rainbow that spans land and sea: one never ends in finding new and intriguing details in this landscape, and yet these do not detract from its dominant impression which is that of the vastness and magical richness of the visible world.

HENDRICK VAN CLEVE III
The Tower of Babel
Anzegem, *Collection of the Comte Phil
Limburg-Stirum*

MAERTEN VAN HEEMSKERCK
Fantastic Panorama (detail from
The Rape of Helen)
Baltimore, The Walters Art Gallery

The Cityscape, Architecture, and Ruins

The new awareness of nature itself was accompanied by the new awareness of the town or city as a phenomenon. In the panoramic landscapes of Patinir, Altdorfer or Heemskerck, against the distant ground of a pure nature arise the countless constructions of a town or vast city, which was conceived as being no less a part of the universe than nature itself.

As with nature, the city was usually not interpreted in terms of its normal appearance. In general, the town as seen by Mannerist artists was an architectural dream, an unfunctional conglomeration of monumental buildings, squares, colonnades, fountains, ruins, arches and

276 monuments. This is certainly true in the panorama of Heemskerck's *Rape of Helen*. It is also
280 true of the cityscape in Antoine Caron de Beauvais' *Massacre of the Triumvirs*, conceived very much as a stage setting. In this painting, despite the very careful delineation of the many architectural monuments, with the exception of the palace at the right, there are no really habitable buildings but rather a proliferation of statues, columns, obelisks and balustrades.

The particularly visionary and dreamlike quality of Mannerist architecture is brought out not only by the unreal juxtaposition of the most unusual monuments and extravagant buildings, but also by the very ambiguous spatial relationships of these architectural settings.

237 In Maerten van Heemskerck's *Momus Finding Fault with the Gods* it is impossible to judge the distance between the foreground and the palace in the background which seems almost to float in space. Relationships are made deliberately ambiguous by placing a huge column base in the foreground which is obviously taller than the figures and yet impossible to really relate proportionally to the background. Likewise one is not sure if the urn at the left is in the same plane as the obelisk or much nearer to the foreground, and thus their relative size remains a

MAERTEN VAN HEEMSKERCK
Mausoleum of Halicarnassus and
Temple of Jupiter
Engravings from series of
The Seven Wonders of the World

mystery. All this enhances the enigmatic quality of the individual monuments and helps to create that aura of fantasy desired by the Mannerist artist. It is, however, in the strange towns 135 of Monsù Desiderio that we see the extreme transformation of the city image into a pure visionary fantasy.

A similar extravagant and imaginative architecture is described in the literature of the sixteenth century. The Palace of Saint John in Canto 34 of Ariosto's *Orlando Furioso* is constructed "within one single, glowing carbuncle." The Palace of Armide in Tasso's *Jerusalem Delivered* is "an immense edifice rearing up from the mountain's summit;" the encircling walls are pierced by a hundred silver gateways swinging upon hinges of pure gold; and within there lies hidden a magic garden. The Abbey of Thélème, constructed specially by Gargantua for Friar John, is described in the following terms by Rabelais: "The said building was a hundred times more magnificent than Bonnivet or Chambord or Chantilly. For it contained nine thousand, three hundred and thirty-two apartments, each one provided with an inner chamber, a closet, wardrobe, and chapel, and each one giving on to a great hall."

The Mannerist image of the city was nourished upon the remaining ruins and descriptions 274 of the architectural wonders of the past. The *Tower of Babel*, the consummate image of the monumental town, in which an entire city is contained in one gigantic edifice, was an architectural theme that particularly appealed to the Mannerist imagination. But it was above all the ruins of classical antiquity which haunted their vision. The ruins of ancient Rome were avidly studied by the artists. Maerten van Heemskerck, for example, during his stay in Rome between 1532 and 1535 spent most of his time sketching the ancient monuments. In the panorama of his 276 *Rape of Helen* it is possible to recognize specific monuments from the Rome of the Caesars, such as Trajan's column, the Baths of Caracalla, and the obelisk of the Circus Maximus. This painting, executed just after his return to the Netherlands, seems a recapitulation of his archaeological orgies in Rome. His phantasmagoria of an ancient city is rendered in terms of imagined, ideal reconstructions together with evocative and deliberate use of ruins. The power of the Mannerist artists to reconstruct the great monuments of the ancient world with the aid of traditional descriptions and a general familiarity with the ruins of the past is

MAERTEN VAN HEEMSKERCK
Colossus of Rhodes and
Pyramids of Egypt
Engravings from series of
The Seven Wonders of the World

COLOSSÆI RO A BARBARIS DIRVTI · PROSPECTVS · I ·

COCK·FECIT·

Previous page:

ANTOINE CARON DE BEAUVAIS
The Massacre of the Triumvirs
Paris, Louvre

COLOSSÆI · RO · ALIVS · PROSPECTVS ·

HIERONYMUS COECK
Ruins of the Colosseum
Engravings

282

278 witnessed by Heemskerck's engravings of the *Seven Wonders of the World* in which the
279 *Mausoleum of Halicarnassus* or the *Colossus of Rhodes* is seen in what he imagined to be its
pristine splendor.

But essentially all these recreations were recreations of ancient Rome itself. The artists
flocked to Rome, but desire to know its ancient treasures was shared by all. Particularly in the
north one craved images of its ruins. Artists did not sketch the ancient monuments exclusively for their own study. They executed drawings and prints after the ancient ruins in order
to satisfy the demand for such images. These works were more true to reality than the imagi-
natively transformed buildings and ruins in their paintings. Hieronymus Coeck, for example,
executed twenty-four prints of Roman ruins, which foreshadow the prints of Piranesi.

HIERONYMUS COECK
Ruins of the Roman Forum
Engraving

Hell and Hades

From the cities of the visible world we pass to those of Hell and Hades. Classical antiquity, Medieval iconography, and the modern sensibility to the world of reality are confounded and woven together in Mannerist art. The theme of Hell and the demons of Hell and temptation, although a traditionally Medieval theme, was a favorite subject of Mannerist art. Of equal fascination to the Mannerist mind, however, was the Underworld or the realm of Hades or Pluto of Classical mythology. The same images of monsters, fires in the night, and strange architectural settings were used for both scenes: the winged devil of Christian iconography 137 appears in the realm of Pluto in the painting reproduced here by Orazio Grevenbroeck. The subjects of Hell and Hades allowed for the creation of the most monstrous fantasies. It is therefore fitting that we close our survey with these themes since they gave the freest possible rein 286 to the diverse expressions of the Mannerist imagination. The print of the *Temptation of Saint Anthony* by Jacques Callot can serve as an example of the summit of the Mannerist ability in the creation of images. Within an immense, natural setting, which contains a small farm house, huge ancient ruins and a view to the distant sea, Callot has created a most frightening vision of the infernal. Horrible monsters and infernal machines invade every part of the ground and sky in a fury of diabolical activity. The achievement of this truly apocalyptic vision represents the two most basic elements of Mannerism, the artistic conquest of reality and the complete freedom of the imagination.

JACOB ISAACSZ VAN SWANENBURGH
Charon Crossing the Styx (detail)
Brussels, Private Collection

JAN BRUEGEL THE ELDER
Juno in the Underworld (detail)
Dresden, Gemäldegaleri

284

JACQUES CALLOT
The Temptation of Saint Anthony
Engraving

Following pages:
Attributed to MONSÙ DESIDERIO
The Inferno (detail)
Besançon, Musée des Beaux-Arts

JAN MANDYN
Monsters
(detail from Saint Christopher)
Munich, Alte Pinakothek

Conclusion

After this panoramic survey of Mannerism and Mannerist painting two impressions must be uppermost in the reader's mind, first that of the richness and diversity of the period and secondly its actuality in terms of modern artistic expression.

From a purely quantitative point of view no other epoch of Western cultural history can offer such a comprehensive list of notable painters, the qualitative level of whose work is very high. The illustrations of this book represent only a very modest sample of the huge creative output of the Mannerist period. But the most striking aspect of this richness is neither its quantity nor high quality but its extraordinary variety. Compared with the High Renaissance or Baroque, Mannerism appears as a perpetual renewal, a limitless source of surprises. This very diversity has been the cause of misunderstanding and the reason why one has so long preferred to ignore this cultural phenomenon which escapes easy definition. But it is precisely its diversity, its openness of mind and imagination which interests us today.

The contribution of the present work has been to present the Mannerist epoch as a whole. We have not tried at all to distinguish individual schools of Mannerist painting. This important work has been carried out by art historians over the past few decades, and their studies and interest have formed the very foundation of our knowledge of the period. We have here rather tried to see the basic common aspects and conceptions of Mannerist art, which show it to be a pan-European movement. Seen as such Mannerism indeed demonstrates itself to be an epoch and an artistic expression of primary importance, not only in the history of art but in the whole history of Western culture.

In this study we have pointed out the ties which, stretching across the brief Classical-Baroque hiatus, unite Mannerism with Romanticism. Melancholy, imagination, a predilection for the sinister, a feeling for nature—these Romantic preoccupations are all equally Mannerist preoccupations. But Mannerism goes further perhaps than Romanticism. Romanticism expended a considerable part of its energies in a reaction to Neo-Classicism, and as a result its revolt remained inevitably linked negatively with Neo-Classicism. The audacities of Mannerism on the other hand—like those of Contemporary art—were far freer, since they were not directed against any particular anterior school. It is for this reason that Mannerism may seem to take the place of Romanticism as the direct precursor of our own era's avant-garde movements. During the course of the present work, we have had occasion when dealing with certain manifestations of Mannerist art, to compare them with Cubism, Expressionism, and Surrealism. These were not meant as superficial comparisons of details. It is a fact that one encounters, between 1520 and 1620, the same boldness, preciosity and even the same vulgarity, the same exacerbated need for novelty and the same interest in archaisms, the same delicate perfume of decadence, even decay, and the same hope in the future of humanity, which have characterized Western culture since the beginning of our own century. These two separate epochs are fundamentally very close to each other. They are both epochs of far-reaching social and spiritual revolution. Each witnessed a sensational expansion of physical horizons. They are both marked by deep anxieties and excessive ambitions, by complex regrets and by an immense confidence in the future. This mutual empathy explains our own fascination with Mannerism.

Selections from
mannerist poetry
IV

Michelangelo Buonarroti   Sonnet to Tommaso de' Cavalieri

D'altrui pietoso e sol di sé spietato
Nas ce un vil bruto, che con pena e doglia
L'altrui man veste, e la sua scorza spoglia,
E sol per morte se può dir ben nato.

Così volesse al mio signor mio fato
Vestir sua viva di mia morta spoglia,
Che, come serpe al sasso si discoglia,
Pur per morte potria cangiar mia stato.

O fussi sol la mia l'irsuta pelle,
Che, del suo pél contesta, fa tal gonna,
Che con ventura stringe sì bel seno,

Ch'i' l'are' pure il giorno; o le pianelle
Che fanno a quel di lor base e colonna,
Ch'i' pur ne porterei due nevi almeno.

Kind to the world, but to itself unkind
A worm is born, that dying noiselessly
Despoils itself to clothe fair limbs, and be
In its true worth by death alone divined.

Oh, would that I might die, for her to find
Raiment in my outworn mortality!
That, changing like the snake I might be free
To cast the slough wherein I dwell confined!

Nay, were it mine, that shaggy fleece that stays,
Woven and wrought into a vestment fair,
Around her beauteous bosom in such bliss!

All through the day she'd clasp me! Would I were
The shoes that bear her burden! When the ways
Were wet with rain, her feet I then should kiss!

Edmund Spenser
The Faerie Queene

Book I, Canto 8 : 420–428

Her craftie head was altogether bald,
And, as in hate of honorable eld,
Was overgrowne with scurfe and filthy scald;
Her teeth out of her rotten gummes were feld,
And her sowre breath abominably smeld;
Her dried dugs, lyke bladders lacking wind,
Hong downe, and filthy matter from them weld;
Her wrizled skin, as rough as maple rind,
So scabby was that would have loathd all womankind.

Her neather parts, the shame of all her kind,
My chaster Muse for shame doth blush to write;
But at her rompe she growing had behind
A foxes taile, with dong all fowly dight ...

Im 1525 Johr nach dem Pfingstag zwischen dem Mitwoch und Pfintztag in der Nacht im Schlaf hab ich dis Gesicht gesehen, wie viel grosser Wassern van Himmel fielen. Und das erste traf das Erdrich ungefähr 4 Meil van mir mit einer sölchen Grausamkeit mit einem ubergrossem Rauschen und Zersprützen und ertrenket das ganz Land. In solchem erschrak ich so gar schwerlich, daß ich doran erwachet, eh dann die andern Wasser fielen. Und die Wasser, die do fielen, warn fast groß. Und der fiel etliche weit, etliche näher, und sie kamen so hoch herab, daß sie im Gedunken gleich langsam fielen. Aber do das erst Wasser, das das Erdrich traf, schier herbeikam, do fiel es mit einer solchen Geschwindigkeit, Wind und Brausen, daß ich also erschrak, do ich erwacht, daß mir all mein Leichnam zittret und lang nit recht zu mir selbs kam. Aber do ich am Morgen aufstund, molet ich hie oben, wie ichs gesehen hätt. Gott wende alle Ding zum besten.

Albrecht Dürer

In the year 1525 after Pentecost between Wednesday and Thursday at night in my sleep I beheld this sight, how many great waters fell from heaven. And the first struck the earth about four miles away with such gruesomeness, with an enormous rushing and splashing and drowned the whole land. This startled me so very greatly that I awoke. And then other waters fell. And the waters that fell then were almost as mighty. And some of them fell at a distance, others closer by, and they came down from so high up that they fell equally slowly in the darkness. And because the first water that struck the earth came so suddenly, fell with such velocity, wind and roaring, I was so startled when I awoke that my whole body shook and I did not quite come to myself for a long time. But when I arose in the morning I painted it here exactly as I had seen it. May God make all things turn for the best.

Albrecht Dürer

Im 1525 Jor noch dem pfingstag zwischen dem ... mitwoch vnd pfintztag Jn der nacht Jm schloff hab jch
dis gesicht gesehen wy fill groser wassren vom hymell fillen vnd das erst traff das ertrich bey 4 meill fon
mir mit einer solchen grausamkeit mit einem ubergrossen rauschen vnd zersprützen vnd ertrenckt
das gantz lant Jn solchem erschrak Jch so gar schrocklich das Jch doron erwachet ... ee dy andern wasser filn
Vnd dy wasser dy do filen dy waren fast groß vnd der fill ettliche weit ettliche neher vnd sy kamen so hoch herab das sy
Jn gedunken gleich longsam filn abee do das erst das das ertrich traff schir herbey kam do fill es mit einer
solchen geschwindikeit wint vnd brausen das jch also erschrak do Jch erwacht das mir all mein leichnam
zitert vnd long nit recht zu mir selbs kom Aber do Jch am morgen auff stund molt Jch sy oben bey Jch
gesehen hett Got wende alli ding zw besten

Albrecht durer

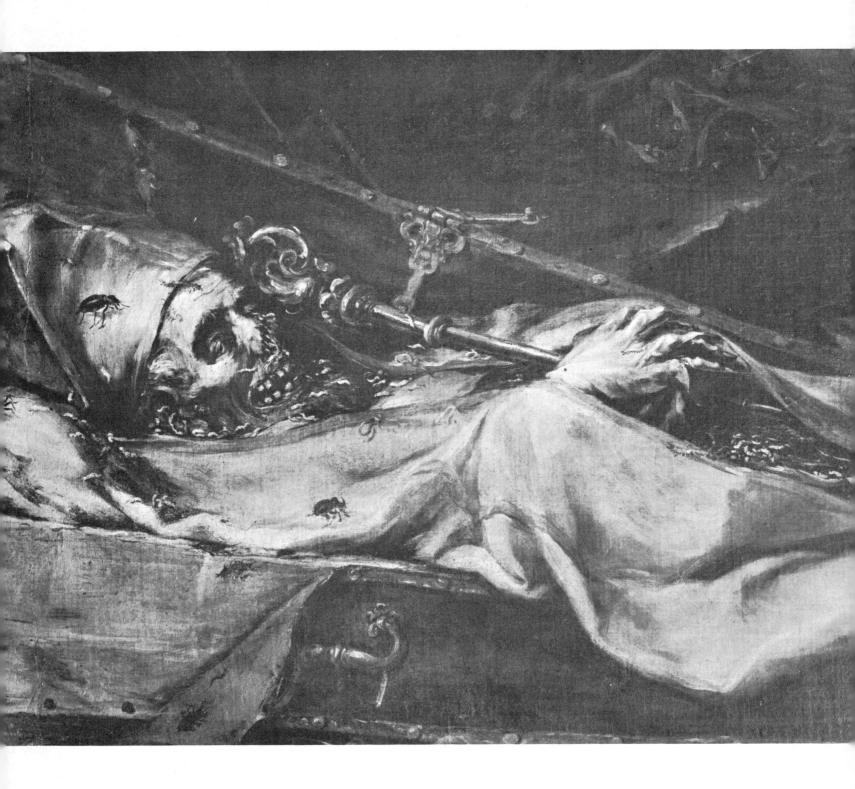

Mortel pense quel est dessous la couverture
D'un charnier mortuaire un corps mangé de vers,
Descharné, desnervé, où les os descouverts,
Depoulpez, desnouez, délaissent leur jointure :

*Le méspris
de la vie et consolation
contre la mort*

Icy l'une des mains tombe de pourriture,
Les yeus d'autre costé destournez à l'envers
Se distillent en glaire, et les muscles divers
Servent aux vers goulus d'ordinaire pasture :

Le ventre deschiré cornant de puanteur
Infecte l'air voisin de mauvaise senteur,
Et le né my-rongé difforme le visage ;

Puis connoissant l'estat de ta fragilité,
Fonde en Dieu seulement, estimant vanité
Tout ce qui ne te rend plus scavant et plus sage. *Jean Baptiste Chassignet*

Imagine, Mortal, that beneath the earthy crust
Of this burial-ground there lies a wormy corpse,
Fleshless, nerveless, while the naked bones,
Shapeless, denuded, are parted from their joints :

*Scorn for life
and consolation in the
face of death*

Here is a hand fallen rotten from its arm,
While, in the head, the eyeballs, all askew,
Are turning into slime, and the divers muscles
Serve as rich pasture for the greedy worms :
The gaping stomach's loud and hideous stench
Infects the surrounding air with pestilence,
And the half-gnawed nose stands horrid in the face ;

Then think well of the frailty of thy state,
Believe in God alone, reject as vanity
All that which does not make thee wise and good.

BIOGRAPHICAL
DICTIONARY

BIBLIOGRAPHY

CATALOGUE
OF SALES

INDEX OF
ILLUSTRATIONS

Biographical Dictionary

The entries in this dictionary include the Mannerist painters and graphic artists discussed in this book, as well as others closely related to them. Also included are certain artists mentioned in the text who have only a limited relationship with Mannerism or who chronologically fall outside the period of Mannerism but were precursors of the style or its belated continuers. The paintings cited as examples of the work of each artist are not necessarily his best known works, but rather those which show most effectively the Mannerist aspects of his style.

AACHEN, Hans von. Cologne 1552–Prague 1616. Worked in Italy (1574–1588), then in Germany, in Cologne, Augsburg, at the Court of Duke William V of Bavaria in Munich, and finally in Prague at the Court of the Emperor Rudolph II from 1597 to 1612. Painter of mythological scenes, he was influenced by the work of Bartholomeus Spranger (q. v.) and Giorgio Vasari (q. v.). One of the most representative figures of the second period of German Mannerism. Typical works: *Bacchus and Ceres* (Vienna); *Bathsheba at the Bath* (Vienna); *Jupiter Embracing Antiope* (Vienna); *The Judgment of Paris* (Graz).

ABBATE, Niccolò dell'. Modena 1512–Fontainebleau 1571. Influenced successively by the style of Correggio (q. v.) and the elongated, elegant figures of Parmigianino (q. v.). Worked mostly in Modena until 1552, when summoned to Fontainebleau, where he became the chief collaborator of Francesco Primaticcio (q. v.). Most of dell'Abbate's frescoes at Fontainebleau were either destroyed (Galerie d'Ulysse) or spoiled by successive restorations (Salle des Cent-Suisses), but contemporary engravings give us some idea of their appearance. Author of very beautiful large landscapes with mythological subjects. Typical works: *The Rape of Proserpine* (Paris, Louvre); *Orpheus and Eurydice* (London, National Gallery).

AERTS, Hendrick. Also called Hendricus a Rijssel, probably after his place of birth (Lille). Worked in the Netherlands c. 1600; painted fantastic palaces.

AERTSEN (or Aertz), Pieter, called Lange Pier. Amsterdam 1508–1575. Pupil of Allaert Claesz at Amsterdam, worked in Antwerp 1535–1556, then in Amsterdam.

A genre painter of distinction. Typical works: *The Kitchen* (Copenhagen); *Dance of the Eggs* (Amsterdam); *Market Scene with the Adulterous Woman* (Frankfurt); *The Meat Stall* (Uppsala).

AGOSTINO VENEZIANO (Agostino Musi). Venice c. 1490–after 1536. Engraver. Pupil of Marcantonio Raimondi (q. v.). Typical works: *The Climbers* (after Michelangelo); *The Skeletons* (after Baccio Bandinelli); *The Carcass* (after Michelangelo or Raphael).

ALDEGREVER, Heinrich. Paderborn 1502–Soest (Westphalia) 1558? Engraver, goldsmith, and painter. Most important Westphalian artist of the 16th c. His early work in Nuremburg was influenced by Dürer's circle, especially the Beham brothers and Georg Pencz. He is most noted for his engravings, of which he did over 300. His heroic figures imitate Michelangelo, but his ornamental designs are very original, based on his early training as a goldsmith. Because of the Italian elements in his work, Aldegrever has been compared with Cranach and Holbein.

ALLORI, Alessandro. Florence 1535–1607. Orphaned at the age of five, adopted and brought up by his uncle Angelo Bronzino (q. v.). Became pupil of Bronzino, and later of Michelangelo Buonarroti (q. v.) in Rome. Author of a treatise on drawing: *Dialogo sopra l'arte del disegnare le figure* (1590). Typically Mannerist works: *The Pearl Fishers* (Florence, Palazzo Vecchio, Studiolo of Francesco I); *The Holy Martyrs* (Florence, Chiesa di S. Spirito); *Venus and Cupid* (Hampton Court).

ALTDORFER, Albrecht. Regensburg (Ratisbon) c. 1480–1538. Painter, engraver, and architect. The foremost exponent of first period German Mannerism. Most important figure of the Danube School. Creator of a rich and imaginative style of landscape painting. Typical works: *The Battle of Issus* (Munich); *St. George in the Forest* (Munich); *The Nativity* (Berlin).

AMBERGER, Christoph. Active Augsburg 1530, d. 1561/62. Perhaps was a pupil of Holbein the Elder (q. v.) and Hans Burgkmair (q. v.); through the latter he may have received some Venetian influence. His works are often attributed to Holbein the Younger (q. v.). He is most famous for his painted portraits, the best example of which is *Charles V* (Berlin).

ANTHONISZ, Cornelis. Amsterdam c. 1499–1553? Painter, woodcutter and etcher, noted for his maps and views of towns. In 1533 he painted a view of Amsterdam, now in the Town Hall. In 1544 he did a series of 12 woodcuts showing plans of the city of Amsterdam.

ARCIMBOLDO, Giuseppe. Milan 1527–1595. Of German origin, he assisted his father Biagio in designing and creating the stained-glass windows of Milan Cathedral. In 1562, entered service of the Emperor Ferdinand I and spent 26 years in Prague where he became one of the favorites of Maximilian II, and more especially, of Rudolph II who made him a Count Palatine. Made innumerable drawings of festivities, costumes and stage-settings for princely entertainments. Commissioned to seek out "curiosities" for the Imperial collections. The most representative painter of metaphorical portraits, which are heads composed of flowers, vegetables, fish, animals, books, etc. according to the allegory represented.

ASPERTINI, Amico. Bologna 1475–1552. A very curious individual, whose eccentricities were recorded by Vasari (q. v.). One of the strangest painters of the 16th c. His work, often arid and expressionist, is reminiscent of Carlo Crivelli (q. v.) and Cosimo Tura (q. v.). From the small part of his work that has survived, one may mention: *The Dispute of St. Augustine* (Hanover); *The Burial of St. Valerius and St. Tibertius* (Lucca, Chiesa di San Frediano); a book of drawings after ancient bas-reliefs (London, British Museum).

AST, Balthasar van der. Middelburg 1590 – Delft after 1656. Worked with his brother-in-law, Ambrosius Bosschaert (q. v.). Painter of flowers and still lifes. Typical works: *Fruits and Haddock* (Brussels); *Haddock* (Hartford, Conn., Wadsworth Atheneum).

BACCHIACCA, Francesco, Ubertini called. Florence 1494–1557. Pupil of Perugino and Andrea del Sarto (q. v.). Typical Mannerist works: *Descent from the Cross*, in which the design of cross and ladder indicate the artist's liking for geometric forms (Florence, Uffizi); *St. Mary Magdalene* (Florence, Pitti); *Leda* (Rotterdam, Van Beuningen Museum).

BALDUNG GRIEN, Hans. Weyersheim, nr. Strasburg c. 1478 – Strasburg 1545. Worked in studio of Albrecht Dürer (q. v.). After about 1520 his style shows influence of Italian Mannerism. Painted strongly modelled nudes against black or very dark backgrounds; preferred macabre themes, scenes of witchcraft. Typical works: *Death and the Maiden* (Basel); *Pyramus and Thisbe*, a night scene (Berlin).

BARBIERE, Domenico, called Domenico Fiorentino. Florence 1506–1565/75. Was a pupil of Rosso Fiorentino (q. v.) and followed him to France to assist in the decoration of the Palace of Fontainebleau. Known chiefly as an engraver. Typical engravings: *Glory* (after Rosso); *Two Anatomical Figures and Two Skeletons* (after Rosso); *A Banquet* (after Primaticcio).

BARLACCHI, Tommaso. Salona (Dalmatia) 16th c. Active Rome, dates unknown. Engraver and publisher who published (perhaps after retouching) a series of engravings of the Marcantonio School in Rome. Among his own engravings is a garland of grotesques in the style of Enea Vico.

BAROCCIO, Federigo. Urbino 1528–1612. Studied under his father Ambrogio, together with Giovanni Battista Franco (q. v.). Much influenced by Correggio. Achieved particularly beautiful effects with transparent colors. A late Mannerist whose religious works (such as *The Beata Michelina*, Rome, Museo Vatican) show an emotional warmth which announces the Baroque.

BASCHENIS, Evaristo. Bergamo 1617–1677. One of a large family of painters. A belated Mannerist, whose work is interesting for its exact construction of volumes. Excelled in the painting of still lifes with musical instruments. Good examples of his paintings are to be found in the Accademia Carrara, Bergamo.

BASSANO, Jacopo da Ponte, called. Bassano 1510/15–1592. Son of Francesco da Ponte the Elder and father of Francesco II, Girolamo, Leandro and Giambattista. In his first works (pure lines and well-defined volumes) showed himself influenced by the Florentine Mannerism of Jacopo da Pontormo (q. v.) and Angelo Bronzino (q. v.): *Decollation of St. John the Baptist* (Copenhagen); *Dives and Lazarus* (Cleveland, Ohio); the very expressionist *St. John* (Bassano Museum). Later, his style is often reminiscent of Tintoretto (q. v.), for example, his *Earthly Paradise* (Madrid, Prado). Particularly known for his many night scenes of the *Adoration of the Shepherds*. His second manner was much imitated and popularized by his four sons, and it is often difficult to distinguish his own work from that of his sons.

BAUGIN (?). Painter of precisely executed still lifes who worked in Paris c. 1630. Not to be confused with Lubin Baugin (c. 1610–1663) or Jean Baugin (active 1640–1660). Only three known works can be attributed to this painter: *The Five Senses* (Paris, Louvre); *Still Life by Candlelight* (Rome, Gall. Spada); *The Dessert of Wafers* (Paris, Louvre).

BAZZI, Giovanni Antonio, see SODOMA.

BEAUVAIS, Antoine Caron de, see CARON.

BECCAFUMI, Domenico di Pace, called Domenico. Valdibiena 1485 – Siena 1551. With Sodoma (q. v.) the most important representative of Sienese Mannerism; one of the great painters of the 16th c., insufficiently acknowledged. His style is characterized by the fluidity of his beautiful and strange color, by a romantic pathos in the expression of his figures, and by a subtle play of dark atmospheres. Typical works: *Christ in Limbo* (Siena, Pinacoteca); *St. Michael* (Siena, Chiesa del Carmine); *Moses Breaking the Tablets of the Law* (Pisa, Cathedral).

BECERRA, Gasparo. Baeza (Andalusia) c.1520–Madrid 1570. Studied in Rome with Michelangelo, Raphael, and Vasari, bringing back to Madrid the Italian taste for huge, fleshy, athletically contorted figures. The High Altar at Astorga Cathedral (1558–1560) is typical of Becerra's style in sculpture, and influenced all Late Mannerist Altars in Castile. While in Rome, he painted frescoes with Daniele da Volterra and Tibaldi at Trinità dei Monti, and executed frescoes after Vasari's designs at the Farnesina. In 1562 he entered the service of Philip II, and painted frescoes of Perseus in the Pardo Palace in a Michelangelesque style.

BEDOLI, Girolamo Mazzuola, known as. Parma c. 1500–1569. Cousin of Parmigianino (q. v.). His style visibly imitated that of his illustrious cousin. Typical works: Cupid Asleep (Chantilly); The Annunciation (Milan, Ambrosiana); Madonna, in the style of Parmigianino (Munich).

BEER, Joost de. Utrecht, d. before 1595. Pupil of Frans Floris (q. v.) and master of Abraham Bloemaert (q. v.) and Joachim Wtewael (q. v.). His work mingled the influences of Floris and of the School of Fontainebleau (q. v.).

BEERT, Osias. Antwerp 1622–after 1678. Continued, during the 17th c., the tradition of Mannerist still lifes, with precise draughtsmanship and lively colors. Typical works: Lobster and Cakes (Brussels); Oysters, Bread, Grapes and Goblets (Madrid, Prado).

BEHAM, Barthel. Nuremberg 1502–Italy 1540. Painter and, especially, engraver. Worked for Duke William IV of Bavaria until 1535, then left for Italy where he remained until his death. He was attracted by themes which were both curious and erotic. Typical engravings: The Three Witches and Death; Women Bathing; Cimon Nourished by his Daughter Perra.

BEHAM, Hans Sebald. Nuremberg 1500–Frankfurt 1550. Elder brother of Barthel Beham (q.v.), and probably a pupil of Albrecht Dürer (q.v.). Painter and engraver, banished from Nuremberg for heresy, settled in Frankfurt. More than 500 of his engravings are known, many of them allegorical subjects, often with very boldly delineated nudes. Typical engravings: Melancholy; The Impossible; The Two Immodest Women and Death; The Buffoon and the Bathers.

BELLA, Stefano della (Etienne de la Belle). Florence 1610–1664. Primarily an etcher, greatly influenced by Callot's (q.v.) lively and elegant style. He was in Paris (1639–1649) where his style changed under the impact of Rembrandt and the Dutch landscapists. He did over 1,000 etchings, depicting all aspects of popular life. He was appointed to the Medicean Court as scenographer, decorator, and costume designer for the festivals of the Grand Duke.

BELLANGE, Jacques. Active Nancy 1602–1616. Painter at the Court of Duke Charles III of Lorraine. Most of his works have not survived, but his prints are sufficiently important to give him a place of honor in the Mannerist movement. Typical graphic works: The Three Marys at the Tomb, elongated figures making stylized gestures; Virgin and Child, etc.

BELLEGAMBE, Jean (Jehan). 1470/80–1535? Worked at Douai. Important painter of the transitional period between the quattrocento and Mannerism. Typical works: The Last Judgment (Berlin); Siren at her Toilet (Douai); Martyrdom of St. Barbara in which the Saint is suspended by her breasts (Vienna, Coll. V. Bloch).

BENSON, Ambrosius. Active Bruges 1519–d. 1550. A considerable number of typically Mannerist works have been attributed to this recently rediscovered painter. Typical works: Judith (Ottawa, National Museum); Lucretia (Genoa. Coll. Marquis de Gentile); Lot (Dusseldorf); After-Supper Concert (Basel, and Paris, Louvre)

BERNAZZANO, Cesare. Active Milan 1536. Probably was a landscape and animal painter who did the backgrounds for Cesare da Sesto's paintings, but there are no certain works attributed to him.

BERTOJA, Jacopo Zanguidi, called. Parma 1544–1574. Pupil of Ercole Procaccini, later adopted the style of Parmigianino. Worked principally for the Farnese family in Parma, Rome and Caprarola. Painter of hazy nudes in soft atmospheres. Typical works: Female Nude (Parma, Galleria Nazionale); Judgment of Paris (Parma, Camera di S. Paolo); Psyche and Cupid, in a hazy atmosphere (Parma, Camera di S. Paolo); Fantastic Landscape (Rome, Galleria Spada).

BEUCKELAER (Beucklaer, Bueckelaer), Joachim. Antwerp 1530?–1573. Pupil of Pieter Aertsen (q. v.), painter of large still lifes which at times include religious scenes. Typical works: Market Place, according to Bryan; The Game Bird Vendor (Vienna); Fish Market (Munich).

BINOIT, Peter. Born Cologne towards end of 16th c. Active Frankfurt c. 1614–1624. Painter of precisely executed still lifes. Typical work: Shellfish, Fish, Delicacies and Fruits (Turin).

BIZELLI, Giovanni. Florence 1556–1612. Pupil of Angelo Bronzino (q. v.). Typical works: The Annunciation, a rather insipid painting which features a charming Virgin (Florence, Uffizi); Martyrdom of St. Agatha (Florence, Chiesa di Sant' Agata).

BLES, Herri (Hendrik) met de, known in Italy as Civetta. Bouvigne (nr. Dinant) 1480?–after 1554. Lived for a long time in Italy. Painter of panoramic landscapes with countless buildings and many human figures; more anecdotic than his contemporary Joachim Patinir (q.v.). Typical works: St. John Preaching (Brussels); The Way to Emmaus (Vienna).

BLOEMAERT, Abraham. Dordrecht 1564–Utrecht 1651. Worked with Hoost de Beer (q. v.) in Utrecht and with Hieronymus Francken in Paris (1580–1583). His style was very typically Mannerist; elongated, elegant figures and nudes, quite similar to those of his compatriot Joachim Wtewael (q. v.); chiaroscuro effects. Toward the end of his life evolved toward the Baroque. Typical works: *The Burning of Troy* (Frankfurt); *Judith with the Head of Holophernes* (Vienna); *Raising of Lazarus*, very close to Wtewael (Valencia); *Daphne* (Breslau).

BLONDEEL, Lancelot. Bruges 1495–1581. Architect, painter, engraver. Father-in-law of the painter Peter Pourbus (q. v.). Surrounded his scenes with elaborate painted frames which are often the most important part of his works. Typical works: *St. Luke Painting the Virgin* (Bruges); *St. George* (Bruges).

BOCK, Hans the Elder. Saverne (Alsace) 1550–Basel 1623. Worked in Basel from 1572 with his pupil Josef Heintz (q. v.), and was the most representative Swiss painter of Mannerism's second phase. Typical works: *Day* and *Night*, sculptural figures synthesizing Michelangelo's monumental style and the strangeness of Hans Baldung Grien (q. v.) (Basel).

BOCKSBERGER, Melchior. 1520?–1587, German engraver. Typical work: *Belshazzar's Feast*, drawing in a very refined chiaroscuro (Oxford, Ashmolean).

BOL, Hans. Mechlin 1534–Amsterdam 1593. Painter of landscapes filled with figures, and watercolor miniatures on wood.

BOLTEN, Arent van. Active in Zwolle before 1637. Dutch goldsmith and engraver. Typical work: an album of drawings of grotesques and monsters (London, British Museum).

BONASONE, Giulio. Bologna c. 1498–c. 1580. Italian engraver, pupil of Marcantonio Raimondi (q.v.). Worked between 1530 and 1574 in Bologna and Rome. Typical engravings: *Young Man and Dragon; Bath Scene.*

BORDONE, Paris. Treviso 1500–Venice 1571. Pupil of Titian. Summoned in 1559 to the Courts of François II and Charles IX of France, then worked in Augsburg for the Fuggers. His style hesitated between classicism and Mannerism. Typical works: *Combat of Gladiators* (Vienna); *Bathsheba* (Cologne, Rheinisches Museum).

BOSCH, Hieronymus. 's Hertogenbosch c. 1450–1516. His family originated in Aachen. Lived throughout his life in 's Hertogenbosch (whence he derived his name). May possibly have belonged to the heretical Adamist sect. In his strange and fantastic visions he is one of the important precursors of Mannerism. His work abounds in Mannerist themes. Typical works: *The Garden of Delights* (Madrid, Prado); *Paradise* and *Hell* (Venice, Palazzo Ducale); *Crucifixion of St. Julia* (Venice); *Carrying of the Cross* (Ghent).

BOSSCHAERT, Ambrosius the Elder. Antwerp c. 1570 – The Hague 1621. The best flower painter of his time.

Had as his pupil his brother-in-law Balthasar van der Ast (q. v.); his sons, Ambrosius II (1610?–1645) and Johannes (1600–?) carried on his manner. Typical works: *Bouquet in a Niche* (The Hague, Mauritshuis); *Flowers in a Vase* (Frankfurt, Historisches Museum).

BOTTICELLI, Sandro. Florence 1445–1510. One of the most important late 15th c. precursors of Mannerism. His style in its purity of line, calligraphic tendency to elongation and expressive deformation, and use of black backgrounds, announce many of the important elements of Mannerist style, as does indeed the strange atmosphere of unreal calm seen in many of his works. Typical works: *The Birth of Venus* (Florence, Uffizi); *Calumny of Apelles* (Florence, Uffizi); *Venus* (Berlin).

BOYVIN, René. Antwerp c. 1530–Rome c. 1598. Engraver. Pupil of the Italian (or Flemish?) engraver Pierre Millan (q.v.); worked in Paris from 1545. His most important engravings were after the paintings of Rosso (q. v.) and Léonard Thiry (q. v.). Typical engravings: the series of the *Story of Jason* (after Thiry), and four different *Nymphs.*

BRACELLI, Giovanni Battista. Genoa 1584–1649. Active from 1624 to 1649 in Florence and Rome. Principally known as an engraver, he seems also to have painted. In 1624 he published a volume of fantastic figures *(Bizzarrie di varie figure)* dedicated to Pietro de' Medici.

BRAMANTINO, Bartolommeo Suardi, called. Born c. 1460, active 1503–1536. Painter and architect. Probably a pupil of Bernardino Butinone in Milano, then a close follower of Bramante. After Leonardo da Vinci and Bramante left Milan in 1499, Bramantino became the leading artist there. Worked in Rome in 1508. In 1525, appointed Court painter and architect by Duke Francesco Maria Sforza in Milan. A few elements of his style, such as the use of abrupt perspective and curiously hard, exaggerated delineation of forms and drapery clearly relate him to the Mannerist current. Typical works: *Crucifixion* (Milan, Brera); *Triptych of St. Michael* (Milan, Ambrosiana); *Ecce Homo* (Lugano, Thyssen Collection).

BRIL (Brill), Paul. Antwerp 1554–Rome 1626. Worked in Antwerp and Lyons, but mainly in Rome. Extremely influential in the development of landscape painting in the late 16th c.: his pupil Agostino Tassi was to become the teacher of Claude Lorrain. Many of his paintings are religious scenes but the figures are very tiny and the works are essentially landscapes. In Rome he executed many important landscape frescoes, among others those of hermit saints in the Sfrondato Chapel in Santa Celia. Produced a great number of small landscape paintings sought after by both his Italian and northern patrons.

BROECK, Crispin van den. Mechlin 1524–Antwerp? 1591. Painter and engraver. Pupil of Frans Floris (q. v.). Travelled in Italy, worked in Middelburg and Antwerp. Typical work: *Last Judgment* (Antwerp).

BRONZINO, Angelo di Cosimo. Monticelli (nr. Florence) 1503–Florence 1572. Pupil of Jacopo da Pontormo (q. v.), also strongly influenced by Michelangelo; appointed Court painter to the Medici Grand Dukes Cosimo I and Francesco I. His style marks the apogee of the deliberately cold and haughty elegance of Florentine Mannerism. Typical works: *Portrait of Ugolino Marteli* (Berlin); *Eleonora of Toledo and her Son Garcia* (Florence, Uffizi); *Admiral Doria* depicted as a naked Neptune (Milan, Brera); *Francesco I* (New York, Frick Coll.); *Venus, Cupid, Time and Folly* (London, National Gallery); *Allegory of Fortune* (Florence, Uffizi); *Passage of the Red Sea* (Florence, Palazzo Vecchio).

BRUEGEL, Jan the Elder, called "Velvet Bruegel." Brussels 1568–Antwerp 1625. Younger son of Pieter Bruegel I, pupil of his grandmother Maria Verhulst (Bessemers), a miniaturist who was the widow of Peter Coecke van Aelst. Went to Milan where in 1516 in service of Cardinal Borromeo. Became Court painter of the Arch Duke Albert of Austria and the Infanta Isabella. Specialized in minutely designed landscapes, allegorical interiors. One of the creators of flower painting as an independent genre. Collaborated often with his friend Rubens. His style was copied by a multitude of followers, notably by his son Jan II (1601–1678). Typical works: *Sense of Smell*, a garden filled with a mass of flowers (Madrid, Prado); *The Fire*, Vulcan's forges in what appear to be ruined Roman thermae (Rome, Doria); *Water*, a great collection of denizens of the ocean (Milan, Ambrosiana); *The Earth or The Earthly Paradise* (Paris, Louvre); *Large Bouquet of Flowers* (Vienna).

BRUEGEL (Brueghel, Breughel, Breugel), Pieter I, the Elder, sometimes also called "Peasant Bruegel." Born (nr. Breda) c. 1525, died Brussels 1569. Pupil of Hieronymus Coeck; visibly influenced by Bosch (q. v.). Travelled in Italy (1552–1553) whence he brought back numerous sketches of landscapes. Worked in Antwerp and Brussels. Married, in 1563, the daughter of Peter Coeck. Typical works: *Triumph of Death*, a multiplicity of cleanly designed details (Madrid, Prado); *Storm at Sea* (Vienna); *Tower of Babel*, an architectural dream (Vienna); *Hunters in the Snow*, a panoramic scene (Vienna).

BRUEGEL, Pieter II, the Younger, called "Hell Bruegel." Brussels c. 1564–Antwerp 1637. Pupil of Gillis van Coninxloo (q. v.). Executed many copies of the work of his father, Pieter Bruegel I; specialized in scenes of conflagration and Hell. Typical works: *Hades* (Florence, Uffizi reserve coll.); *Orpheus in Hades* (Brussels, Coll. Mme. Vergote de Lantsheere); *Burning of Sodom* (Lucca); *Virgil and Dante in Hell* (Dresden).

BRUEGEL, Pieter III. b. Antwerp 1589. Son of Pieter "Hell" Bruegel. Typical work: *The Advocate of Bad Causes*, with a huge clutter of legal papers (Antwerp).

BUGIARDINI, Giuliano. Florence 1475–1554. Pupil of Domenico Ghirlandaio together with his friend Mi-

chelangelo, but developed an entirely different style. He painted tender, milky flesh in an atmosphere of expertly executed chiaroscuro. Typical works: *Martyrdom of St. Catherine* (Florence, Santa Maria Novella); *Virgin Suckling the Infant Jesus* (Florence, Pitti).

BUNEL, François II. Blois c. 1522–Paris after 1595. Son of François Bunel I. Towards the end of his life became Court painter and "valet de chambre" of Henri de Navarre (later Henri IV). A certain number of paintings of the School of Fontainebleau have been attributed to him; most of these are very precisely modelled female nudes with strongly erotic undertones. His brother Jacob Bunel (1551–1614) collaborated with Toussaint Dubreuil (q. v.) in decorating the Louvre. Works attributed to him include: *Gabrielle d'Estrées and the Duchess of Villars in the Bath* (Paris, Louvre); *Lady at her Toilet* (Dijon); *Sabina Poppea* (Geneva); *Italian Actors* (Béziers).

BURGKMAIR, Hans the Elder, Augsburg 1473–1531. Painter and engraver who worked under Martin Schongauer at Colmar. He probably travelled in Italy as his work shows Venetian influence, and he was influential in introducing the Italian style to Augsburg. His woodcuts and paintings exerted a strong influence on his German contemporaries, Hans Holbein the Younger (q. v.) and Christoph Amberger (q. v.).

BUTTERI, Giovanni Maria. Active Florence 1567, d. 1606. Pupil of Angelo Bronzino (q. v.), collaborated with Giorgio Vasari (q. v.). Typical work: *The Glass Blowers* (Florence, Palazzo Vecchio, Studiolo).

BUYTEWECK, Willem. Rotterdam c. 1590–1630. Genre painter, engraver. Typical engravings: series of *Seven Young Nobles of Seven Countries*, of extreme preciosity.

CALCAR, Jan Stefan van. Kalkar (Cleves) 1499–Naples 1546. Eloped with a young girl of Dordrecht, fled to Italy, where he became a pupil of Titian and friend of Giorgio Vasari (q. v.). Known especially for his anatomical drawings for Andreas Vesalius' *De humani corporis fabrica*, Basel, 1543.

CALLOT, Jacques. Nancy 1594–Paris 1635. Worked in Rome and Florence (in service of Duke Cosimo II), then in Nancy in service of Duke of Lorraine. A late Mannerist of great imagination. His paintings are rare, and he is known chiefly as an etcher. Typical works (etchings): *The Temptation of St. Anthony*, the "Capricci," and *Les Grandes misères de la guerre*.

CALVAERT, Denys, called Dionisio Fiammingo. Antwerp c. 1540 – Bologna 1619. Went to Italy when still very young and settled in Bologna. Typical work: *Danaë* (Lucca).

CAMBIASO, Luca. Moneglia (Liguria) 1527–Madrid 1585. Pupil of his father Giovanni Cambiaso, painter and decorator. Worked at Genoa as painter of frescoes and as a sculptor. Summoned, in 1583, by Philip II to Spain, where he executed the rather mediocre frescoes in the Escorial choir. One of the most original painters of the 16th c.; a master of night scenes lighted by a candle: *Madonna and Child, Saint Ann and Saint Joseph* (Genoa, Palazzo Bianco). His drawings reveal a developed cubist vision of form.

CAMPI, Bernardino. Cremona 1522–Reggio 1592. Originally a goldsmith, later turned to painting; pupil of his uncle Giulio Campi. Typical works: *St. Cecilia and St. Catherine* (Cremona, San Sigismondo); *Decollation of St. John the Baptist* (Cremona, Cathedral).

CAMPI, Vincenzo. Cremona before 1532–1591. Younger brother of Giulio Campi and cousin of Bernardino Campi (q. v.). Specialized in scenes of market stalls heaped high with fish, poultry, fruit, etc. Typical works: *The Fishmonger; The Fruit Seller; Woman Selling Poultry* (all at Mindelheim, Schloß Kirchheim); *Woman with Fruits* (Milan, Brera); *Woman with Fish* (Milan, Brera).

CAMPIN, Robert. See Master of Flémalle.

CANDIDO (Candid), Pietro, Pieter de Witte called. Bruges *c.* 1548–Munich? *c.* 1628. Lived in Florence 1570–1586, where he worked for the Medicis. Influenced by Giorgio Vasari (q. v.). Ended his career in Munich, at the Court of the Dukes of Bavaria. Typical works: *Fall of the Rebel Angels* (Vienna); *Madonna* (Oldenburg, Landesmuseum).

CARAGLIO, Gian-Jacopo. Parma or Verona *c.* 1500–Parma 1570. Engraver, pupil of Marcantonio Raimondi (q. v.). Worked in Rome, and in Poland for Sigismund I. Made engravings after Parmigianino (q. v.) and Rosso (q. v.).

CARAVAGGIO, Cecco del. See CECCO del Caravaggio.

CARAVAGGIO, Michelangelo Merisi da. Caravaggio (nr. Milan) 1573–Porto d'Ercole 1610. Greatest Italian painter of the early years of the 17th c. In many ways his mature works fall outside the Mannerist movement, but his early works such as the *Bacchus* (Florence, Uffizi) are quite clearly in the Mannerist tradition. His realistic paintings of night scenes had a great influence on other artists. Many of his followers, particularly the northerners such as Cecco del Caravaggio or Georges de La Tour, developed his style in a manner that was still largely in the Mannerist tradition.

CARIANI, Giovanni de' Busi called. Venice 1485–1547/48. Typical works: *Woman in a Landscape*, a semi-nude woman in a twilight atmosphere, technique close to that of Dosso Dossi (Berlin); *Lot and his Daughters* (Milan, Castello Sforza).

CARON, Antoine, called Caron de Beauvais. Beauvais *c.* 1529–Paris *c.* 1599. Worked at Fontainebleau with Francesco Primaticcio (q. v.) for some years prior to 1550; painter to the Court of Catherine de Medici from 1559, assigned to design decorations for court banquets and triumphal entries. His allegorical scenes often reflect the fêtes, processions, and ballets popular at the Court of the Valois. Typical works: *The Emperor Augustus and the Tiburtine Sibyl; Massacre Under the Triumvirate* (both Paris, Louvre); *Death of Semele* (Paris, Coll. Jean Ehrenmann).

CARPI, Ugo da. Carpi *c.* 1480–1532. Painter, but mainly engraver. Invented the technique of chiaroscuro woodcut, which he used to recreate many works by Parmigianino (q. v.) among others.

CASINE, Vittorio. Florentine painter; evidence of his activity between 1567 and 1572. Collaborated with Giorgio Vasari (q. v.) in the decoration of the Studiolo of Francesco I in the Palazzo Vecchio in Florence, where he painted a *Vulcan's Forge* which is rather clumsy in execution but notably Mannerist in the elongation of the bodies.

CASTELLO, Giovanni Battista, called El Genovese. Genoa 1547–1637. Pupil of Luca Cambiaso (q. v.); a miniaturist who followed his master to Spain and the Court of Philip II. Typical work: *Madonna and Child*, miniature on parchment (Genoa, Palazzo Bianco).

CAVALORI, Mirabello (Salincorno de Mirabello). Florence 1510/20–1572. A collaborator of Giorgio Vasari; helped prepare the decorations for the obsequies of Michelangelo. Typical works: *Wool Spinners* and *Lavinia at the Altar* (Florence, Palazzo Vecchio, Studiolo).

CECCO del Caravaggio, Francesco, called. A follower of Caravaggio who worked in Rome about 1615, probably a Frenchman. Took the painting of realistic night scenes illuminated by strong contrasts of light from Caravaggio, but his insistent and hard delineation of forms gives an almost archaic quality to his painting. Typical work: *Resurrection of Christ* (Chicago).

CESARI, Giuseppe (Cavaliere d'Arpino). Rome 1560/68 to 1640. A late Mannerist artist who worked in Rome and Naples. Held an important place among the artists in Rome from about 1585 through the first quarter of the 17th c. His style is rather dry, lifeless and classicizing. Typical works: Mosaic decoration of the cupola, St. Peter's, Rome; frescoes, Cappella Paolina, Santa Maria Maggiore, Rome; ceiling frescoes of choir of San Martino, Naples.

CHIMENTI, Jacopo, called Jacopo da Empoli. Empoli (nr. Florence) 1551(?)–1640. A belated Mannerist. Painted many religious works but also some admirable still lifes. Typical works: *Bathsheba* (Vienna); two *Still Lifes* (Florence, Pitti); *Drunkenness of Noah* (Florence, Uffizi).

CIRCIGNANO, Niccolò, see POMARANCIO.

CLAESZ, Pieter. Steinfurt (Westphalia) 1597–Haarlem 1661. Painter of still lifes. Typical works: *Still Life* with *Cheeses* (Haarlem); *Still Life by Candlelight* (Stockholm, Coll. Hedberg).

CLEVE, Hendrick III van. Antwerp 1525–1589. Landscape painter and engraver. Pupil of his father Willem and of Frans Floris (q. v.). After a trip to Italy, he entered the guild at Antwerp in 1551. Painted landscape backgrounds in paintings by Floris.

CLEVE, Joos van. Became a master at Antwerp in 1511, d. there 1540. Specialized in royal portraits, working in Paris for François I, probably also worked in Genoa and Cologne. In his religious paintings, he was influenced by Leonardo, Dürer, the Master of Flémalle, Gerard David, Quentin Massys, and the stylizations of the Antwerp Mannerists. Typical work: *Henry VIII* (Hampton Court).

CLOUET, François, known as Jehannet or Janet. Tours 1516/20–Paris 1572. Son of Jean Clouet (Brussels c. 1486–Paris 1541). In 1541 succeeded his father as Painter in Ordinary to the King. Known chiefly as a portraitist, he also painted nudes and mythological scenes in the usual style of the School of Fontainebleau. Typical work: *Diana of Poitiers Bathing* (Richmond, Coll. Cook).

CLOVIO, Giulio, called Macedo. Grisane (Croatia) 1498–Rome 1578. Painter and miniaturist, illuminated choirbooks and missals for Cardinal Marino Grimani and Cardinal Allesandro Farnese. Taken prisoner by the Spaniards during the Sack of Rome in 1527. When he returned from Spain he entered the Monastery of Saint Ruffino in Mantua. Clovio greatly admired Michelangelo and tried to imitate him in miniature, copying figures from the Sistine Ceiling in a Psalter of 1542 (Paris, Bibliothèque Nationale).

COECK, Hieronymus. Antwerp c. 1510–1570. Painter and engraver. Made two stays in Italy; was the teacher of Pieter Bruegel I, and one of the greatest engravers of the mid 16th c. Typical engravings: 13 landscapes (after Bruegel), and 14 landscapes with Biblical or mythological scenes (after Mathys Cock), as well as a series of Roman ruins.

COECK, Peter. Aelst 1502–1550. Pupil of Bernard van Orley. Travelled in Italy, Constantinople, Tunis. Senior official of the Antwerp Guild in 1537. Married the miniaturist Maria Verhulst. Typical work: *The Last Supper*, with fine details of still life (Brussels).

CONINCK, Kerstiaen de. Master in Antwerp 1580, d. after 1630. Typical work: *Panoramic Landscape with Mary Magdalene* (Ghent).

CONINXLOO, Gillis van. Antwerp? 1544–1607. Left Amsterdam in 1585 for religious reasons, worked in Frankenthal, then in Amsterdam. Painter of wooded landscapes which adhere closely to a "three tone" scheme of warm brownish foreground, green middle distance, and blue distance. Typical works: *A Wood* (Vienna, Liechtenstein Gallery); *Wooded Landscape with Elijah* (Brussels).

COPPI, Jacopo, called del Meglio. Peretola 1523–Florence 1591. One of Giorgio Vasari's collaborators in the decoration of the Studiolo of Francesco I in the Palazzo Vecchio, Florence, for which he executed *The Invention of Gunpowder* and *Alexander and the Family of Darius*.

CORNELISZ, Cornelis, van Haarlem. Haarlem 1562–1638. Pupil of Pieter Pietersz. Worked in Antwerp, in France (1579) and chiefly in Haarlem where, with Karel van Mander (q. v.) and Hendrick Goltzius (q. v.) he founded the Haarlem Academy. Typical works: *The Flood*, a mass of Mannerist nudes (Nuremberg); *Lot and his Daughters* (Rome, Coll. Zeri); *Allegory of Fortune* (Geneva, Coll. Baszanger); *Marriage of Peleus and Thetis* (Haarlem); *Bathsheba* (Amsterdam), Rijksmuseum).

CORNELISZ, Lucas, known as Lucas de Kok. Leyden 1493/95–London 1552. Son of Cornelis Engelbrechtsz, brother of Cornelis and Pieter, pupil of his father. Worked in England, painting many portraits for Henry VIII.

CORREGGIO, Antonio Allegri, called. Correggio (nr. Modena) 1489 or 1494–Parma 1534. One of the greatest Italian painters of the 16th c. Worked mainly in Parma. In his fresco decorations of the cupola of the Cathedral of Parma he shows himself to be a precursor of the Baroque. He was a great master of the *sfumato* technique and his works were often characterized by an extreme voluptuousness. Typical works: *Danaë* (Rome, Galleria Borghese); *Education of Cupid* (London, National Gallery); *Jupiter and Io* (Vienna).

COSIMO, Piero di. See PIERO di Cosimo.

COSSA, Francesco. Ferrara c. 1435–Bologna 1477. Along with Cosimo Tura (q. v.) and Ercole di' Roberti (q. v.), the other important members of the School of Ferrara, he was a 15th c. precursor of Mannerism. In some of his frescoes in the Palazzo Schifanoia, Ferrara, his strange vision is surrealistic in character.

COTAN, Juan Sanchez. See SANCHEZ COTAN, Juan.

COUSIN, Jean the Elder. Sens c. 1490–Paris c. 1560. Established in Paris; did not apparently work at Fontainebleau, but his style was nevertheless clearly influenced by Rosso (q. v.). He was the author of a *Livre de Perspective* (1560). Typical works: *Eva Prima Pandora*, an elongated reclining nude in a dreamlike landscape (Paris, Louvre); *Charity* (Montpellier).

COXIE, Michiel. Mechlin 1499–1592. Pupil of Bernard van Orley (q. v.). Worked in Rome, Mechlin and Brussels. Strongly Italianate in style. Typical work: *The Departure of Psyche* (Paris, Coll. Maximo Sciolette).

CRANACH, Lucas the Elder. Kronach (Franconia) 1472–Weimar 1553. Court Painter to the Electors of

Saxony in Wittenberg; friend of Martin Luther, took an active part in the Reformation. His manner was copied so well by his three sons and by his pupils that it is often difficult to distinguish his work from that of his imitators. Painted a great many nudes in landscape settings or against a black background. Typical works: *Venus and Cupid* (Munich); *Judgment of Paris* (Karlsruhe).

CRIVELLI, Carlo. Venice? *c.*1435–*c.*1495. The wiry outline bounding his figures, a certain reserved haughtiness combined with an expressionism which occasionally verges on caricature, a taste for fantastic architectures *(The Annunciation,* London, National Gallery), the richly designed frameworks of flowers, fruits, even vegetables, set out in rows or else strung up in heavy garlands, combine to make Crivelli an immediate precursor of Mannerism.

CRONENBURG, Adriaen van. Pietersbiern (Friesland) 1552–after 1590. Portrait painter. His works are arresting for their pure and simple color schemes selected with great discretion. Typical works: four full-length portraits of ladies and young girls (Madrid, Prado).

DELAUNE, Etienne. Paris 1518–Strasburg 1583. Engraver and goldsmith. A Huguenot, he fled from Paris in 1572 and took refuge in Strasburg. Made engravings after Francesco Primaticcio, Giorgio Ghisi, Luca Penni, Jean Cousin, and from his own designs.

DERUET, Claude. Nancy 1588–1660. Court painter of Duke Henry II of Lorraine and of Louis XIII of France. An intimate friend of Jacques Callot (q.v.) who etched his portrait. Typical works: four allegories of the elements (Orleans); that of *Air* is a scene of the Duchess of Lorraine at the hunt.

DESIDERIO, Monsù. This is a name which seems to cover at least three artists, the principal among whom is François Nomé, Metz *c.*1590–*c.*1650. Worked in Rome 1612, Naples 1620. He specialized in fantastic landscapes of fantastic abandoned towns and ruins seen at night, weirdly illuminated by fire or the moon. His style possibly owes much to Mannerist stage design.

DEUTSCH, Nikolaus Manuel. Berne 1484–1530. Together with Urs Graf (q.v.) the most representative figure of the first phase of Swiss Mannerism—was also an important magistrate in Berne, as well as being a diplomat and taking an active part in the Reformation movement. Typical works: *Decollation of St. John,* very beautiful tapestry-like landscape in an atmosphere of rich, heavy twilight; *Martyrdom of the Ten Thousand,* extremely cruel scene of martyrs impaled (both Basel).

DOSSI, Dosso, Giovanni Luteri, called. Ferrara 1479?–1542. Pupil of Lorenzo Costa. Lived in Rome, Venice and Ferrara. Worked for the Dukes of Este. A friend of Ariosto. Artist of great imagination, his landscape settings are rich in color and romantic in mood. He was particularly fond of strange subjects of sorceresses and enchantresses. Typical works: *Circe* (Washington, D.C., National Gallery); *Diana and Calypso; Circe* (both Rome, Galleria Borghese).

DUBOIS, Ambroise. Antwerp 1542/43–Fontainebleau 1614. Flemish, but naturalized French in 1601. Succeeded Toussaint Dubreuil (q.v.) as Painter in Ordinary to Henri IV; was one of the representative figures of the second School of Fontainebleau (q.v.). Typical work: *Clorinda Baptised by Tancred* (Paris, Louvre).

DUBOIS, François. Amiens 1529–Geneva 1584. Fled to Geneva to escape religious persecution. His painting, *Triumvirate as Oppressor of the Roman Republic* (Lausanne) is an allegory on the Massacre of the Huguenots.

DUBOIS, Jean the Elder. Avon 1604–Fontainebleau 1676. Pupil of his father, Ambroise (q.v.). Became court painter in 1636; appointed overseer of paintings at Fontainebleau in 1651. He finished four of his father's paintings in the High Chapel and decorated many of the palace rooms with paintings.

DUBREUIL, Toussaint. Paris 1561–Paris 1602. Painter in Ordinary to Henri IV; one of the representative figures of the second School of Fontainebleau (q.v.). Typical work: *A Sacrifice* (Paris, Louvre).

DUCERCEAU, Jacques Androuet the Elder. Paris *c.*1520–Switzerland after 1584. Architect and engraver. None of his architectural work is known to survive. Even in his own time he was principally known as an engraver. He engraved ornaments, architectural motifs and grotesques. His best known works are his two volumes on *Les plus excellents Bastiments de France* published 1576 and 1579.

DÜRER, Albrecht. Nuremberg 1471–1528. Painter and engraver. Made two voyages to Italy, in 1494 and 1505, and visited the Netherlands in 1520/21. Worked for the Emperor Maximilian I 1512–1519. The influence of Dürer on European Mannerism is equalled only by that of Michelangelo (q.v.). Typical Mannerist works: *Madonna,* with a background of ruins and dark foliage (London, National Gallery); *Women Bathing,* an expressionist drawing (Bremen, Kunsthalle); engravings such as *Melancholy, The Knight and Death, The Desperate Man,* etc.

DUVET, Jean. Langres 1485–after 1561. Engraver. Worked in Langres and Dijon. His over-detailed engravings were certainly influenced by the work of Albrecht Dürer (q.v.). Typical engravings: *The Stag Hunt;* **Unicorn.**

ELSHEIMER, Adam. Frankfurt 1578–Rome 1610. He was in Venice before 1600 and then in Rome where he worked for about ten years. Painted small and imaginative landscapes, often on copper. His landscapes in their strong light contrasts reveal the influence of Caravaggio. His style had an important influence on the development of landscape painting in the north.

EMPOLI, Jacopo da, see CHIMENTI.

ENGELBRECHTSZ, Cornelis. Leyden 1468?–1533. Was the teacher of Lucas van Leyden (q. v.). Introduced Mannerist elements (elongation, tortuous attitudes) into an art still basically 15th c. in conception. Typical works: *Crucifixion* (Leyden, Lakenhal); *Constantine and Helen* (Munich); *Temptation of St. Anthony* (Dresden).

ES, Jacon Fopsen van. c. 1596–Antwerp 1666. Painter of still lifes. A belated 17th c. exponent of Mannerist tradition. Typical works: *Bowl of Lemons* (Doetinchem, Coll. A. Vromen); *Crabs, Prawns, Lemon* (Nancy); *Marine Deities among a Heap of Fish* (Vienna, Schönbrunn).

EWORTH, Hans. A painter from Antwerp (his name was originally Ewoutsz) who worked in London from 1545/49? until his death in 1574. Succeeded Hans Holbein as Henry VIII's Court painter; sophisticated and involved Mannerist imagery. Typical work: *Elizabeth Confounding Juno, Minerva and Venus* (Hampton Court).

FANTUZZI, Antonio da Trento, called. c. 1510–1550. Italian engraver; pupil of Parmigianino. Worked in Rome, Bologna and Fontainebleau. Along with René Boyvin (q. v.) and Domenico del Barbiere he executed many engravings after the works of Rosso at Fontainebleau.

FEI, Alessandro, known as del Barbiere. Florence 1543–1592. Disciple of Giorgio Vasari. He worked in the Studiolo of Francesco I in the Palazzo Vecchio, Florence, executing the scene of *The Goldsmith's Shop*.

FIGUEIREDO, Christovão de. See MASTER of the "Paraizo."

FINSONIUS (Finson), Ludovicus. Bruges before 1580 – Arles 1632. Worked in Naples with Caravaggio (q. v.), then in Aix. Interpreted the magic realism of Caravaggio with the Flemish taste for detail. Typical works: copy after Caravaggio of the *Penitent Magdalen* (Marseilles) signed and dated 1612; *Still Life with Flute Player* (Oxford, Ashmolean Museum).

FLORIS, Frans (Frans de Vriendt). Antwerp 1516?–1570. Pupil of Lambrecht Lombart (q. v.). Worked in Italy and Antwerp, where he became a prominent Italianizer. Influenced by Michelangelo and Vasari; style very derivative. Typical works: *Banquet of the Sea Gods* (Stockholm).

FLOTNER, Peter. d. Nuremberg 1546. Sculptor and wood engraver. The author of an erotic series in the manner of Giulio Romano (q. v.).

FONTAINEBLEAU, School of. This designates the painters who worked at the Palace of Fontainebleau at the court of the Valois kings, and the other painters in France who came directly under the influence of this style. The style of painting and stucco decoration of the School of Fontainebleau was developed by Rosso Fiorentino (q. v.) (who was called to Fontainebleau in 1530) and carried on by the host of artists and helpers he gathered around him. Rosso was followed at Fontainebleau by two other Italians: Primaticcio and Niccolò dell'Abbate, who also contributed greatly to the stylistic formation of French artists. The most important French artists of the first School of Fontainebleau were Antoine Caron de Beauvais and Jean Cousin the Elder. The decorative style of the School of Fontainebleau was widely diffused through engravings and had a tremendous influence in France and throughout Europe.

FONTANA, Lavinia. Bologna 1552–Rome 1614. Daughter and pupil of Prospero Fontana (q. v.). Typical works: *Noli me tangere* (Florence, Uffizi); *Solomon and the Queen of Sheba* (Dublin).

FONTANA, Prospero. Bologna 1512–1597. Worked in Rome, at Fontainebleau and in Genoa. Typical work: *St. Alexis Succoring the Beggars* (Bologna, San Giacomo Maggiore).

FRANCKEN, Ambrosius the Elder. Herenthals 1544–Antwerp 1618. Younger brother of Frans I Franken. Pupil of Frans Floris (q. v.). A Flemish Italianizer, fond of depicting tortures and executions. Typical work: *Martyrdom of St. Crispin and St. Crispinian* (Antwerp).

FRANCKEN, Frans I. Herenthals 1542–Antwerp 1616. Elder brother of Ambrosius Francken (q. v.) and father of Frans II Francken (q. v.). Typical work: *Belshazzar's Feast* (Poitiers).

FRANCKEN, Frans II. Antwerp 1581–1642. Son of Frans I Francken (q. v.), nephew of Ambrosius Francken (q. v.) and father of Frans III Francken. Painter of genre scenes and lively landscapes. Typical work: *Passage of the Red Sea* (Besançon).

FRANCO, Giovanni Battista, called Il Semolei. Udine 1498–Venice 1561. A very Mannerist painter of limited talent. Typical works: *The Battle of Montemurlo* (Florence, Pitti); *Christ in Limbo* (Rome, Galleria Colonna).

FRATTINI, Giovanni, called del Mio. Active Vicenza c. 1556. A Venetian plainly influenced by the Florentine manner. His rondels, Libreria Sansoviniana, Venice, represent curious Mannerist nudes.

FREMINET, Martin. Paris 1567–1619. Studied in Italy 1592–1600, where he was influenced by the works of Parmigianino and Michelangelo. On his return to France, in 1600, appointed painter to Henri IV, and became one of the masters of the Second School of Fontainebleau.

FURINI, Francesco. Florence 1600–1646. One of the principal painters of the Florentine Baroque. The insistent sensuality of his female figures, however, witnesses a continuation of a typically Mannerist theme. Typical work: *Ila and the Nymphs* (Florence, Pitti).

GALLE, Philipp. Haarlem 1537–1612. Head of a family of engravers which included his sons Theodore (1571–1633) and Cornelius I (1576–1650) and numerous grandchildren. Principal work: *The Seven Wonders of the World* after Maerten van Heemskerck (q.v.).

GAROFALO, Benvenuto Tisi, called. Ferrara 1481–1559. Influenced successively by Boccaccio Boccaccino in Cremona, by Lorenzo Costa in Bologna, by Dosso Dossi in Ferrara, by Michelangelo, and especially by Raphael in Rome, without succeeding in creating for himself a personal *maniera*. Works tending towards Mannerism: *Mars and Venus; Bacchanale* (both in Dresden).

GEEL, Jacob Jacobsz van. *c.* 1585 – after 1638. Worked in Middelburg, Delft and Dordrecht. Painted old trees with tormented, gnarled shapes. Typical work: *Trees* (Amsterdam, Rijksmuseum).

GEERTGEN tot Sint Jans (Geertgen of Haarlem). Leyden *c.* 1465 – *c.* 1493. Pupil of Albert van Ouwater. Accredited painter of the Knights of St. John, in Haarlem (his name means "Little Gerard of the Brethren of St. John"). This late 15th c. artist was the first painter of night scenes and so deserves to be classed among the immediate predecessors of Mannerism. Typical work: *Nativity*, a night scene (London, National Gallery).

GENGA, Girolamo. Urbino 1476–1551. His works offer a good example of a transitional style between the classicism of *c.* 1500 and Mannerism. He was equally influenced by Raphael and Dürer. Particularly interesting for his drawings. Typical work: *Martyrdom of St. Sebastian* (Florence, Uffizi).

GERUNG, Mathias. Nordlingen *c.* 1500–Lavingen 1569. Worked for the Cardinal-Archbishop of Augsburg; a rather clumsy but curious artist who was fond of very complicated compositions. Typical work: *Lot and his Daughters* (Vienna) with an extremely lewd Lot.

GHERARDI, Cristofano, called Doceno. Borgo S. Sepolcro 1500–1556. Decorator; friend of Giorgio Vasari with whom he collaborated on works in the Palazzo Vecchio, Florence.

GHEYN, Jacob II de. Antwerp 1565–The Hague 1629. Pupil of his father, an artist in stained-glass and engraver, and of Hendrick Goltzius (q.v.). Made engravings after his own drawings, and after Abraham Bloemaert, Cornelis Cornelisz van Haarlem, Jan Mander, Hendrick Goltzius (all of which q.v.), etc. Typical drawings: *Witches' Kitchen* (Oxford, Ashmolean); *Scene of Sorcery in a Cave* (Berlin, Kupferstichkabinett). Original engravings: *Witches' Sabbath; The Cross-Bowman;* series of *The Four Elements.*

GHEYN, Jacob III de. Leyden 1596–Utrecht 1644. Engraver; son and pupil of Jacob II de Gheyn (q.v.). Typical engravings: series of *The Seven Sages of Greece; St. Peter and St. Paul; Triton.*

GHISI, Giorgio. Mantua *c.* 1520–1582. Engraver; pupil of Giulio Romano (q.v.). Made engravings after Raphael, Francesco Primaticcio, Luca Penni and Bernardino Campi (all q.v.). Typical engraving: "*Dream of Raphael,*" (after Luca Penni).

GIORGIONE, Giorgio Barbarelli, called. Castelfranco 1476/78–Venice 1510. His career is almost entirely mysterious; we know that he lived in Venice around 1495, worked there for fifteen years and died of the plague. Only a few paintings generally agreed to be attributable to him have survived. Not properly a Mannerist, many of the paintings ascribed to him witness a liking for strange and obscure themes and a taste for evocative atmospheric effects which make him a precursor of many elements of the Mannerist style.

GIULIO Romano, Giulio Pippi called. Rome 1492/99–1546. Pupil of Raphael. Worked first in Rome (Sala di Costantino, Vatican) and from 1524 in Mantua in the service of Federigo Gonzaga, for whom he built and decorated the Palazzo del Tè, Mantua. He developed the classical idiom of Raphael into a strongly Mannerist style. His frescoes of the *Fall of the Titans* in the Palazzo del Tè are filled with huge figures and falling masonry and represent an exaggerated and brutal piece of Mannerist illusionism. His paintings are often very erotic in tone and he is noted for having illustrated Pietro Aretino's work on erotic pleasures.

GOES, Hugo van der. Goes (Zeeland) 1440–Brussels 1482. One of the most important Flemish painters of the 15th c. In his expressionistic deformations and extreme precision of contours he can be considered a precursor of Mannerism.

GOLTZIUS, Hendrick. Mühlbracht (nr. Venlo) 1558–Haarlem 1617. Strongly influenced by Bartholomeus Spranger (q.v.). With Cornelis Cornelisz van Haarlem, the founder of the Haarlem Academy (1587). Goltzius began his career as a painter late in life; he was above all an engraver of superb virtuosity, and in his own original designs he showed superb imagination. Paintings: *The Golden Age* (Arras); *Allegory of Vanity* (Basel). Original engravings: *The Magician; Roman Heroes; Hercules,* with monstrous muscle development; *Pygmalion; Bacchus, Ceres and Venus.* Engravings after other artists: *Mars and Venus* and *The Marriage of Cupid and Psyche* (after Spranger); *Tantalus, Icarus, Phaeton, Ixion* (after Cornelisz).

GOLTZIUS, Hubert. Wurzburg 1526–Bruges 1583. Distant cousin of Hendrick Goltzius (q.v.). Painter, engraver, printer and numismatist. He was a pupil of Lambert Lombard (q.v.) at Liège, and founded a printing house in Bruges in 1562. Travelled in Germany, Switzerland, Italy and France from 1558–1567, and again to Italy in 1574–1576. Very few of his paintings are known.

GOSSAERT, Jan. See MABUSE.

GOURMONT, Jean de. Carquebut (Manche) c. 1483–1551. Painter and engraver; brother of the Parisian printers Robert and Gilles Gourmont; worked with them in Paris until 1520, then settled in Lyons.

GOVAERTS, Abraham. 1589–Antwerp 1626. Landscapist in the tradition of Joachim Patinir, Herri met de Bles, Pieter Bruegel the Elder.

GRAF, Urs. Soleuvre c. 1485–Basel 1527. Swiss goldsmith, artist in stained-glass, engraver, draughtsman and printer. In 1512 signed on as a mercenary in the service of France for the Milanese campaign; his escapades cost him various spells of exile or prison. His drawings (the paintings are nearly all lost) are as truculent and disrespectful as he was himself; his subjects were often quite coarse and vulgar.

GRANACCI, Francesco. Florence 1477–1543. Pupil of Domenico Ghirlandaio and friend of Michelangelo. Typical work: *Martyrdom of St. Apollonia*, with elongated figures (Florence, Accademia).

GRECO, Domenikos Theotokopoulos, called El Greco. Crete 1541–Santo Domingo, Spain, 1614. Great mystic painter, one of the most outstanding figures of the whole 16th c. Worked in Venice where he was much influenced by Tintoretto (q.v.) and Bassano (q.v.) and then in Rome, from 1577 on in Toledo. Typical works: *Laocoön* (Washington, Nat. Gall.); *View of Toledo* (New York, Met. Mus. and Madrid, Condesa de Oñate Coll.); *The Burial of Count Orgaz* (Toledo, Santo Tomé).

GREUTER, Matthäus. Strasburg 1564/66–Rome 1638. Engraver who was active in Strasburg (1587–1593), Lyon (1594–1602), and Avignon. By 1604, his workshop was established in Rome where he engraved works after Aldegrever, Dietterlin, H. de Clerck and Raphael, as well as images of saints, portraits, book illustrations, plans and maps of Rome. His later works show intricate allegories in a typical Mannerist style.

GREVENBROECK, Orazio. Identification of this painter is uncertain. He is sometimes considered identical with Charles-Laurent Grevenbroeck who was active as a painter of landscapes and seascapes in Paris in the early 18th c. But it is possible that Orazio is another painter who was born in Milan in 1678, son of the Dutch painter Jan Grevenbroeck I who was working in Italy and in 1695 returned to Dordrecht. Although Orazio's style is that of the late 17th and 18th c., his imagery, as seen in the *Rape of Persephone* (Brussels), reproduced in this volume, is in the Mannerist tradition.

GRIEN, Hans Baldung. See BALDUNG GRIEN.

GRIMMER, Jacob. Antwerp c. 1526–after 1589. Landscapist in the tradition of Herri met de Bles (q.v.). Typical work: *The Four Seasons* (Antwerp).

GRÜNEWALD, Matthias (Neithardt-Gothardt) Würzburg c. 1455–Halle 1528. His mature works are clearly Mannerist in inspiration. His great masterpiece, the large altarpiece painted for the church of Isenheim (finished c. 1515) and now in the Colmar Museum is a work of a powerful expressionism.

GUNDELACH, Matthäus. Kessel? 1566–Augsburg 1653. Typical work: *Allegory of Mineral Wealth* (Dortmund).

HAARLEM, Cornelis van. see CORNELISZ.

HAARLEM, Geertgen van. see GEERTGEN tot Sint Jans.

HAMEN Y LEON, Juan van der. Madrid 1596–1631. Pupil of his father, the Brussels painter Juan van der Hamen, who had settled in Madrid. Painted still lifes of the Flemish type of a table set with food. He was also influenced by the Spanish type of still life, sparse in objects and arranged with careful symmetry, often set in a niche or window frame.

HEEMSKERCK, Maerten van. Heemskerck 1498–Haarlem 1574. Painter and engraver. Pupil of Jan van Scorel (q.v.). Lived in Italy 1532-1536. Justly nicknamed the "Michelangelo of the North." Heemskerck may be considered, by the richness of his imagination, his extraordinary mastery of design, and the splendor of his coloring, to be one of the very important painters of the 16th c. Typical works: *St. Luke Painting the Virgin and Child* (Haarlem); *Descent from the Cross* (Brussels); *Crucifixion* (Ghent); *Momus Finds Fault with the Gods*, strange figures in a fine architectural setting (Berlin); *The Rape of Helen*, a panorama of towns, ruins, mountains, and coastlines (Baltimore, Walters Art Gallery).

HEERE, Lukas de. Ghent 1543–Paris? 1584. Pupil of Frans Floris (q.v.). Worked in France at the Court of Catherine de Medici, in Ghent and in England. Typical works: *The Seven Arts in Time of War* (Turin, Galleria Sabauda); *Wise and Foolish Virgins* (Copenhagen).

HEINTZ, Josef I. Basel 1564–Prague 1609. Pupil of Hans Bock (q.v.) in Basel, studied in Rome. In 1591 appointed court painter to Rudolph II in Prague. Typical works: *Satyrs and Nymphs* (Munich); *Diana and Actaeon* (Vienna).

HEMESSEN, Jan (Sanders) van. b. Hemixem (nr. Antwerp) date unknown, d. Haarlem 1556. Senior officer of the Antwerp Guild in 1548. Specialized in genre scenes. Typical works: *A Brothel* (Berlin); *The Girl and the Customer* (Karlsruhe); *The Prodigal Son* (Brussels).

HILLIARD, Nicholas. Exeter? c. 1547–London 1619. The first important English painter of whose career and works we have any degree of knowledge, and along with Isaac Oliver (q.v.) England's finest miniaturist. Recorded in the Goldsmiths Company in 1570, by which time he had already been appointed Limner and Goldsmith to Queen Elizabeth. James I, on his accession, granted him a 12-year monopoly of royal portraiture. In France c. 1577, attached to the Duc d'Alençon. Author of the *Arte of Limning*. Typical works (all miniatures): *Portrait of a Young Dandy*, full-length, leaning against a tree among roses; *Portrait of a Young Man*, bust, with a background of flames (both London, Victoria and Albert Museum).

HOEFNAGEL, Joris. Antwerp 1542–Vienna 1600. Miniaturist. Fled from Antwerp after the sack of the town in 1576. Stayed for some time in Rome, where he worked for Cardinal Farnese; then in Innsbruck in the service of the Archduke Ferdinand; and in Prague at the court of Rudolf II. Engraved albums of minutely studied plants and animals.

HOLBEIN, Hans, the Younger. Augsburg 1497/98–London 1543. Holbein was the outstanding portrait painter of the North, noted for a precise realism and simplification of form. Pupil of his father Hans the Elder, then active in Basel (1514–1526). After a first stay in London (1526–1528), Holbein settled there permanently in 1532, and was appointed Court Painter to King Henry VIII. He became the leading portrait painter of England, but also did wall decorations, and designs for books, costumes, and jewelry.

HONDECOETER, Gillis Claesz d'. Active Amsterdam 1610–1638. Painted landscapes, often with many animals, in a style close to that of Roland Jacobsz Savery (q.v.) and Gillis van Coninxloo (q.v.). Typical work: *Orpheus with the Animals* (Stockholm).

HONTHORST, Gerrit. Utrecht 1590–1656. Pupil of Abraham Bloemaert. Worked in Italy 1610–1620; then in Utrecht and The Hague where he was court painter; 1628 he went to England, worked for King Charles I. In Italy he was strongly influenced by the works of Caravaggio (q.v.) and painted night scenes lighted by a candle or a torch, for which he earned the name of Gherardo delle Notti. Abandoned this style after returning to the North and in later years devoted himself to portraiture.

HUBER, Wolf. c. 1490–1533. Painter and engraver. Pupil of Albrecht Altdorfer (q.v.). Painted numerous landscapes of the Tyrol. Typical works: *Erection of the Cross* (Vienna); *Portrait of Jacob Ziegler* (Vienna).

HULSDONCK, Jacob van. Antwerp c. 1582–1647. Worked in Middelburg and Antwerp. Painter of still lifes in an extremely precise and sober style. Typical work: *Ham and Herring* (The Hague, Gall. A. Nijstad).

JACOBZ, Jacob. See GEEL, Jacob Jacobsz van.

JACONE, Jacopo da Sandro, called. Florentine painter, d. 1553. Pupil and collaborator of Andrea del Sarto (q.v.). Giorgio Vasari (q.v.) describes him as a typical bohemian; his idleness possibly explains the rarity of his works. There exists by this artist a *St. Lucy* (Florence, Santa Lucia).

JAMNITZER, Wenzel. Vienna 1508–Nuremberg 1586. Goldsmith and engraver. Author of *Perspectiva Corporum Regularium*, 1563, with engravings of attractive and complicated polyhedrons.

JANSSENS, Abraham. Antwerp 1575–1632. A painter who continued into the 17th c. the Italianizing trend of the Flemish artists known as "Romanists." A good painter of strong sculptural style, eclipsed by his great contemporary Rubens, who created a new Baroque style while Janssens essentially continued in the Mannerist tradition. Typical work: *Allegory of Voluptuousness* (Brussels).

KESSEL, Jan van. Antwerp 1626–1679. His mother was a daughter of Jan Bruegel the Elder, and his teacher was his uncle, Jan Bruegel the Younger, whose style he followed in his minutely detailed landscapes and his bouquets of flowers. Typical works: *Insects* (Strasburg); *Insects and Lizards* (Bonn); *Study of Flowers and Insects* (Oxford, Ashmolean Museum).

LAPPOLI, Giovanni Antonio. Arezzo 1492–Rome 1552. His first master was Domenico Pecori of Arezzo; he then went to Florence and studied with Pontormo (q.v.). He was influenced by his friends Rosso (q.v.) and Perino del Vaga (q.v.). Was imprisoned by the Spanish during the sack of Rome of 1527. Worked mainly in Arezzo.

LA TOUR, Georges de. Vic-sur-seille (Lorraine) 1593. Nothing is known of his earliest training. His youthful paintings show influence of the Mannerists of Lorraine, particularly Jacques Bellange. But his art was really formed on the style of Caravaggio and his followers. It is highly probable that La Tour was in Rome sometime between 1610 and 1618. After 1618 he seems to have settled in Lorraine. Famed for his beautiful night scenes lighted by a single candle, which earned him the title of Painter to King Louis XIII (1639). He was the most original and important of the French painters who came under the influence of Caravaggio. The brilliance of his artificial lighting which accented the pure, almost abstract volumes of his forms is still connected with the Mannerist style. He was active in the religious movement directed by the Franciscans in Lorraine and his religious works are of a profound and moving simplicity. Typical works: *The Penitent Magdalen*; *Saint Jerome in his Cell* (both Paris, Louvre).

LEAL. See VALDÉS LEAL, Juan de.

LEONARDO da Vinci. Vinci (near Florence) 1452–Château de Cloux (near Amboise) 1519. This great Italian Renaissance painter anticipated in many ways both the style and temperament of the Mannerist period. He was the creator of the *sfumato*, painter of enchanted distant landscapes, with a taste for dark atmospheric settings, and a strong interest in the strange and grotesque. All this and the strong current of erotic perversity in his world make him one of the immediate precursors of Mannerism.

LEYDEN, Lucas. See LUCAS van Leyden.

LIGOZZI, Jacopo. Verona 1547–Florence 1626. Studied in Venice. From 1575 onward worked at the court of the Medici in Florence, where he became keeper of the Ducal collections. Typical works: *The Virgin Appearing to St. Francis*, with an interesting landscape (Florence, Pitti); *The Rape of the Sabines* (Rome, private coll.).

LINARD, Jacques. c. 1600–Paris 1645. Painter of still lifes, particularly bouquets of a great variety of flowers executed with an archaic precision. Typical work: *Basket of Flowers* (Paris, Louvre).

LLANOS, Hernando de. La Mancha before 1480–after 1525. Collaborated with Hernando Yañez de la Almedina (q. v.) in the decoration of Valencia Cathedral; far more academic than Yañez. Typical work: *Flight into Egypt* (Valencia, Cathedral).

LOMAZZO, Giovanni Paolo. Milan 1538–1600. A late Mannerist painter and theorist. Author of the *Trattato dell'arte della pittura* (1584) and the *Idea del tempio della pittura* (1590). Among his few surviving paintings is the *Transfiguration* (Milan, Ambrosiana).

LOMBART, Lambrecht. Liège 1506–1566. Pupil of Mabuse (q. v.). Travelled in Germany and Rome during 1537/38. Was the teacher of Frans Floris (q. v.) and Hendrick Goltzius (q. v.). An academic Italianizer.

LOPEZ, Gregorio. See MASTER of the "Paraizo" of Lisbon.

LORENZO di Credi, called Barducci. Florence 1459–1537. Pupil of Verrocchio, and one of the precursors of Mannerism. Typical work: *Venus*, against a black background (Florence, Uffizi).

LUCAS van Leyden. Leyden 1494–1533. Pupil of Cornelis Cornelisz van Haarlem (q. v.). Became acquainted with Albrecht Dürer (q. v.) in Antwerp, where they were both staying briefly, and with Mabuse (q. v.) with whom he travelled in Ghent, Mechlin and Antwerp. Typical works: *The Last Judgment*, sculptural nudes in beautiful attitudes (Leyden, Lakenhal); *Fortune*, against a black background (Strasburg); *Lot and his Daughters*, a scene of incest against an apocalyptic background (Paris, Louvre). He was also one of the finest engravers of the 16th c. Typical engravings: *Woman with Dog*; *The Virtues*; *Abraham and the Three Angels*; *Mars, Venus and Cupid*.

LYTENS, Gysbrecht. 1586?–Antwerp 1627? Lytens is perhaps the artist known hitherto as the "Master of the Winter Landscapes". Specialized in great bare trees of strange shapes, rime-covered or in snowy landscapes. Typical works: *Winter Landscape* (Nancy); *Winter Landscape* (Vienna).

MABUSE, Jan Gossaert, called. Maubeuge c. 1478–Middelburg 1535. Influenced initially by Quentin Massys. Visited Italy for a year in 1508; on his return to the Netherlands worked for the nobility (Eleanor of Austria, Philip of Burgundy, Adolphe of Burgundy, etc.). One of the most important of the Italinate artists. Typical works: *Christ on the Mount of Olives*; *Neptune and Amphitrite* (all Berlin).

MACCHIETTI, Girolamo. Florence c. 1535–after 1564. Pupil and collaborator of Giorgio Vasari (q. v.). Typical works: *The Baths of Pozzuoli* and *Medea and Aeson* (Florence, Palazzo Vecchio, Studiolo).

MANDER, Karel van. Meulebeke (nr. Coutras) 1548–Amsterdam 1606. Pupil of Lukas de Heere (q. v.) in Ghent. Was in Rome between 1573 and 1577, where he met Bartholomeus Spranger (q. v.) who strongly influenced him. He settled in Haarlem where he opened an academy with Hendrick Goltzius (q. v.) and Cornelis Cornelisz van Haarlem (q. v.). Was also a poet and art critic; author of the *Schilderboek* (1604), which is the best early source of information on northern painters. Typical work: *Landscape with St. John the Baptist Preaching* (Hanover).

MANDYN, Jan. Haarlem 1500–Antwerp 1560. Typical Antwerp Mannerist painter. He settled in Antwerp in 1530, where among his many pupils was Bartholomeus Spranger (q. v.).

MANTEGNA, Andrea. Padua 1431–Mantua 1506. A very important painter and engraver of the Italian Renaissance. In his use of extreme foreshortening (*Dead Christ*, Milan, Brera), his fantastic landscapes, and the expressive preciseness and hardness in the delineation of his forms, he can be considered a precursor of Mannerism.

MARINUS van Reymerswaele. Born Zeeland. Active 1509?–after 1567? Excelled in the precise depiction of crumpled materials, plush, waste paper, melted wax, wrinkled faces. Typical works: *St. Jerome* (Madrid, Prado); *The Calling of St. Matthew* (Ghent); *The Money-Lenders* (London, Nat. Gall.).

MASSYS (Matsys), Jan. Antwerp 1510?–1575. Banished as a Protestant in 1544. Worked in Italy and France. His very white nudes are close to the style of the School of Fontainebleau though they have an additional element of perversity which relates them to Lucas Cranach (q. v.). Typical works: *Venus*, a large, pearly nude (Stockholm); *Courtesan and Old Man*, very expressionistic (Stockholm); *Susanna* (Brussels); *Bathsheba* (Paris, Louvre).

MASSYS (Matsys), Quentin. Louvain c. 1465/66–Antwerp 1530. One of the most important Antwerp Mannerists. His works reveal influence of Dürer, Patinir and Leonardo. His Madonnas, portraits and genre scenes had an important influence on Flemish painting.

MASTER OF FLORA. The painter thus designated is the presumed author of a series of works of the School of Fontainebleau: *The Triumph of Flora* (Zurich,

Coll. Dr. W. Feilichenfeldt); *Flora* (Montpellier); *Birth of Cupid* (New York, Met. Mus.); *Lot and his Daughters* (New York, Seligman Gall.).

MASTER OF THE HALF-LENGTH PORTRAITS OF WOMEN: A Netherlandish master of the first half of the 16th c. Typical works: *Venus and Cupid* (Berlin); *Neptune and Thetis* (Berlin); *Three Female Musicians* (London, Nat. Gall.); *Lucretia* (Rome, Galleria Colonna).

MASTER OF THE "PARAIZO" OF LISBON. The Master thus designated was a Portuguese artist of the first half of the 16th c., author of the *Madonna and Child and Angels* now in the museum at Lisbon but originally in the Convent of the "Paraizo." He is sometimes identified with Christovão de Figuieredo or, alternatively, with Gregorio Lopez. The same style is to be found in an *Immaculate Conception* (Lisbon).

MATHAM, Jakob. Haarlem 1571–1631. Engraver. Pupil and son-in-law of Hendrick Goltzius (q. v.). Made engravings after the work of Goltzius, Pieter Aertsen (q. v.) and Roland Jacobsz Savery (q. v.).

MAZZOLA, Francesco, see PARMIGIANINO.

MAZZUOLI, Francesco, called Maso da San Friano. c. 1532–1571. An artist of great imagination and marvelous technique. For the Studiolo of Francesco I in the Palazzo Vecchio, Florence, he painted the *Diamond Mine* and the *Fall of Icarus*.

MICHELANGELO Buonarroti. Caprese (near Florence) 1475 – Rome 1564. This most powerful personality of the whole Italian Renaissance is generally recognized as having been the model for many Mannerist artists. But he himself, through his concern with clarity of design, his use of the *linea serpentina*, the elongation of his figures, his love of the nude, his rare color effects, may quite clearly be classed among the Mannerists.

MILLAN, Pierre. d. 1551. An Italian or Flemish engraver who worked in Paris. The teacher of René Boyvin (q. v.). Typical work: *The Nymph of Fontainebleau*, after a painting by Rosso Fiorentino (q. v.) and a frame by Francesco Primaticcio (q. v.).

MINGA, Andrea del. Florence c. 1540–1596. Collaborator of Giorgio Vasari (q. v.). Typical works: *Deucalion and Pyrrha* (Florence, Palazzo Vecchio, Studiolo).

MOMPER, Joos de. Antwerp 1564–1635. Travelled in Italy and Switzerland. Painter of landscapes in the tradition of Pieter Bruegel the Elder. Father of Frans de Momper who was also a landscapist. Typical work: *Mountainous Landscape* (Vienna).

MONOGRAMMIST ⚮. Italian engraver of the early 16th c. Creator of a few known prints of stereographic forms conserved in Hamburg, Florence and Vienna.

MORALES, Luis de. Badajoz c. 1510–1568. Painter of graceful Madonnas in an extremely soft *sfumato* technique. Typical works: *Madonna and Child* (Madrid, Prado); *Madonna and Child* (New York, Hispanic Society).

MOREELSE, Paulus. Utrecht 1571–1638. Painter and architect. Visited Italy before 1604. Perhaps a pupil of Michiel van Mierevelt at Delft. Painted mythological and religious scenes mixing the late Mannerism of Utrecht with the influence af Caravaggio. Also painted portraits. Had many pupils of whom Dirck van Baburen is the best known. Typical work: *Vanitas* (Amsterdam).

MULLER, Jan. Amsterdam 1571–1628. Draughtsman and engraver. Worked in Augsburg and in Amsterdam; made engravings after Hendrick Goltzius (q. v.), Bartholomeus Spranger (q. v.), the sculptors of the School of Prague, and his own drawings. Typical engravings: *Belshazzar's Feast*, after Melchior Bocksberger (q. v.); *Lot and his Daughters*, after Spranger; *The Three Fates*, after Cornelis Cornelisz van Haarlem (q. v.); *Creation of the World*, seven plates after Goltzius.

NALDINI, Giovanni Battista, called Matteo. Florence 1537–1590. One of the artists employed in decorating the Studiolo of Francesco I in the Palazzo Vecchio, Florence, for which he executed *Harvest of the Gray Amber* and an *Allegory of Sleep*.

NEER, Aert van der. Amsterdam 1603/04–1677. Landscape painter specializing in moonlight effects, usually showing the canals and rivers around Amsterdam.

NOMÉ, François. See DESIDERIO, Monsù.

OLIVER, Isaac. Rouen before 1568 – London 1617. Miniaturist. Pupil of Nicholas Hilliard; rivalled his teacher. Visited Venice in 1596. Painted portraits of Queen Elizabeth, Mary Queen of Scots, James I, and others of the court.

ORLEY, Bernard (Barent) van. Brussels c. 1495–1542. Is supposed to have made two visits to Italy, and to have known Raphael personally. Court Painter to the Spanish Governors of the Netherlands. The host of Albrecht Dürer (q. v.) during the latter's visit to Brussels. As a Protestant, involved in the persecutions of 1527, escaped the Inquisition thanks to the protection of Margaret of Austria. Typical works: *The Trials of Job* (Brussels); cartoons for the tapestries of *Maximilian's Hunting-Parties*.

ORSI, Lelio. Reggio 1511 – Novellara 1587. Pupil of Correggio and Michelangelo. Worked in Reggio, Novellara, Venice (1553), Rome (1554–1556) and Parma. Painter of night scenes (*Martyrdom of Saint Catherine*, Modena, Galleria Estense), and creator of turbulent storm effects (*Way to Emmaus*, London, Nat. Gall.). He had a highly personal and expressive style.

PAGNI, Benedetto. Born Pescia early 16th c., died c. 1570. Known as *Pagni da Pescia*. Pupil of Giulio Romano (q.v.) **in** Rome. Painter and decorator of a precise and elegant style. In service of Francesco IV Gonzaga in Mantua. Typical works: *Allegory of the Fame of the Medici* (Sarasota, Ringling Museum).

PALMA, Giovane, Jacopo di Antonio Negretti, called. Venice 1544–1628. Painter and engraver; grandnephew of Palma Vecchio. This Venetian late Mannerist was a follower of Guidubaldo d'Urbino in Urbino, then active in Rome under the influence of Michelangelo and other Mannerists. Returned to Venice where his style was based on the late Titian, Tintoretto (q.v.), Salviati (q.v.), and Alessandro Vittoria.

PARMIGIANINO, Francesco Mazzola, called. Parma 1503–Casal Maggiore 1540. Influenced in his youth by Correggio (q.v.), then by Michelangelo (q.v.). Worked in Parma, Rome and Bologna. One of the most important of Italian Mannerist painters. In his works are seen clearly developed some of the most typical characteristics of the Mannerist style, such as the elongation of figures, supple lines, and studied and graceful attitudes. Typical works: *The Madonna of the Long Neck* (Florence, Uffizi); *Madonna and Child, Portrait in a Convex Mirror* (both Vienna).

PATINIR (Patenier, Patinier), Joachim. Dinant c. 1485–Antwerp 1524. Was perhaps a pupil of Gerard David. Worked in Antwerp. A painter of importance for the creation of the landscape considered as an independent entity. Typical works: *The Styx*, a mysterious river between the meadows and copses of Paradise and the towering walls of Hell (Madrid, Prado); *Temptation of St. Anthony*, fantastic rocks, vast panorama (Madrid, Prado); *Lot Fleeing Sodom*, with the town in flames and sinking into the Dead Sea (Nuremberg, Coll. Praun). Had a large number of disciples whose work is often difficult to distinguish from his own.

PEETERS, Clara. Antwerp. Active second quarter of 17th c. Still life painter. Her tables set with food are executed with a rigidity of composition and an extreme precision and dryness of detail. Typical work: *Still life with Tart and Olives* (Madrid, Prado).

PENCZ, Georg. German painter and engraver, active Nuremberg 1500–1550. Was probably a pupil of Albrecht Dürer, and collaborated with the Behams (q.v.). Made several journeys to Italy and may have attended the studio of Marcantonio Raimondi (q.v.). Typical works: *Cimon in Prison Nourished by his Daughter Perra* (Warsaw); *Judith* (Munich). Engravings: *Abraham Caressing Agar, Lot and his Daughters, Bathsheba, Susanna*.

PENNI, Luca. Florence 1500?–France 1556. Painter and print designer. Pupil of Raphael at Rome, worked with Perino del Vaga in Genoa and Lucca. Perhaps worked in England for Henry VIII. Lived in France from 1530–1556, where he collaborated with Rosso and Primaticcio at Fontainebleau.

PERINO DEL VAGA, Pietro Buonaccorsi, called. Florence 1500–Rome 1547. Pupil of Raphael. In 1527 to Genoa where he executed and directed the decorations of the Palazzo Doria. Returned to Rome where he executed important frescoes in Castel Sant'Angelo for Pope Paul III.

PERUZZI, Baldassare. Siena 1481–Rome 1536. Pupil of Pinturicchio; also influenced by Sodoma (q.v.). Worked in Rome and Siena. Typical works: trompe-l'œil decorations in the Villa Farnesina, Rome; *Venus emerging from the Bath* (Rome, Galleria Borghese).

PIERO DI COSIMO, Piero di Lorenzo, called. Florence 1462–1521. His strange themes and predilection for the bizarre make him an important precursor of Mannerism. Typical works: *Perseus Liberating Andromeda from the Sea Monster* (Florence, Uffizi); *Death of Procris* (London, Nat. Gall.).

POMARANCIO, Niccolò Circignani, called. 1516–1596. A late Mannerist painter who was the favorite artist of the Jesuits in Rome during the 1580's and 1590's. Worked in a rather dull and passionless style executing frescoes of the cruelest martyrdoms for the English Jesuit College of San Tomaso di Canterbury, Rome (frescoes destroyed) and for the church of the German Jesuit College, Santo Stefano Rotondo, Rome. A typical example of a late Mannerist artist who actively served the cause of the Counter-Reformation.

PONTORMO, Jacopo da, Jacopo Carucci, called. Pontormo 1494–Florence 1557. Pupil of Andrea del Sarto (q.v.) in Florence. One of the most important figures of the first phase of Florentine Mannerism. Was first influenced by Michelangelo, but also, through Dürer's engravings, by the northern style. His hallucinated vision, his strong and imaginative draughtsmanship which at times leads to distortion of images, his liking for sharp and pallid colors all combine to make him the most vigorous and inspired exponent of Florentine Mannerism. Typical works: *The Supper at Emmaus* (Florence, Uffizi); *Joseph in Egypt* (London, Nat. Gall.); *Descent from the Cross* (Florence, S. Felicita); frescoes of the Medici Villa at Poggio a Caino (near Florence).

POPPI, Francesco Morandini, called. Poppi 1544?–Florence 1597. Pupil of Giorgio Vasari (q.v.). Typical works: *The Three Graces* (Florence, Uffizi); *Charity* (Florence, Accademia); *Alexander, Campaspe and Apollo* (Florence, Palazzo Vecchio, Studiolo).

POZZOSERRATO, Ludovico, Lodewijk Toeput, called. Mechlin c. 1545–Trieste c. 1604. Lived for a long time in Venice. The name Pozzoserrato is the Italian translation of Toeput ("blocked well"). He painted fantastic panoramas filled with endless detail. Typical works: three *Landscapes*, with dramatic lighting and coloring (Hanover).

PRIMATICCIO, Francesco. Bologna 1504–Paris 1570. In 1526 worked under Giulio Romano on the decorations of the Castello and the Palazzo del Té at Mantua. In 1532 summoned to France by François I. Perhaps Primaticcio is as much or more responsible than Rosso for the creation of the decorative style of Fontainebleau which so effectively combined painting and stucco. Executed a great many decorations at Fontainebleau (Salle du Roi, Salle de la Reine, Pavillon de Pomone) which have all, unfortunately, been destroyed or disfigured. His style can be clearly seen, however, in his drawings and the many engravings after his decorations at Fontainebleau. This style, at once delicate and elegant, had a great influence in France.

PROCACCINI, Giulio Cesare. Bologna c. 1570–Milan 1625. About 1585 he established himself in Milan with his father Ercole Procaccini the Elder and his brothers Camillo and Carlo Antonio. His artistic culture is based on Correggio and the chiaroscuro of the Lombard school. In 1618 transferred his residence to Genoa and had an influence on many young Genovese artists of the earlier 17th c. At Genoa he knew the young Rubens whose richness and fluidity of color influenced Procaccini's later works. Typical work: Mary Magdalen (Milan, Brera).

RAIMONDI, Marcantonio. Bologna 1480–1534. Worked first of all in Venice, where he copied and published engravings of Albrecht Dürer; then in Rome, where he made prints after the work of Raphael and Giulio Romano (q.v.). Was the head of a whole school of artists whose prints were very influential in spreading his school throughout Europe.

RAPHAEL (Raffaello Sanzio). Urbino 1483–Rome 1520. The greatest exponent of the classical High Renaissance style. His latest works, however, show many incipient Mannerist stylistic elements. This is particularly true in the last of his frescoes for the Vatican Palace, those of the Stanza dell' Incendio, which show Mannerist tendencies in the complication of composition and the treatment of space, as well as in the use of certain studied figures and poses to become common among his followers. His many pupils and disciples all showed themselves to be Mannerist to a greater or lesser extent.

REVERDY, Georges. Born near Lyons at the beginning of 16th c. Painter and engraver. Active Lyons 1529–1565. Typical work: Adoration of the Shepherds (Paris, Ecole des Beaux Arts).

REYMERSVAELE (Roymerswaele, etc.), Marinus Claeszon van. See MARINUS van Reymerswaele.

RING, Ludger Tom the Younger. Munster 1522–1583. Son of Ludger Tom Ring the Elder, and brother of Hermann Tom Ring. Painted in a style of great precision of line and detail, portraits, scenes with figures and many still life objects, and also pure still lifes such as the two paintings of A Vase of Flowers (Munster).

ROBERTI, Ercole de'. Ferrara 1456–1496. Like his fellow artists of Ferrara, Cosimo Tura (q.v.) and Francesco

Cossa (q.v.) his style was strange and expressionistic. Worked with these other artists of the school of Ferrara in the frescoes of the Palazzo Schifanoia at Ferrara and together with them was one of the important 15th c. precursors of Mannerism.

ROMANO, Giulio. See GIULIO Romano.

ROSSO FIORENTINO, Giovanni Battista Rosso, called. Florence 1494–Fontainebleau 1540. Pupil of Andrea del Sarto (q.v.) and Jacopo da Pontormo (q.v.). Worked in Florence, and then in Rome. Fled from Rome at the sack of Rome in 1527 and spent three years moving from place to place. In 1530 was summoned to France by François I where he took over the direction of the decoration of the palace of Fontainebleau. His works of the Italian period are strongly emotional and monumental (Descent from the Cross, Volterra, Pinacoteca). At Fontainebleau he developed a style of decoration combining painting and stucco which had a tremendous influence in France and even elsewhere in Europe. His principal work remaining at Fontainebleau is the Galerie François I, but unfortunately even this has been much altered.

ROTTENHAMMER, Hans. Munich 1564–Augsburg 1625. Visited Rome and Venice; on his return to Germany worked for the Dukes of Bavaria, then for the Emperor Rudolph II in Prague. Influenced by Bartholomeus Spranger (q.v.). Typical works: Bath (Dessau, Castle); Fall of the Damned (Vienna).

SALMEGGIA, Enia, called Il Talpino. Bergamo c. 1550–Milan 1626. Religious themes of the Counter-Reformation treated with typically Mannerist sensual ambiguity; beautiful chiaroscuro effects. Typical works: Martyrdom of St. Catherine, a luminous nude in thick shadows (Rome, Colonna); Martyrdom of St. Agatha (Bergamo, Carmine).

SALIMBENI, Ventura. Siena c. 1567–1613. Pupil of his father Arcangelo Salimbeni and of his half-brother Francesco Vanni. His paintings are characteristic of the religious Mannerism of the Counter-Reformation, while his engravings have affinities with the style of Hendrick Goltzius (q.v.). Typical works: Annunciation (Budapest); Diana (Florence, Uffici).

SALVIATI, Francesco de' Rossi, called. Florence 1510–Rome 1563. Pupil of Andrea del Sarto; close friend of Giorgio Vasari (q.v.), with whom he frequently collaborated. Worked on large-scale decorations in Rome (Vatican), Venice (Palazzo Grimaldi and Libreria Vecchia) and Florence (Palazzo Vecchio). Assumed the name of his patron, Cardinal Salviati.

SANCHEZ COTAN, Juan. Orgaz 1561–Granada 1627. Monk in the Carthusian Monastery of Paular, then in that of Granada. Painter of religious subjects. Is chiefly known today for his beautiful still lifes consisting of a very few vegetables and fruits such as cabbages, melons, cardoons or cucumbers. His objects, set upon or hung in a window frame, appear against a dark background and are sharply illuminated by a strong shaft of light revealing all the beauty of their forms. Typical work: *Still Life Melon, Cabbage, Quince and Cucumber* (San Diego, Fine Arts Gallery).

SANDRO, Jacopo da. See JACONE.

SARTO, Andrea del, Andrea Angeli di Francesco, called. Florence 1486–1531. Pupil of Piero di Cosimo (q.v.); influenced by Fra Bartolommeo. His earlier paintings are in the classical style of the High Renaissance but his later works admit many elements of the Mannerist style. Teacher of Jacopo da Pontormo, Francesco Salviati and Giorgio Vasari. Typical works: *Miracle of St. Philip Benizzi* (Florence, Annunziata); *Holy Family* (Florence, Pitti).

SAVERY, Roland Jacobsz. Courtrai 1576–Utrecht 1654. Pupil of Hans Bol (q.v.) in Amsterdam. Worked in Paris, then in Prague at the court of Rudolph II and later of Mathias I. Settled in the Netherlands in 1616. Painter of flowers, *Earthly Paradises, Noah's Arks,* and mountain forests. His rich, dense and imaginative landscapes are typical of the early seventeenth century Mannerist landscape painting in the north.

SAVOLDO, Girolamo. Brescia *c.* 1480–1548. A painter very important for his rich color, fine landscapes with romantic light effects, and excellent portraits. Typical works: *Tobias and the Angel* (Rome, Galleria Borghese); *Portrait of a Man,* perhaps Gaston de Foix (Paris, Louvre).

SCARSELLINO, Ippolito. Ferrara 1571–1620. Pupil of Girolamo da Carpi. Influenced by Bassano (q.v.), Dosso Dossi (q.v.) and Correggio. His works are rich in color with fine effects of twilight. Typical work: *Venus and Cupid* (Parma, Galleria Nazionale).

SCHIAVONE, Andrea Meldolla, called. Zara (in Dalmatia, whence his name) 1522–Venice 1563. Painter of elongated figures in a misty atmosphere. Typical works: *Diana and Actaeon* (Oxford, Christ Church); *Two mythological Scenes,* drowned in a golden mist (Dublin); *Antiope* (Leningrad, Hermitage).

SCHIAVONE, Giorgio Chiulinovich, called. Dalmatia 1434–1504. A precursor of Mannerism. Framed his Madonnas with wreaths of fruit and arches sculpted in the style of Carlo Crivelli (q.v.) and Cosimo Tura (q.v.). Typical work: *Madonna* (London, Nat. Gall.).

SCHÖN, Erhard. b. *c.* 1495, d. Nuremberg after 1543. Painter and engraver. Possibly a pupil of Albrecht Dürer. Specialized in anamorphic designs. Typical prints: *Was siehst du?,* anamorphosis; *Heraus, du alter Tor!,* anamorphosis. *Turks Carrying Off Christian Prisoners.*

SCHOOTEN, Floris Gerritz van. Painter of still lifes. Active Haarlem early 17th c. Typical work: *Still Life with Herrings, Oysters and Bread* (Haarlem).

SCOREL, Jan van. Scorel (near Alkmaar) 1495–Utrecht 1562. A great traveller, worked in Utrecht in the studio of Mabuse, (q.v.), in Cologne, in Basel, in Nuremberg in the studio of Albrecht Dürer, (q.v.), in Carinthia, in Venice, in Rhodes; visited Jerusalem, stayed some time in Rome, then returned to the Netherlands by way of France; finally settled in Utrecht where he became the teacher of Maerten van Heemskerck (q.v.). Typical works: *Lucretia,* white nude against a black background (Berlin); *Baptism of Christ* (Haarlem); *The Flood* (Madrid, Prado).

SELLAER, Vincent. Active Mechlin 1538 – died before 1589. Contemporary of Michiel Coxie (q.v.) but his paintings belong to an older style of Leonardesque Mannerism established by Massys (q.v.) in Antwerp, where Sellaer probably learned it. He mixed Lombard elements with Raphael and the Florentine styles of Sarto and Bacchiacca.

SIGNORELLI, Luca. Cortona *c.* 1441/50–1523. This artist may be considered one of the immediate precursors of Italian Mannerism by virtue of the hardness of outline, sharp foreshortenings of the figures, illusionistic perspective, and the insistent sculptural quality of his work. Typical work: Frescoes in the Cathedral of Orvieto.

SINT JANS, Geertgen tot. See GEERTGEN tot Sint Jans (Geertgen of Haarlem).

SODOMA, Giovanni Antonio Bazzi, called. Vercelli 1477–Siena 1549. Possibly a pupil of Leonardo, but in any case an admirer of the master's work. Worked in Rome (Vatican, Villa Farnesina) and especially in Siena. His paintings are bathed in a dark and heavy atmosphere. His pictures often reproduce the equivocal type of figure to be found in Leonardo's work. Typical works: *Sacrifice of Abraham,* with a very effeminate Isaac (Pisa cathedral); *St. Sebastian,* also very effeminate, in a beautiful landscape at dusk (Florence, Pitti); *Christ in Limbo* (Siena, Pinacoteca).

SOLIS, Virgel. Nuremberg 1514–1562. Engraver. Worked in Nuremberg. In addition to original engravings executed many prints after other artists.

SOREAU, Jean. Active Frankfurt 1615, d. after 1638. Painter of still lifes characterized by a clearly defined line. Typical work: *Still Life with Flowers, Basket and Plate of Fruit* (Oxford, Ashmolean).

SPRANGER, Bartholomeus. Antwerp 1546–Prague 1611. Pupil of Jan Mandyn (q.v.) and Frans Mostaert. Worked in Paris 1565, then in Italy. Employed by the Austrian Court, first at Vienna with Maximilian II, then, after 1581, at Prague with Rudolph II, where he became the principal figure of the School of Prague. His style expressed a synthesis of Flemish, French and Italian Mannerism. Typical works: *Susanna and the Elders* (Nuremberg); *Hermaphrodite and the Nymph Salmacis* (Vienna); *Hercules and Omphale Disguised* (Vienna).

STOER, Lorenz. Nuremberg? before 1540–after 1620. Goldsmith and engraver. Worked in Nuremberg and

Augsburg. His *Geometria et Perspectiva*, 1567, contains a series of woodcuts of geometrical landscapes.

STOSKOPFF, Sebastian. Strasburg 1597–1657. Painter of still lifes with a few objects carefully delineated. His *Still Life with a Basket of Glasses* (Strasburg) is particularly admirable.

STRADANO, Giovanni, Jan van der Straet, known in Italy as. Bruges 1523–Florence 1605. Master in Antwerp, worked for some time in Lyons, then in Italy, where he worked successively in Venice, Rome, Naples, and finally Florence where he was one of the collaborators of Giorgio Vasari (q. v.). One of the artists employed in the Studiolo of Francesco I in the Palazzo Vecchio, Florence, for which he executed the *Distillers' Workshop*.

SWANENBURGH, Jacob Isaacsz van. Leyden *c.* 1571–1638. Worked for many years in Venice and Naples. Typical works: *Pharaoh crossing the Red Sea* (Leyden); *The Rape of Persephone* (Leyden).

TAVARONE, Lazzaro. Genoa 1556–1641. Pupil of Luca Cambiaso (q. v.), whom he accompanied to Spain to the court of Philip II; after the death of Cambiaso, completed the paintings which the Master had left unfinished in the Escorial. Worked in Genoa cathedral on a chapel decoration featuring the life of St. Lawrence. Typical work: *Christ Stripped of his Garments* (Sestri Levante, Rizzi Coll.).

TEMPESTA, Antonio. Florence 1555–1630. Pupil of Santi di Tito (q. v.), then of Giovanni Stradano (q. v.). Known chiefly as an engraver (with more than 1,800 known prints to his credit). Not to be confused with Pieter Mulier the Younger, known as the Cavaliere Tempesta (Haarlem 1637–Milan 1701). Typical works of Antonio Tempesta: forty-six engravings for the *Trattato degl' istrumenti di martirio* by Father Antonio Gallonio (Rome, 1591).

THIRY, Leonard. b. the Netherlands, d. Antwerp 1550. Pupil of Rosso Fiorentino (q. v.). Active Fontainebleau 1536–1550. His work has been engraved by René Boyvin, Jacques Ducerceau and Léon Davent.

TIBALDI, Pellegrino. Puria (Vasolda) 1527–Milan 1596. Painter, sculptor, architect. Worked first in Bologna, where he was influenced by Parmigianino (q. v.); went to Rome in 1550 and joined the group of artists around Daniele da Volterra (q. v.); returned to Bologna in 1552, where he executed, notably, the frescoes of the Palazzo Poggi; in 1586 was summoned by Philip II of Spain to the Escorial where, among other works, he painted the frescoes in the cloister. His frescoes in the Palazzo Poggi of scenes from the Odyssey are powerful and imaginative and use illusionistic architectural settings and strong foreshortening.

TINTORETTO, Jacopo Robusti called. Venice 1518–1594. By reason of his distortion of space and his predilection for visionary effects of color and flicker-

ing light, Tintoretto must be considered the principal representative of Venetian Mannerism. Typical works: *The Last Supper*, with an entirely unreal perspective of the table and equally unreal lighting effects (Venice, S. Giorgio Maggiore); *Removal of the Body of St. Mark* (Milan, Brera); *Venus and Vulcan* (Munich); *The Flight into Egypt*, a tapestry universe (Venice, Scuola di S. Rocco); *St. Mary of Egypt*, nocturnal landscape; *Paradise*, huge canvas of myriad figures (Sala del Gran Consiglio, Palazzo Ducale, Venice).

TITO, Santi di. Borgo S. Sepolcro 1536–Florence 1603. Pupil of Angelo Bronzino (q. v.); worked in Rome and Florence. For the Studiolo of Francesco I in the Palazzo Vecchio, Florence, executed the scene of *Phaeton's Sisters Turned into Poplar Trees*.

TOUR, Georges de La. See LA TOUR, Georges de.

TURA, Cosimo. Ferrara 1432–1495. Along with the other members of the School of Ferrara, Francesco Cossa (q. v.) and Ercole de' Roberti, with whom he worked in the Palazzo Schifanoia, Ferrara, he may be considered one of the precursors of Mannerism. His works show a brittle and metallic sense of form, the utilization of bizarre details, and expressionist distortions.

UDINE, Giovanni da, Giovanni Ricamatore, called. Udine 1487–Rome 1564. Printer, painter, stuccoworker, and architect. Pupil of Giovanni Martini da Udine (1502) and Giorgione (1510/11). Entered Raphael's studio in Rome and did the stucco decoration of the Vatican Loggie (1517–1519) and in Raphael's frescoes of the Villa Farnesina. In 1532 did stuccoes in the Medici Chapel in San Lorenzo in Florence. At first his grotesque stucco decorations were in the style of Pinturicchio and Signorelli, then under the influence of the antique he created a new style.

VAGA. See PERINO DEL VAGA.

VALCKENBORCH (Valckenburgh, etc.), Lucas van. Louvain *c.* 1530–Frankfurt 1597. May have been a pupil of Pieter Bruegel the Elder. A Protestant who took part in the revolts against the Spaniards and had to flee to Germany, where he entered the service of the Arch-Duke Mathias. His landscapes, which are often busy panoramas or Towers of Babel, show the clear influence of Pieter Bruegel the Elder. His brother Martin (1535–1562) and his sons Frederick (1570–1623) and Gillis (born *c.* 1580) worked in a very similar style, so that it is sometimes difficult to distinguish their production. Typical works: *Building of the Tower of Babel* (Munich); *The Four Seasons* (Vienna). Martin van Valckenborch: *Tower of Babel* (Dresden). Frederick van Valckenborch: *Foundry at the Edge of a River* (Wuppertal). Gillis van Valckenborch: *The Siege of Jerusalem* (Braunschweig).

VALDÉS LEAL, Juan de. Seville 1622–Seville 1690. An important painter of the Baroque in Spain. For the frequent use of the theme of death in his works he has been called "the painter of the dead". Although his style is Baroque, the complicated symbolism of these allegories of death and the frightening gruesomeness of his skeletons and corpses are in the Mannerist tradition. Typical works: *Finis gloriae Mundi* and *In Ictu Oculi* (Seville, Hospital de la Caridad).

VASARI, Giorgio, Avezzo 1511 – Florence 1574. Distant cousin of Luca Signorelli (q. v.). Pupil of Michelangelo in Florence. Worked in Rome for Cardinal Farnese and for Pope Julius III, then worked mainly in Florence. Held a most important position at the court of the Medici as director of all main artistic undertakings in which he participated with his many disciples, above all the decorations of the Palazzo Vecchio. He also directed the decorations for the marriage of Francesco I de' Medici and those for the funeral of Michelangelo. His frescoes are often extremely erudite in subject matter, crowded with figures in complicated compositions and often rather unpleasant in color. A few of his smaller paintings such as the *Perseus and Andromeda* (Florence, Palazzo Vecchio, Studiolo), are quite elegant and of beautiful color. Vasari had a great influence on Florentine art of the second half of the 16th c. He was the creator of the Accademia del disegno, founded in 1561, and also the author of what is perhaps the most important source book of the history of art ever written: *Le Vite de' più eccellente architetti, pittori e scultori italiani* (1550).

VENEZIANO, Agostino. See AGOSTINO, Veneziano.

VENUSTI, Marcello. Como 1515 – Rome 1579? Pupil of Perino del Vaga; influenced by Michelangelo. Typical works: *Holy Family* with elongated figures, *Christ Driving the Money Changers from the Temple* (both London, Nat. Gall.).

VERHAEGT (Van Haecht), Tobias. Antwerp 1561–1631. Landscape painter. Typical work: *Panorama with river* (Munich).

VERONESE, Paolo Caliari, called. Verona 1528 to Venice 1588. To Venice in 1530. In Rome 1560. One of the greatest Venetian painters of the 16th c. Many characteristics of his works are clearly Mannerist: above all the distorted and unstable balance of his figures, and the ambiguous treatment of space with large figures on a high foreground and several inexplicable levels and planes containing figures in the background. Typical of his Mannerist works is the *Saint John Preaching* (Rome, Galleria Borghese).

VICO, Aenea. Parma c. 1520–1563/67. Engraver and illustrator. Worked in Florence for Duke Cosimo, then in Venice. Typical engravings: *Leda and Jupiter* (after Perino del Vaga); *Mars and Venus* (after Parmigianino); a *Rhinoceros*.

VINCENZO da San Gimignano (Tamagni, Vincenzo di Benedetto di Michele). San Gimignano 1492 – c. 1530?

Probably a pupil of Sebastiano Mainardi in the circle of Ghirlandaio. In 1505/06, he painted frescoes in Monte Oliveto at Chiusuri with Sodoma, where his style changed under the latter's influence. In 1517, he was in Rome assisting Raphael, and his style underwent another change. After his return to Tuscany, he began painting again in his earlier manner of Ghirlandaio. Typical work: *Madonna and Child with Saints* (fresco in San Gimignano, Palazzo Pratellesi).

VINCI, Leonardo da. See LEONARDO da Vinci.

VISET, Jean. Known as an etcher. Active Fontainebleau 1536.

VOLTERRA, Daniele Ricciarelli, called Daniele da. Volterra 1509 – Rome 1566. Pupil of Sodoma (q. v.); influenced by Michelangelo. Worked mostly in Rome (Vatican; Sta. Trinità dei Monti). His style is characterized by accentuation of volumes and a tendency to geometric forms. Typical works: *Beheading of St. John the Baptist* (Rome, Sta. Trinità dei Monti); *David and Goliath*, a double picture with a painting on each side of the canvas (Paris, Louvre).

VOS, Marten de. Antwerp 1532–1603. Pupil of his father, Peter de Vos, and of Frans Floris (q. v.). Stayed some time in Italy. His work shows alternately the influence of Frans Floris and of Tintoretto (q. v). Many of his drawings were engraved by the Sadelers. Typical works: *Apollo and the Muses*, (Brussels); *Jonas* (Berlin); *Temptation of St. Anthony*, in which the monsters are most precisely delineated (Antwerp).

VRIES, Hans Vredeman de. Leeuwarden 1527 – c. 1606. Worked in Germany, Antwerp, Amsterdam, The Hague, and at the court of Rudolph II in Prague. Painter of fantastic architectures. Typical work: *Palace* (Berlin).

WEDIG, Gotthardt von. Cologne 1583–1641. Painter of still lifes. Typical work: *Meal by Candlelight* (Darmstadt).

WEYDEN, Roger van der (Rogier de la Pasture). Tournai c. 1399 – Brussels 1464. 1450 to Italy where he visited in particular Rome and Ferrara. His workshop in Brussels was the most important in the Low Countries. This important 15th c. artist, in the angular expressionistic distortions of his figures and his extreme calligraphic elegance was a major precursor of Mannerism.

WIERIX. The name of a family of engravers. There were three Wierix brothers: JAN (Amsterdam 1550 to The Hague c. 1617), HIERONYMUS (Amsterdam 1551–1621), ANTHONIS (Amsterdam c. 1555–?).

WINGHE or WINGHEN, Jodocus (Joos). Brussels 1544 – Frankfurt 1603. Studied in Rome and Paris. In 1568 in Brussels as court painter to Alessandro Farnese, Duke of Parma. In 1585 left Brussels for religious reasons and settled in Frankfurt. Did many drawings for engravings executed by Thomas de Bry, the Sadelers and Hendrick Goltzius. Typical works: *Diana* (Budapest); *Jupiter and Ceres* (Leningrad, Hermitage); *Lot and his Daughters* (Gotha).

WITTE, Peter de. See CANDIDO, Pietro.

WOLFVOET, Victor. Antwerp 1612–1652. Pupil of his father, then of Rubens. Master in Antwerp Guild in 1644. Typical works: *Melchizedek and Abraham*; *Fall of the Manna* (The Hague, Mauritshuis); *Medusa Head* (Dresden Gallery).

WTEWAEL, Joachim. Utrecht *c.* 1566–1638. Pupil of Joost de Beer (q. v.). Travelled in France and Italy. With Abraham Bloemaert (q. v.) the most important member of School of Utrecht. Typical works: *The Flood* (Nuremberg); *Marriage of Thetis and Peleus* (two versions, Braunschweig and Munich); *Lot and his Daughters* (The Hague, Coll. H. C. van Maasdijk); *The Judgment of Paris* (London, Coll. C. D. Rotch).

YANEZ de la Almedina, Hernando. La Mancha before 1480–1536. May possibly have been a pupil of Leonardo in Florence in 1505. Worked 1506–1513 in Cathedral of Valencia in collaboration with Hernando de Llanos, then worked alone in the Cuenca Cathedral in 1526. The most original of the Spanish Mannerists. Typical work: *Adoration of the Kings* (Cuenca, Cathedral).

ZAMBRANO, Juan Luis. Cordoba before 1590–Seville 1639. Pupil of Pablo de Cespedes. Active in Seville.

Typical works: *Martyrdom of St. Stephen* (Cordoba, Cathedral); *David with the Head of Goliath* (Cordoba, Museum).

ZUCCARO (Zuccari, Zuccheri), Federigo. San Angelo in Vado 1542–Acona 1609. Younger brother, pupil and collaborator of Taddeo Zuccaro (q. v.). Worked in Rome (Sala Regia, Vatican); Florence (cupola of Cathedral); London (portraits, some of dubious attribution, but certainly by him is a drawing of Queen Elizabeth in the British Museum); Venice; Spain (the Escorial). Founded the Accademia de' San Luca in Rome. Author of the *Idea de' Pittori, Scultori ed Architetti* (1607), an important treatise on the idealist aesthetic of late Mannerism.

ZUCCARO, Taddeo. San Angelo in Vado 1529–Rome 1566. Elder brother of Federigo Zuccaro (q. v.). Worked for the Duke of Urbino (frescoes in the cathedral), for Popes Julius III and Paul IV (Sala Regia, Vatican), and above all for Cardinal Alessandro Farnese. His frescoes in the Palazzo Farnese at Caprarolo are typical of his accomplished but rather academic style.

ZUCCHI, Jacopo. Florence *c.* 1541–Rome or Florence 1589/90. Pupil and collaborator of Giorgio Vasari (q. v.). Worked first in Florence for the Medici, then from 1567 onwards in Rome. Painted small pictures which are elegantly graceful and full of precious detail. Typical works: *The Coral Fishers* (Rome, Borghese); *Cupid and Psyche* (Rome, Borghese); *The Golden Age* (Florence, Uffizi).

Catalogue of Sales of Mannerist Paintings from 1930 to 1963

The letters and numbers which follow the titles indicate the currency and price; in parenthesis, the letter refers to the place of sale and the numbers correspond to the day, month, and year of the sale—eg.: £300 (s. 26. II. 58) = 300 English pounds (Sotheby, London, 26 February 1958).

AACHEN, Hans von
Judith; £300 (s. 26. II. 58)
School:
Adoration of the Kings; sch. 12,000 (D. 5.–9. XII. 60)

ABATE, Niccolò dell'
Allegory of Life; £105 (C. I. VI. 51)

Abbreviations:

DM	German marks
£	English pounds
gns.	English guineas
$	American dollars
ffr.	old French francs
nffr.	new French francs
fb.	Belgian francs
fs.	Swiss francs
fl.	Dutch florins
sch.	Austrian schillings
kr.	Swedish kroners
C.	Christie's, London
S.	Sotheby, London
A.	Anderson, New York
Char.	Galerie Charpentier, Paris
M.	J. de Mul, Brussels
F.	Fischer, Lucerne
K.	Karl und Faber, Munich
L.	Lempertz, Cologne
D.	Dorotheum, Vienna

AERTSEN, Pieter
Kitchen Scene with Feast in the House of Simon;
£22 (s. 8. VII. 30)
Kitchen Scene with Mary Magdalen Annointing Christ's Head; £50 (s. 8. VII. 30)
Pietà; $625 (A. 27. III. 30)
Calvary; £44 (1935)
Christ at Emmaus; £11 (1935)
Peasant Gathering; fb. 32,000 (G. 19. XI. 55)
Landscape with the Multiplication of the Loaves;
sch. 40,000 (Vienna, 12. IX. 58)
Street Musicians; fb. 18,000 (Brussels, 23. II. 59)
The Fruit Seller; fb. 210,000 (Brussels, 7.–8. XII. 60)

ALDEGREVER, Heinrich
Madonna; £56 (s. 16. VII. 30)

ALTDORFER, Albrecht
The Magi; £54 (C. 10. III. 30)
Crucifixion; $800 (A. 27. III. 30)
Gentleman by the Water; £441 (Char. 11. VII. 30)
Engravings:
Judith; £6 (C. 17. XII. 29)
St. George; fs. 1250 (Gutekunst-Klipstein, Berne, 28. IV. 55)
Paris; fs. 300 (Berne, 15. VI. 60)
Resurrection; DM 1950 (Munich, 1. XI. 59)

ARCIMBOLDO, Giuseppe
Pair of Landscapes; fs. 1050 (F. 25. XI. 52)
Landscape; fs. 1100 (F. 12. VI. 56)
Peninsula in Form of Man's Head; fs. 2950 (F. 24. XI. 59)

AST, Balthasar van der
Flowers, Shell-Fish; gns. 6500 (C. 27. VI. 58)
Flowers and Fruit; ffr. 2,000,000 (Char. 10. XII. 59)

Peaches, Plums, and Shell-Fish; gns. 2000 (C. 27. XI. 59)
Vase of Flowers; fb. 500,000 (Brussels, 7.–8. XII. 60)
Flower Still Life; fl. 23,000 (P. Brandt, Amsterdam, 6.–8. VI. 61)

BALDUNG GRIEN, Hans
Magicians; £46 (London, 26. IV. 27)
Adam and Eve; $700 (New York, 5. II. 42)
Crucifixion; DM 8000 (L. 27. IV. 49)
Engraving:
Madonna; DM 4400 (K. 29. II. 53)
Pen Sketches:
Reclining Nymph; fs. 1200 (Berne, VI. 60)

BAROCCIO, Federigo
Flight into Egypt; £25 (C. 14. III. 30)
Christ and Disciple; £10 (1931)
Rest in Egypt; £5 (1931)
Two drawings:
Woman's Head; Kneeling Woman; £10 (s. 19. II. 30)

BASCHENIS, Evaristo
Two *Still Lifes;* lire 30,000 (Milan, Galeria, 1. VI. 49)
Still Life; DM 3800 (Bad Kissingen, 10. VII. 60)

BASSANO, Jacopo da Ponte, called
Christ in the House of Mary and Martha; £5 (1931)
Flight into Egypt; £13 (1935)
Christ at Emmaus; £21 (1935)
Market; £18 (1934)
Peasant; ffr. 25,000 (Paris, 16. III. 49)
Landscape with Portrait; fs. 1500 (F. 21. VII. 60)
Attributed to Bassano:
Supper at the House of Mary and Martha; ffr. 13,000 (Paris, XII. 44)
School of Bassano:
The Evil Rich Man; ffr. 1350 (5. V. 33)
The Prodigal Son; ffr. 360 (17. III. 33)

BECCAFUMI, Domenico
Madonna in the Clouds; £21 (C. 2. XI. 34)

BEHAM, Barthel
Gentleman and his Wife; £1102 (C. 27. VI. 30)
Gentleman in Black; £200 (London, 9. VI. 32)

BEHAM, Hans Sebald
Moses and Aaron; £4 (s. 19.–20. V. 30)
Pen Sketches:
The Communal Bath; ffr. 11,200 (Paris, 28. XI. 28)
Engravings:

Madonna; DM 410 (K. 2. V. 60)
Young Woman and Death; DM 135
(Heidelberg, 12. XI. 59)

BELLANGE, Jacques
Engravings:
The Three Marys; fs. 9200 (Berne, 15. VII. 60)
The Virgin and Child with Saints; fs. 4300

BELLEGAMBE, Jean
Judith; £ 2400 (s. 6. III. 57)

BENSON, Ambrosius
Mary Magdalen; £ 1300 (s. 11. X. 55)

BEUCKELAER, Joachim
Fruit and Vegetable Merchant (pair); £ 152 (A. 20. II. 30)
Kitchen Scene (pair); £ 115 (A. 20. II. 30)

BINOIT, Peter
Spring Flowers; £ 5200 (18. XI. 59)
Still Life; DM 2900 (Munich, 5. XII. 56)

BLES, Herri met de
The Magi; £ 52 (C. 10. III. 30)
Holy Family with Saints; £ 4500 (A. 27. III. 30)
Landscape; DM 12,000 (Weinmüller, Munich,
10.–11. VI. 59)

BLOEMAERT, Abraham
Crowning of David; £ 70 (s. 27. X. 29)
Woman Caressing a Child; £ 10 (1931)
Diana and Acteon; ffr. 120,000 (Me. Ader, Paris, 29. II. 50)
Shepherd and Cow; £ 240 (s. 11. XI. 59)
Peasant Woman; ffr. 500 (Paris, 8. XII. 38)

BOCK, Hans the Elder
Portrait of a Man; ffr. 42,100 (Paris, 3. XII. 41)

BORDONE, Paris
Reclining Venus; fs. 10,000 (F. 21.–27. VI. 60)

BOSCH, Hieronymus
Garden of Delights, coll. Derain; ffr. 4,090,000
(Char. 28. III. 55)
Two Pharisees; £ 6500 (s. 10. V. 61)

BOSSCHAERT, Ambrosius the Elder
Plums; £ 25 (C. 4. XII. 30)
Flowers in a Basket; £ 17 (C. 17. IV. 35)
Flowers in a Glass Vase; £ 44 (1934)
Flowers in a Vase; £ 11 (1935)
Vase of Flowers in a Niche; £ 10 (1935)
Bouquet; fb. 30,000 (Brussels, 14. V. 58)
Tulips; gns. 2000 (C. 27. XI. 59)
Flowers; DM 2500 (Paris, 6. V. 60)
Flowers; ffr. 650,000 (Char. 3. XII. 59)
Flowers in a Vase; fl. 36,000 (P. Brandt, Amsterdam,
24.–25. V. 60)

BRIL, Paul
Creation; £ 7 (1931)
Four Paintings:

*Flight into Egypt, Healing of the Woman, Jairus,
Temptation;* £ 16 (1931)
Landscape with Flowers; fs. 520 (F. 17. V. 49)
Landscape; DM 10,000 (L. 4. V. 55)
Mountainous Landscape; fl. 2000 (Amsterdam, 23. X. 56)
Landscape; fs. 900 (N. Rauch, Geneva, 13.–15. VI. 60)
Landscape; fb. 24,000 (Brussels, 12. IV. 60)
Drawing:
Landscape; £ 10 (s. 19. II. 30)

BRONZINO, Angelo di Cosimo
Lady Holding a Book; £ 84 (Char. 25. VII. 30)
Lady Caressing her Child; £ 120 (Char. 26. V. 30)
Man in Black; £ 370 (s. 16. VII. 30)
Young Man Holding Gloves; £ 577 (Char. 1. V. 30)
Mars, Venus, and Cupid; £ 7 (Char. 19. VII. 31)
Venus and Cupid; £ 18 (1931)
Lady with a Vase; £ 8 (1931)
Seated Gentleman; £ 11 (1931)
Man in Black; £ 63 (1931)
Bianca Capello; £ 504 (1935)
Lady in Yellow; £ 24 (1935)
Pietro de' Medici; £ 70 (1935)

BRUEGEL, Jan the Elder
Massacre of the Innocents; $ 450 (A. 27. II. 30)
The Twelve Months; £ 546 (C. 18. VII. 30)
Flora; £ 19 (1930)
Flowers; £ 52 (C. 26. VII. 35)
Wooded Landscape; £ 15 (1934)
Mountainous Landscape; £ 10 (1935)
Summer; fb. 35,000 (Brussels, 12. X. 42)
Attributed to Jan Bruegel:
Circe; ffr. 66,000 (Paris, 11. I. 43)
School of Jan Bruegel:
Garden of Eden; ffr. 28,000 (1947)
Landscape; DM 2500 (L. 6. V. 53)
Allegory; fb. 240,000 (Brussels, 8. X. 58)
Creation of Eve; fb. 90,000 (Brussels, 29. V. 58)
Basket and Bouquet of Flowers; fb. 180,000
(Brussels, 29. V. 58)
Landscape with Travellers; £ 4400 (s. 9. XII. 59)
Flowers; £ 4200 (s. 18. XI. 59)
The Sense of Smell; fb. 475,000 (Brussels, 7.–8. XII. 60)
The Sense of Hearing; fb. 650,000 (Brussels, 7.–8. XII. 60)
Jonah and the Whale; £ 3500 (s. 17. V. 61)
Floral Still Life; £ 10,500 (s. 21. VI. 61)

BRUEGEL, Pieter the Elder
The Sermon on the Mount; $ 2200 (1930)
Winter; £ 340 (s. 8. XII. 48)
Hermit in a Landscape; fb. 270,000 (Brussels, 1. III. 57)

BRUEGEL, Pieter the Younger
Massacre of the Innocents; $ 1600 (1931)
Inferno; £ 17 (s. 13. II. 35)
Portrait of an Artist; ffr. 200,000 (V. 45)
Alchemist; ffr. 1,000,000 (Char. 28. III. 55)
Town in Winter; nffr. 58,000 (Paris, 20. VI. 61)

BURGKMAIR, Hans the Elder
Presentation of the Virgin; £ 5500 (s. 4. XI. 53)
Engravings:
Lovers and Death; DM 6300 (K. 19. XI. 53)

CALLOT, Jacques
Italian Carnival (6 paintings); £ 577 (C. 14. III. 30)
Engravings:
Temptation of St. Anthony; fs. 5000 (Berne, 6. XI. 58)
Slave Market; fs. 550 (Berne, 4. VI. 57)
Fantasies (14 sheets); (Berne, 4. VI. 57)
Impruneta; fs. 1650 (Berne, 4. VI. 57)
Miseries of War (7 plates); DM 460 (Berlin, 1. XII. 59)

CAMBIASO, Luca
Pen Sketches:
Saint John; ffr. 260 (Paris, 23. X. 42)
Annunciation; ffr. 120 (Paris, 29. III. 43)
Drawings:
Annunciation; £ 18 (s. 26. XI. 29)
Sacrifice of Abraham (pair); (Gutekunst-Klipstein, Berne, 11. III. 54)
Two Angels; fs. 700 (Lucerne, 21. VII. 60)
Holy Family Before the Temple; DM 450 (Berne, 1. XII. 59)

CARAVAGGIO, Michelangelo Merisi da
Two Ladies as Mercury and Justice; £ 6 (1931)
Young Peasant; £ 9 (1935)
Attributed to Caravaggio:
Sepia:
Venus and Amour: ffr. 260 (Paris, 30. VI. 43)
Man with a Spur; ffr. 28,000 (Me. Baudoin, 30. XII. 48)

CHIMENTI, Jacopo, called Jacopo da Empoli
Drawing:
Interior; £ 21 (s. 16. VII. 30)

CLAESZ, Pieter
Currant Tart; ffr. 138,000 (Char. 30. V. 49)
Still Lifes:
Dessert; ffr. 170,000 (Char. 7. XI. 50)
Ham; ffr. 520,000
Crabs; ffr. 350,000 (coll. Katz, Paris, M. Albinet, 17. XII. 48)
Still Life; £ 1050 (s. 7. XII. 60)

CLEVE, Joos van
The Magi, Annunciation, Shepherds; £ 42 (C. 14. III. 30)
Man in Green and Woman in Red; £ 1102 (C. 25. VII. 30)
Madonna, St. Catherine and St. Joseph; £ 2415 (C. 20. VI. 30)
Rest in Egypt; £ 36 (1934)
Infant Bacchus; £ 27 (1935)
Rest in Egypt; £ 36 (C. 2. XI. 34)
Portrait of a Young Man; £ 5200 (s. 14. VI. 61)

CLOUET, François
Charles V; £ 120 (C. 11. VII. 30)
François I; £ 157 (C. 11. VII. 30)
Henry II *of Navarre*; £ 21 (C. 14. II. 30)
Eleanor, Wife of François I; £ 21 (1934)
Mary of Scotland; £ 50 (1934)

CLOVIO, Giorgio Giulio
The Last Judgment; £ 39 (C. 11. VII. 30)

CONINXLOO, Gillis van
Virgin and Child; £ 84 (C. 25. VII. 30)

Madonna; £ 69 (C. 29. IV. 35)
Landscape with Stag Hunt; fb. 36,000 (Brussels, 26. X. 59)
Christ and His Disciples; $ 2000 (s. 14. VI. 61)
Landscape; fb. 70,000 (Brussels, 25.–27. IV. 61)

CORNELISZ, Cornelis, van Haarlem
Acts of Charity; £ 11 (C. 16. III. 30)
Feast of the Gods; £ 50 (C. 14. II. 30)
Baptism of Christ; £ 5 (1931)
Death of Procris; £ 10 (1931)
Aphrodite; sch. 20,000 (D. 9. VI. 59)
Life and Death; fl. 900 (Amsterdam, 3. XI. 59)

COXIE, Michiel
Adam and Eve; DM 300 (Munich, 10. X. 56)

CRANACH, Lucas I
Adam and Eve; £ 50 (s. 27. XII. 29)
Duke of Saxony; £ 1890 (C. 11. VII. 30)
Feast of the Gods; £ 14 (Puttick's, 28. V. 30)
Luther and his Wife; £ 220 (s. 29. I. 30)
Bust of a Young Woman; DM 43,000 (1931)
Cleopatra; £ 16 (1931)
Lucretia; £ 21 (1931)
Judith; £ 36 (1931)
Salome; $ 600 (1931)
Salome; £ 714 (C. 26. VII. 35)
Luther; $ 125 (A. 4. I. 35)
Female Nude; ffr. 8,500 (Paris, 26. X. 42)
Adam and Eve (2 panels); ffr. 16,000 (VI. 45)
Head of a Woman; fs. 2900 (F. 16. XI. 48)
Eve; ffr. 95,000 (Paris, Me. Engelmann, 27. VI. 49)
Adoration of the Magi; £ 1,800 (s. 17. V. 61)
Samson and Delilah; £ 11,000 (s. 14. VI. 61)
Portrait of a Young Woman; £ 1,900 (s. 14. VI. 61)
Engravings:
St. Christopher; DM 3100 (K. 19. II. 53)
St. Catherine; ffr. 920,000 (Char. 24. III. 55)
Virgin and Child; fl. 32,000 (F. Muller, Amsterdam, 9. II. 54)
Ecce Homo; DM 26,000 (Hamburg, 24. XI. 56)
Landscape with Hunter; gns. 2400 (C. 1. IV. 60)

DERUET, Claude
Engraving:
Rest on the Flight into Egypt; sch. 25,000 (Vienna, 3. XII. 59)

DESIDERIO, Monsù
Church Interior; £ 9 (1931)
Square (Stage Setting); £ 420 (s. 28. II. 51)
Ruins; £ 399 (C. 16. VII. 54)
Martyrdom of St. Peter; £ 900 (s. 7. XII. 60)

DEUTSCH, Nikolaus Manuel
Salome; £ 10 (Willis's, 23. X. 30)

DOSSI, Dosso
Jacob's Dream; $ 375 (A. 18. XII. 29)
Holy Family; £ 42 (1931)
Lucretia Borgia; £ 57 (C. 17. V. 35)
Noah Entering the Ark; £ 18 (1931)
Attributed:
Madonna; fs. 1500 (Lucerne, 24. XI. 59)

DÜRER, Albrecht
Pen Sketch:
Studies of Hands; fl. 1000 (F. Muller, Armstad, 2. III. 54)
Engravings:
Cavalier and Death; fs. 2900 (Gutekunst-Klipstein, Berne, 28. IV. 55)
Large Fortune; DM 1700 (Dr. Ernst Hauswedell, Hamburg, 4. II. 55)
St. Hubert; DM 1150 (Heidelberg, 8. X. 58)
Jealousy; DM 6600 (K. 27. IV. 59)
St. Jerome in the Desert; DM 11,000 (Berlin, 23. IX. 59)
Jealousy; DM 10,000 (Berlin, 23. IX. 59)
Melancholy; DM 2950 (Berlin, 23. IX. 59)
Knight, Death, and the Devil; DM 14,000 (Berlin, 23. IX. 59)
Apocalypse; fs. 65,000 (Rauch, Geneva, 2. III. 53)

ELSHEIMER, Adam
Ariadne and Nymphs; £ 21 (C. 30. V. 30)
Interior; £ 21 (S. 16. VII. 30)

ENGELBRECHTSZ, Cornelis
Triptych (Nativity, etc.) £ 900 (1958)
Triptych (Nativity, etc.) £ 580 (S. VII. 59)

EWORTH, Hans
Gentleman Holding a Scale; £ 27 (C. 9. XII. 29)
Lady Hopton; £ 50 (C. 11. VI. 30)

FINSONIUS, Ludovicus
David and Goliath; £ 33 (Puttick's, 26. VII. 30)

FLORIS, Frans
Mount of Olives; £ 16 (1931)
Martyrdom of St. Justina; ffr. 4500 (Paris, 11. II. 43)
Kneeling Nude Woman with Flowers; fs. 4700 (Zurich, 25. II. 55)
August (peasant); DM 9800 (Wuppertal-Elberfeld, 4. IX. 58)
Mary Magdalen; kr. 1900 (Stockholm, 11. XI. 59)

FONTANA, Lavinia
Lady; $ 1000 (1931)

FRANCKEN, Frans I
Susanna; £ 7 (1931)
The Poor and the Rich; fb. 22,000 (Brussels, 12. X. 42)
Belshazzar's Feast; ffr. 26,100 (I. 45)

FRANCKEN, Frans II
Return of the Prodigal Son; $ 300 (A. 27. III. 30)
Crucifixion; DM 5000 (Cologne, 5.–8. II. 60)

FRANCO, Giovanni Battisto
Pen Sketch:
A Warrior; ffr. 800 (I. 45)

GAROFALO, Benvenuto Tisi
St. Catherine; £ 39 (C. 24. IV. 31)
Madonna; £ 183 (C. 20. XII. 29)
Birth of Christ; £ 430 (S. 20. VII. 60)

GERUNG, Mathias
Melancholy; ffr. 420,000 (Burton Sale, Nice, 7. VII. 43)

GIORGIONE, Giorgio Barbarelli, called
Romantic Landscape; £ 157 (C. 1. VII. 30)
Landscape; £ 25 (1930)
(School of) Pen Sketch:
Figures of a Man and Woman; ffr. 1550 (Paris, 29. III. 43)
David with the Head of Goliath; gns. 850 (C. 25. II. 60)

GIULIO Romano
Madonna; £ 25 (C. 11. VII. 30)
Dancing Children; £ 3 (London, 1931)

GOLTZIUS, Hendrick
Engravings:
Noël de la Faille and his Wife; DM 320 (Hollstein and Puppel's, 7. II. 30)
Danae; kr. 2300 (Gal. Bukowskis, Stockholm, 11. IV. 35)
Head of a Woman; ffr. 1900 (Paris, 4. V. 43)
Pietà; $ 45 (Parke-Bernet, New York, 17. IV. 56)
Hercules; DM 100 (Munich, 13. XI. 57)

GRAF, Urs
Standard Bearer; DM 5500 (1958)

GRANACCI, Francesco
Resurrection of Lazarus; £ 72 (S. 26. II. 29)

EL GRECO, Domenikos Theotocopoulos, called
St. Bartholomew; nffr. 30,000 (Char. 31. III. 60)
St. Paul; £ 5000 (S. 7. XII. 60)

HEEMSKERCK, Maerten van
Jacob and Esau; £ 11 (C. 14. III. 30)
Hercules and Omphale; £ 105 (1931)
Portrait of a Senator; fb. 105,000 (Palais des Beaux Arts, Brussels, 26. IV. 53)
Peasants' Street Festival; DM 1350 (L. 26.–29. IV. 61)
Pen Sketch:
Susanna; DM 2400 (Munich, 16. X. 59)

HEERE, Lukas de
Gentleman; $ 800 (A. 10. IV. 30)
Jane Grey; £ 787 (C. 28. II. 30)
Queen Mary; £ 9 (1934)
Diana Sleeping By the River; £ 55 (Paris, 10. V. 61)

HEMESSEN, Jan Sanders van
(attributed):
The Brawl; ffr. 29,000 (Paris, Me. Boisgirard, 10. XI. 48)
Madonna and Child; DM 13,000 (L. 4. XII. 52)

HILLIARD, Nicholas
Henry VIII; ffr. 25,000 (Me. Bellier, 6. XII. 48)
Miniature; £ 5000 (S. 11. X. 55)
Anne of Denmark; gns. 380 (C. 21. I. 60)

HOLBEIN, Hans the Younger
Sir Thomas More; £ 78 (C. 4. VII. 30)
Nobleman with a Pink; £ 31 (1931)

HONTHORST, Gerrit
Adoration of the Shepherds; £ 5 (1931)
Card Players; £ 37 (1931)
Portrait of a Man; fs. 650 (F. 17. V. 49)
Croesus and Solon; fb. 210,000 (Brussels, 7. XII. 57)

Young Girl Lighting a Candle; sch. 180,000
(D. 3.—5. XII. 59)

HUBER, Wolf
Engraving:
Nativity; DM 480 (K. 18. II. 55)
Drawing:
Raising of the Cross; DM 600 (Munich, 16. III. 60)

KESSEL, Jan van
Artist's Studio; £49 (Knight, Frank, Rutley, 25. XII. 29)
Venus at the Forge of Vulcan; $450 (A. 27. III. 45)
Summer; fb. 29,000 (Brussels, 25. I. 43)
Flowers; fl. 3200 (P. Brandt, Amsterdam, 25. V. 58)
Beach with Aquatic Animals (pair); fb. 70,000
(Palais des Beaux-Arts, M. I. III. 56)
Butterflies; fb. 28,000 (M. 5. VI. 57)
Insects (four sheets); fs. 3200 (Stuber, Berne,
10.—16. II. 60)

LOMBART, Lambrecht
Multiplication of the Loaves and Fishes; £1750
(S. 9. XII. 53)
St. John Preaching; gns. 800 (C. I. IV. 60)

LUCAS van Leyden
Judgment of Solomon; £31 (1931)
Golgotha; kr. 7000 (Stockholm, 15.—17. IV. 59)

MABUSE, Jan Gossaert, called
Triptych: Madonna and Saints; £80 (S. 25. VII. 30)
Madonna, Child, Saints, and Angels; £80 (1931)
The Magi; £17 (1935)
Attributed:
Infant Jesus and Saint John; ffr. 380,000
(Dansette Sale, 16. II. 42)
Mars, Venus and Love; ffr. 3,900,000 (Char. 3. VII. 59)
Virgin and Child; ffr. 600,000 (Char. 10. VII. 59)

MARINUS van Reymerswaele
St. Jerome Meditating; $500 (A. 18. XII. 29)

MASSYS, Jan
Mary Magdalen; $3000 (A. 27. III. 30)
Lucretia; £121 (C. 19. VII. 31)
Merry Company; (Brussels, 30. X. 56)
Susanna at the Bath; fl. 2500 (Amsterdam, 3. XI. 59)
Praying Saint; gns. 1500 (C. 13. XI. 59)
Susanna and the Elders; fl. 2400 (Amsterdam, 13. VI. 61)

MASTER OF THE HALF-LENGTH PORTRAITS
OF WOMEN
Mary Magdalen Writing; ffr. 5,000,000 (Char. 3. XII. 59)
Mary Magdalen; nffr. 16,500 (Char. 31. III. 60)

MOMPER, Joos de
Mountain Landscape; fl. 750 (Müller, Amsterdam,
31. V. 49)
Mountainous Landscape; ffr. 930,000
(Char. I.—20. II. 59)
Panorama; DM 20,000 (Munich, 18.—19. III. 59)
Summer; fb. 120,000 (Brussels, 7.—8. XII. 60)

MORALES, Luis de
Madonna; DM 3800 (1930)

NEER, Aernout van der
Moonlight; £14 (S. 10. XII. 30)
Moonlit Landscape; fs. 8800 (F. 13.—17. VI. 61)

OLIVER, Isaac
Gouache:
Madonna and Child; £550 (S. 18. XI. 59)
Miniature:
James I; gns. 280 (C. 21. I. 60)

ORLEY, Bernard van
Holy Family; £420 (C. 18. VII. 30)
Holy Family and Saints; £420 (C. 19. VII. 31)
Last Judgment; ffr. 90,000 (27. VI. 45)
David and Bathsheba; £4200 (S. 29. VI. 53)
Half-Length Portrait of a Young Girl; ffr. 2,500,000
(Char. 3. XII. 59)

PARMIGIANINO, Francesco Mazzola, called
Madonna; $250 (A. 4. I. 35)
Madonna; £10 (S. 27. V. 35)
Marriage of St. Catherine; £4 (C. 26. VII. 35)
Drawing:
Leda; £10 (S. 10. VII. 31)
Pen Sketch:
Female Dancer and Two Figures; ffr. 4200 (I. 45)

PATINIR, Joachim
Agony in the Garden; $2700 (A. 27. III. 30)
St. John Preaching; £136 (C. II. VII. 30)
St. Jerome in the Desert; ffr. 180,000 (XII. 46)
St. Jerome; fb. 36,000 (F. 4. V. 56)
Calvary; £750 (S. 8. VII. 59)

POELENBURG, Cornelis van
Venus and Nymphs; £6 (C. 30. VII. 30)
Arcadia; DM 900 (Cassierer, Berlin, 20. IX. 30)

PONTORMO, Jacopo da
Holy Family; £24 (C. 22. II. 35)
St. Sebastian; £15 (C. 15. III. 35)
Attributed:
David Holding the Head of Goliath; ffr. 600
(Paris, 24. III. 47)
Virgin and Child; ffr. 32,000 (Paris, 30. VI. 47)

PROCACCINI, Giulio Cesare
(Attributed) Pen Sketch
Episode from the Life of Diana; ffr. 2900 (XI. 46)

RING, Ludger Tom the Younger
Gentleman; $1100 (A. 10. IV. 30)

ROTTENHAMMER, Hans
Mars and Venus Taken by Vulcan; £22 (C. 19. VII. 31)
Toilet of Venus; £4 (C. 19. VII. 31)
Perseus and Andromeda; £6 (1935)
Last Judgment; £7 (1935)
Adam and Eve in the Garden of Eden; Original Sin
(pair); fb. 35,000 (Brussels, 8. XII. 59)
Mythological Scene (pair); fb. 21,000
(Brussels, 7.—8. XII. 60)

SALIMBENI, Ventura
Holy Family; £12 (Dowell's, 8. II. 30)

SALVIATI, Francesco de' Rossi
Annunciation; £54 (C. 18. VII. 30)

SAVERY, Roland Jacobsz
Orpheus; fs. 8500 (Lucerne, 21. VII. 60)

SCHIAVONE, Andrea Meldolla, called
Life of a Saint; £48 (C. 31. VII. 30)
Death of Adonis; £21 (C. 12. VII. 31)
Tancred and Clorinda; £9 (C. 2. XI. 34)

SCHOOTEN, Floris Gerritz van
Kitchen Scene; nffr. 5800 (Char. 21. VI. 60)

SCOREL, Jan van
Isaac and Jacob; $300 (A. 27. III. 30)
Young Woman; ffr. 1,020,000 (Char. 7. VI. 55)

SODOMA, Giovanni Antonio Bazzi, called
Head of Christ; £11 (s. 19. II. 30)

SPRANGER, Bartholomeus
Poseidon and Amphritrite; fs. 500 (Lucerne, 24. XI. 59)

TIBALDI, Pellegrino
Madonna and Saints; £19 (C. 13. XII. 29)

TINTORETTO, Jacopo Robusti, called
Magi; £90 (s. 11. III. 31)
Christ and his Disciples; £15 (C. 13. III. 31)
The Philosopher; sch. 30,000 (D. 10. IX. 53)
Portrait of a Young Girl; $14,000 (Parke-Bernet, 19. X. 60)

VALCKENBORCH, Lucas van
Icarus; fb. 110,000 (Brussels, 6. III. 59)
Landscape with Hermit; fb. 100,000 (Brussels, 4. III. 60)
Winter; fb. 24,000 (Brussels, 14. VII. 60)

VASARI, Giorgio
Pen Sketch:
Figure of a Woman; ffr. 3000 (XII. 44)
Attributed:
Adoration of the Shepherds; ffr. 15,000 (XII. 44)
Portrait of an Italian Poet; $3100 (s. 17. V. 61)

VENUSTI, Marcello
Fortune; £18 (C. 20. XII. 29)
Madonna in Mauve; £6 (1935)

VERHAEGT, Tobias
Mountainous Landscape; fb. 120,000 (Brussels, 17. XII. 57)

VOS, Marten de
The Manna, Abraham and Melchizedek (pair); £21 (1931)
Mythological Scene; $50 (1931)

VRIES, Hans Vredeman de
Palace Court with Solomon and the Queen of Sheba; £13 (1931)

ZUCCARO, Federigo
Lady in Embroidered Gown; £16 (C. 19. VII. 31)
Queen Elizabeth; £9 (Williq's Room, 23. IV. 31)

Bibliography

I. OLD SOURCES

A. BIOGRAPHIES:

C. VAN MANDER
Het schilder-Boeck, Haarlem, 1604. English edition: C. van de Wall, *Dutch and Flemish Painters*, New York, 1936.

F. PACHECO
Arte de la Pintura, su antiguedad y grandeza, Seville, 1649.

J. VON SANDRART
Teutsche Akademie, Nuremberg, 1675–79. Modern edition edited by A. Peltzer, Munich, 1925.

G. VASARI
Le vite de' più eccellenti pittori, scultori ed architetti, Florence, 1550. English edition: A. B. Hinds and G. du C. de Vere, *Lives of the Most Eminent Painters, Sculptors, and Architects*, London, 1912.

B. ESTHETIC TREATISES:

A. ARMENINO
De' veri precetti della pittura, Ravenna, 1587.

M. BIONDO
Della nobilissima pittura, Venice, 1549.

R. BORGHINI
Il Riposo, Florence, 1584.

V. DANTI
Primo libro del trattato delle perfette proporzioni, Florence, 1567.

A. DÜRER
Underweysung der Messung mit dem Zirkel und Richtscheyt in Linien, Ebenen und ganzen Körpern, 1525. *Vier Bücher von menschlicher Proportion*, Nuremberg, 1528. English edition: W. M. Conway, *The Writings of Albrecht Dürer*, London, 1958.

A. A. GILIO
Due Dialoghi, Camerino, 1564.

LEONARDO DA VINCI
Trattato della Pittura, edit. H. Ludwig, Vienna, 1882. English edition: A. P. McMahon, *Treatise on Painting*, Princeton, 1956.

G. P. LOMAZZO
Trattato dell'arte della Pittura, Milan, 1584. *Idea del Tempio della Pittura*, Milan, 1590.

G. MANCINI
Considerazioni sulla pittura, edit. by A. Marucchi & L. Salerno, Rome, 1956–57.

MICHELANGELO
Correspondance, edit. by G. Milanesi, Florence, 1875. English edition: E. H. Ramsden, *The Letters of Michelangelo*, Stanford Univ., 1964.

P. PINO
Dialogo di Pittura, Venice, 1548.

B. VARCHI
Due Lezioni sopra la pittura e scultura, Florence, 1546.

F. ZUCCARO
L'Idea de' Pittori, Scultori ed Architetti, 1607.

C. EXTRACTS AND ANALYSES OF ESTHETIC TREATISES:

A. BLUNT
Artistic Theory in Italy: 1450–1600, Oxford, 1940.

E. G. HOLT
Literary Sources of Art History, Vol. II, Princeton, 1958.

F. J. SANCHEZ CANTON
Fuentes literarias para la historia del arte español, Madrid, 1923.

J. VON SCHLOSSER
Die Kunstliteratur, Vienna, 1924, pp. 305–404.

L. VENTURI
La critique d'art en Italie à l'époque de la Renaissance, Rieti, 1928.

I. L. ZUPNICK
"The Aesthetics of the Early Mannerists," *Art Bulletin*, XXXV, December, 1953, pp. 302–306.

D. TRAVEL DIARIES AND MEMOIRS:

B. CELLINI
La vita scritta da lui medesimo (1558–1566). English edition: R. H. H. Cust, *The Life of Benvenuto Cellini*, London, 1910.

A. DÜRER
Das Tagebuch der Reise in die Niederlande, edit. Leitschuc, 1884. English edition: R. Fry, *Records of Journeys to Venice and the Low Countries*, Boston, 1913.

L. GUICCIARDINI
Descrizione di tutti i Paesi Bassi, Antwerp, 1567.

MONTAIGNE
Journal de voyage en Italie par la Suisse et l'Allemagne en 1580 et 1581, posthumous edit. Rome, 1774.

F. MORYSON
Itinerary, edit. Glasgow, 1907.

II. EUROPEAN CIVILIZATION AT THE TIME OF MANNERISM

P. J. BLOK
Geschiedenis van het Nederlandsche Volk, vol. III, Groningen, 1892.

J. BURCKHARDT
The Civilization of the Renaissance in Italy, London, 1944.
The Cambridge Modern History, vol. I, *The Renaissance*, Cambridge, 1902–11.

C. DIMIER
Le Château de Fontainebleau et la cour de François Ier, Paris, 1930.

R. EHRENBERG
Das Zeitalter der Fugger, 2 vols., Berlin, 1896.

J. VAN DER ELST
L'Age d'or Flamand, Paris, 1951.

A. GINDELY
Rudolf II und seine Zeit, 1600–1612, 2 vols., Prague, 1863–65.

G. HANOTAUX
La Cour de François Ier, Paris, 1888.

A. HAUSER
The Social History of Art, vol. I, London, 1951.

H. HAUSER
La modernité du XVIe siècle, Paris, 1930.
La Prépondérance espagnole (Peuples et Civilisations), Paris, 1946.

H. JANITSCHEK
Die Gesellschaft der Renaissance in Italien und die Kunst, Stuttgart, 1879.

J. JANSSEN
Geschichte des deutschen Volkes beim Ausgang des Mittelalters, 8 vols., Freiburg im Breisgau, 1881–94. English edition: *History of the German People at the Close of the Middle Ages*, 16 vols., London, 1900–10.

J. KULISCHER
Allgemeine Wirtschaftsgeschichte, vol. II, *Die Neuzeit*, Munich, 1929.

A. LEFRANC
La vie quotidienne au temps de la Renaissance, Paris, 1939.

R. MOUSNIER
Les XVIe et XVIIe siècles, vol. 4 of *L'Histoire générale des Civilisations* by M. Crouzet, Paris, 1953–1957.

H. PIRENNE
Histoire de Belgique, vol. 3, Brussels, 1923.

A. RENAUDET
Les Débuts de l'âge moderne (Collection Peuples et Civilisations), Paris, 1946.

H. ROY
La vie, la mode et le costume au XVIIe siècle, époque Louis XIII, étude sur la cour de Lorraine, Paris, 1924.

H. SEE
Les origines du capitalisme moderne, Paris, 1926.

W. SOMBART
Der moderne Kapitalismus, vol. I, Leipzig, 1902.

J. STRIEGER
Jakob Fugger der Reiche, Leipzig, 1926.
Das reiche Augsburg, Munich, 1938.

A. SYMONDS
Renaissance in Italy, 7 vols., London, 1886.

III. MANNERIST PHILOSOPHY AND LITERATURE

E. B. BAX
Rise and Fall of the Anabaptists, London, 1898 (Part 3 of *The Social Side of the Reformation in Germany*).

L. BLANCHET
Campanella, Paris, 1920.

O. H. BRANDT
Thomas Münzer, sein Leben und seine Schriften, Jena, 1932.

R. BRAY
La préciosité et les précieux, Paris, 1948.

E. BREHIER
Histoire de la Philosophie, vol. I, Part 3, Paris, 1926–1932.

H. BUSSON
*Les sources et le developpement du rationalisme dans
la littérature française de la Renaissance*, Paris, 1922
The Cambridge History of English Literature, vols.
IV–VII, Cambridge, 1908–1931.

D. CANTIMORI
Eretici Italiani del Cinquecento, Florence, 1939.

E. CASSIRER
*Individuum und Kosmos in der Philosophie der Ren-
aissance*, Leipzig, 1927.

J. R. CHARBONNEL
*La pensée italienne au XVIe siècle et le mouvement
libertin*, Paris, 1917.

V. COUSIN
Vanini, ses écrits, sa vie et sa mort, Paris, 1843.

H. CYSARZ
Deutsche Barock Dichtung, Leipzig, 1924.

C. DEJOB
*De l'influence du Concile de Trente sur la littérature
et les beaux-arts chez les peuples catholiques*, Paris,
1884.

L. FEBVRE
Le Problème de l'Incroyance au XVIe siècle, Paris, 1942.

G. G. FERRERO
Marino e i marinisti, Milan, 1954.

W. FRAENGER
The Millenium of H. Bosch, Chicago, 1951.

J. FREDERICH
De secte der Loisten of Antwerpsche libertijnen,
Ghent, 1891.

H. J. C. GRIERSON
Metaphysical Lyrics and Poems of the XVIIth Century,
Oxford, 1921.

G. R. HOCKE
Manierismus in der Literatur, Rowohlts deutsche
Enzyklopädie, vols. 82/83, Hamburg, 1959.

LEGOUIS and CAZAMIAN
L'Histoire de la Littérature Anglaise, Paris, 1924.

E. MÂLE
L'Art religieux après le Concile de Trente, Paris, 1932.

A. MORET
Le lyrisme allemand au XVIIe siècle, Paris, 1935.

G. DE RUGGERO
*Storia della Filosofia, Rinascimento, Riforma e Con-
trariforma*, Bari, 1930.

A. M. SCHMIDT
L'Anthologie des Poètes du XVIe siècle.
La poésie scientifique en France au XVIe siècle, Paris,
1938.

P. SMITH
History of Modern Culture, vol. I, "The Great Renewal," New York, 1930.

R. STAMM
"Über Manierismus bei Shakespeare," *Der Bund*, vol. 3,
1958.

L. P. THOMAS
Le lyrisme et la préciosité cultiste en Espagne, Paris,
1909.
*Gongora et le gongorisme considérés dans leurs rap-
ports avec le marinisme*, Paris, 1911.

G. TOFFANIN
"Cinquecento," *Storia letteraria d'Italia*, Milan, 1929.

J. TORTEL
Le préclassicisme français, Paris, 1952.

L. G. WALTER
Thomas Münzer et les luttes sociales, Paris, 1929.

R. WOLKEN
Die Lieder der Wiedertäufer, Berlin, 1903.

IV. MODERN LITERATURE ON MANNERISM

G. S. ADELMANN AND G. WEISE
*Das Fortleben gotischer Ausdrucks- und Bewegungs-
motive in der Kunst des Manierismus*, Diss. Tübin-
gen, 1946.

D. ANGULO INIGUEZ
Pintura del Renacimiento (vol. 12 of *Ars Hispaniae*),
Madrid, 1954.

F. ANTAL
"Zum Problem des niederländischen Manierismus,"
Kritische Berichte zur kunstgesch. Literatur, 2, 1928–29,
pp. 207–256.

H. BADERON
L'Ecole de Fontainebleau, Geneva, 1944.

C. H. BAKER and W. G. CONSTABLE
English Painting of the XVI and XVII Centuries, Florence, 1930.

J. BALTRUSAITIS
Aberrations, Paris, 1957.
Anamorphoses ou perspectives curieuses, Paris, 1955.

A. BARTSCH
Le Peintre-Graveur, 21 vols., Vienna, 1803–1821; completed by J. D. Passavant, 6 vols., Leipzig, 1860–1864.

F. BAUMGART
"Zusammenhänge der niederländischen mit der ita-
lienischen Malerei in der zweiten Hälfte des 16. Jh.,"
Marburger Jb. für Kunstwiss., 13, 1944, pp. 187–250.

L. BECHERUCCI
Manieristi Toscani, Bergamo, 1944.

S. BEGUIN
L'Ecole de Fontainebleau, Paris, 1960.

W. BERNT
Die Niederländischen Maler des 17. Jahrhunderts, Munich, 1948.

A. BLUNT
Art and Architecture in France, 1500–1700 (Pelican History of Art) London and Baltimore, 1953.

G. BRIGANTI
Il manierismo e Pellegrino Tibaldi, Rome, 1945.
Italian Mannerism, Princeton, 1962.

F. BURGER
Die deutsche Malerei vom ausgehenden Mittelalter bis zum Ende der Renaissance, Berlin, 1913–1921.

K. H. BUSSE
Manierismus und Barockstil, Ein Entwicklungsproblem der florentinischen Seicento Malerei, Diss. Leipzig, 1911.

M. L. CATURLA
"El manierismo," *Rivista de Ideas Esteticas*, 2, 1944, pp. 3–16.

K. CHYTIL
Die Kunst in Prag zur Zeit Rudolf II, Prague, 1904.

L. COLETTI
"Intorno alla storia del concetto di manierismo," *Convivium*, 1948, pp. 801 ff.
"La crisi manieristica nelle pitture veneziana," *Convivium*, 13, 1941, pp. 109–126.

E. R. CURTIUS
Europäische Literatur und lateinisches Mittelalter, Bern, 1953.

L. DIMIER
French Painting in the Sixteenth Century, New York, 1904.

M. DVORAK
"El Greco and Mannerism," *Magazine of Art*, 46, Jan. 1953.
Geschichte der italienischen Kunst im Zeitalter der Renaissance, vol. 2, "Das 16. Jh.," Munich, 1928.

G. N. FASOLA
"Storiografia del manierismo," *Scritti di Storia dell'arte in onori di L. Venturi*, 1, pp. 429–447, Rome, 1956.

S. J. FREEDBURG
Painting of the High Renaissance in Rome and Florence, 2 vols., Princeton, 1961.

J. G. FREEMAN
The Maniera of Vasari, London, 1867.

D. FREY
Gotik und Renaissance als Grundlage der Modernen Weltanschauung, Augsburg, 1929.

M. J. FRIEDLÄNDER
Die Altniederländische Malerei, 14 vols., Berlin, 1924–1937.
"Die Antwerpener Manieristen von 1520," *Jb. d. Preuss. Kunstslgen.*, 36, 1915, pp. 65–91.
Mannerism and Anti-Mannerism in Italian Painting, New York, 1957.

L. FRÖHLICH-BÜM
Parmigianino und der Manierismus, Vienna, 1921.

G. R. HOCKE
Die Welt als Labyrinth, Rohwolts deutsche Enzyklopädie, vols. 50/51, Hamburg, 1957.

M. HOERNER
"Manierismus," *Zeitschrift für Ästhetik und allgemeine Kunstwissenschaft*, Stuttgart, 1924.
"Der Manierismus als künstlerische Anschauungsform," *Ibid.*, Stuttgart, 1928.
"Holbein, Erasmus und der frühe Manierismus des 16. Jahrhunderts," *Ibid.*, Stuttgart, 1929.

H. HOFFMANN
Hochrenaissance, Manierismus, Frühbarock in der italienischen Kunst des 16. Jahrhunderts, Zurich and Leipzig, 1939.

F. W. HOLLSTEIN
Dutch and Flemish Etchings, Engravings, and Woodcuts, ca. 1450–1700, Amsterdam, 1949, ff.
German Engravings, Etchings and Woodcuts, ca. 1400–1700, Amsterdam, 1954, ff.

G. ISARLO
"Les manieristes neerlandais," *L'Art et les artistes*, 148, June, 1934.
La Peinture en France au XVIIe siècle, Paris, 1960.

N. IVANOFF
Stile e maniere, Venice, 1957.

G. IVEN
Versuch einer Deutung des Manierismus, Diss. Köln, 1938.

H. KAUFFMANN
"Der Manierismus in Holland und die Schule von Fontainebleau," *Jb. d. Preuss. Kunstslgen.*, 44, 1923, pp. 184–204.

H. KEHRER
Greco als Gestalt des Manierismus, Munich, 1939.

H. LADENDORF
Catalogue de la Collection Grzimek, Cologne, 1960.

I. LAVIN
"Observation on Medievalism in Early XVIth Century Style," *Gazette des beaux-arts*, série 6, vol. 50, Sept. 1957.

A. LINZELER and J. ADHÉMAR
Inventaire du fonds français, Graveurs du XVIe siècle, Paris, 2 vols., 1932 and 1938.

R. LONGHI
"Comprimari Spagnoli della maniera italiana," *Paragone*, 43, 1953, pp. 3–11.

H. LOSSOW
"Zum Stilproblem des Manierismus in der italienischen und deutschen Malerei," *Beiträge zu den Kulturbeziehungen zwischen Nord und Süd, Festschrift W. Waetsold 1940*, Berlin, 1941, pp. 192–208.

K. OBERHUBER
Die stilistische Entwicklung im Werk B. Sprangers, Diss. Vienna, 1959.

E. PANOFSKY
Idea, Leipzig and Berlin, 1924.

F. G. PARISET
Jacques Callot et les peintres et graveurs lorrains du 17ème siècle.

N. PEVSNER
"Tintoretto and Mannerism," *Architectural Review*, III, June, 1952, pp. 360–365.
"Gegenreformation und Manierismus," *Repertorium für Kunstwissenschaft*, 1925, pp. 243 ff.

W. PINDER
"Zur Physiognomik des Manierismus," *Festschrift Ludwig Klages*, Munich, 1932.

V. DE RUVO
"La concezione estetica di G. Vasari," *Studi Vasariani*, Florence, 1952, pp. 183–185.

R. DOS SANTOS
L'Art portugais, Paris, 1938.

C. H. SMYTH
Mannerism and Maniera, New York, 1963.

W. SYPHER
Four Stages of Renaissance Style, Garden City, 1955.

A. VENTURI
Storia dell'arte italiana, la Pittura del Cinquecento, vol. IX, 1–6, Milan, 1925–1933.

A. M. VOGT
Grünewald, Meister gegenklassischer Malerei, Zürich, 1957.

H. VOSS
Die Malerei der Spätrenaissance in Rom und Florenz, Berlin, 1920.

E. K. WATERHOUSE
Painting in Britain, 1530–1790 (Pelican History of Art), London and Baltimore, 1953.

W. WEISBACH
"Gegenreformation, Manierismus, Barock," *Repertorium für Kunstwiss.*, 49, 1928, pp. 16–28.
"Zum Problem des Manierismus," *Studien zur Deutschen Kunstgeschichte*, 1934.
Manierismus in Mittelalterlicher Kunst, Basel, 1942.

G. WEISE
"La doppia origine del concetto di manierismo," *Studi Vasariani*, Florence, 1952, pp. 183–185.
"Maniera und Pellegrino, zwei Lieblingswörter der italienischen Literatur der Zeit des Manierismus," *Romanistisches Jahrbuch*, 3, 1950, pp. 321 ff.

F. WÜRTENBERGER
Der Manierismus, der Europäische Stil des sechzehnten Jahrhunderts, Vienna, 1962.

F. ZERI
Pittura e Contrariforma, l'arte senza tempo di Scipione da Gaeta, Turin, 1957.

V. MANNERIST EXHIBITION CATALOGUES SINCE 1950

The Art of Mannerism, Arcade Gallery, London, 1950.
Aufgang der Neuzeit, Deutsche Kunst und Kultur von Dürers Tod bis zum Dreißigjährigen Krieg, 1530–1630, Ger. Museum, Nuremburg, 1952.
Fontainebleau e la maniera italiana (studies by B. Molajoli, F. Bologna, R. Causa), Naples, 1952.
Manieristi piemontesi e lombardi, Turin, 1954.
Pontormo to Greco, the Age of Mannerism, Indianapolis, 1954.
Mostra di disegni dei primi manieristi italiani, Uffizi, Florence, 1954 (catalogue by L. Marcucci).
Le Triomphe du Manierisme européen de Michelange au Greco, Council of Europe, Amsterdam, 1955 (studies by J. Adhémar, R. van Luttervelt, B. Molajoli, C. Sterling, B. Thomas, H. Weihrauch).
The Art of Mannerism, Delius Gallery, London, 1955.
Mostra del Pontormo e del primo manierismo fiorentino, Palazzo Strozzi, Florence, 1956.

VI. MONOGRAPHS ON MANNERIST PAINTERS

ARCIMBOLDO:
B. Geiger, *Giuseppe Arcimboldi*, Florence, 1954.
C. Legrand and F. Sluys, *Arcimboldo et les arcimboldesques*, Paris, 1955.

BECCAFUMI:
M. Gibellino-Krasceninnikowa, *Il Domenico Beccafumi*, Florence, 1933.

BLOEMAERT:
G. Delbanco, *Der Maler A. Bloemaert*, Strasbourg, 1928.

BOSCH:
J. Combe, *Jerome Bosch*, Paris, 1947.
W. Fraenger, *The Millenium*, Chicago, 1951.
W. Vogelsang, *Hieronymus Bosch*, Amsterdam, 1951.

BRONZINO:
A. M. Comb, *Angelo Bronzino, His Life and Works*, Cambridge, 1928.
A. Emiliani, *Bronzino*, Busto Arsizio, 1960.
M. Tinti, *Bronzino*, Florence, 1920.

P. BRUEGEL THE ELDER:
F. Grossmann, *Tutta la pittura di Brueghel*, Florence and London, 1956.
C. de Tolnay, *Brueghel*, Brussels, 1935.

CAMBIASO:
B. Suida Manning, "The Nocturnes of Luca Cambiaso," *Art Quarterly*, Detroit, 1952–53.
Luca Cambiaso e la sua fortuna, Exhibition Catalogue, Palazzo dell'Accademia, Genoa, 1956.

CARAVAGGIO:
Caravaggio, Exhibition Catalogue, Milan, 1951.
W. Friedlaender, *Caravaggio Studies*, Princeton, 1955.
G. Isarlo, *Caravage et les Caravagistes européens*, Aix-en-Provence, 1941.
M. Marangoni, *Caravaggio*, Florence, 1922.

CORNELIS CORNELISZ:
W. Stechow, "Cornelis van Haarlem in de Hollandse laatmanieristische Schilderkunst," *Elsevier's Maandschrift*, XLV, 1935, pp. 73 ff.

CORREGGIO:
B. Bodmer, *Il Correggio e gli Emiliani*, Novara, 1943.

DÜRER:
E. Panofsky, *The Life and Art of Albrecht Dürer*, Princeton, 1955.

GIORGIONE:
G. Isarlo, *Les Indépendants dans la peinture ancienne*, Paris, 1956.

GIULIO ROMANO:
P. Carpi, *Giulio Romano ai servigi di Federigo II Gonzaga*, Mantua, 1921.
F. Hartt, *Giulio Romano*, New Haven, 1958.

GRÜNEWALD:
W. K. Zülch, *Grünewald*, Munich, 1949.

HEEMSKERCK:
L. Preibisz, *M. van Heemskerck*, Leipzig, 1911.

LUCAS VAN LEYDEN:
N. Beets, *Lucas de Leyde*, Brussels and Paris, 1913.

MICHELANGELO:
M. Brion, *Michel-Ange*, Paris, 1937.
L. Goldscheider, *Michelangelo; Paintings, Sculpture, Architecture*, London, 1953.
H. Thode, *Michelangelo und das Ende der Renaissance*, 3 vols., Berlin, 1908–1913.
C. de Tolnay, *Michel-Ange*, Paris, 1951.

ORSI:
R. Salvini and A. M. Chiodo, *Catalogue of the Lelio Orsi Exhibition*, Reggio Emilia, 1950.

PARMIGIANINO:
S. J. Freedberg, *Parmigianino*, Cambridge, 1950.
L. Fröhlich-Bum, *Parmigianino und der Manierismus*, Vienna, 1921.

PONTORMO:
G. N. Fasola, *Pontormo o del Cinquecento*, Florence, 1947.
E. Toesca, *Il Pontormo*, Rome, 1943.

PRIMATICCIO:
L. Dimier, *Le Primatice*, Paris, 1960.

ROSSO:
P. Barocchi, *Il Rosso Fiorentino*, Rome, 1950.

SAVERY:
Roeland Savery, 1576–1639, Exhibition Catalogue, Musée des Beaux-Arts, Ghent, 1954.

SCOREL:
E. Houtzager and G. J. Hoogewerff, *Catalogue of the Jan van Scorel Exhibition*, Central Museum, Utrecht, 1955.

TIBALDI:
G. Briganti, *Il manierismo e Pellegrino Tibaldi*, Rome, 1945.

TINTORETTO:
E. Newton, *Tintoretto*, London, 1952.

Index of Illustrations

*All illustrations are
listed in sequence by page*

* *indicates a plate
in full color*